MADE IN AMERICA

THE HIDDEN HISTORY OF HOW THE U.S. ENABLED COMMUNIST CHINA AND CREATED OUR GREATEST THREAT

XI VAN FLEET
AND YU JIE

NEW YORK NASHVILLE

Center Street
Hachette Book Group
1290 Avenue of the Americas, New York, NY 10104
centerstreet.com
@CenterStreet/@CenterStreetBooks

First Edition: January 2026

Center Street is a division of Hachette Book Group, Inc. The Center Street name and logo are registered trademarks of Hachette Book Group, Inc.

The publisher is not responsible for websites (or their content) that are not owned by the publisher.

Center Street books may be purchased in bulk for business, educational, or promotional use. For information, please contact your local bookseller or the Hachette Book Group Special Markets Department at special.markets@hbgusa.com.

Library of Congress Cataloging-in-Publication Data has been applied for.

ISBNs: 9781546009344 (hardcover), 9781546009368 (ebook)

Printed in the United States of America

LSC-C

Printing 1, 2025

To President Donald J. Trump and those—
leaders and citizens alike—who not only recognize
the threat posed by the Chinese Communist Party,
but have the resolve to fight back

CONTENTS

INTRODUCTION

In 2022, I made a life-altering decision: I quit my job to write a book—something I had never imagined myself doing. This wasn't just a passion project; it felt like a calling. A fire had been lit in me.

I knew I had to tell my story—of surviving one of the most brutal Communist regimes in history and living through Mao's Cultural Revolution. It wasn't just about what I endured; I was driven to sound the alarm for the American people of the cultural Marxist Revolution now sweeping across America.

My book, *Mao's America: A Survivor's Warning*, laid out the parallels between Mao's Cultural Revolution and America's Woke Revolution. Through meeting audiences and hearing feedback on social media, I have been told by many people that my book was an eye-opener—helping them understand, often for the first time, what is really happening in America. The book also led to interviews with countless conservative media outlets, including the Tucker Carlson Network. The video with Carlson was retweeted by Elon Musk on X, reaching tens of millions of people.

But more questions still beg for answers.

As we battle the spread of Marxist woke ideology here at home, we also face an unprecedented threat from Communist China—a regime determined to replace the United States as the world's leading power, and well on its way to achieving that goal.

How is it that the United States—the world's sole superpower, once triumphant over the evil empire of the Soviet Union—now finds itself challenged by an even greater Communist threat, rising from what was once dismissed as a backward wasteland: the People's Republic of China (PRC)?

The situation is dire.

America is under assault by Communism—both from within and from without.

It was with that same sense of urgency that I embarked on the journey of writing this book—*Made in America: The Hidden History of How the U.S. Enabled Communist China and Created Our Greatest Threat*—to uncover a little-known but critically important history of the past century. In it I hope to reveal the pivotal role the United States played in the rise of the Chinese Communist Party. This is the first book of its kind to tell the full story—from the CCP's birth to its emergence as a formidable global power in the world today.

It is an extraordinary story: how a fringe movement, led by a handful of radicalized professors and students in China, evolved into the most dangerous adversary America has ever faced. What's even more extraordinary—and troubling—is that the United States was part of that story *every step of the way*.

It has been a tremendous undertaking to trace more than a century of history in order to shed light on America's role in enabling and empowering the CCP. I'm deeply grateful for my collaboration with Yu Jie—a well-known Chinese dissident, prolific author, and leading expert on the Chinese Communist Party. We both hail from Chengdu, Sichuan, and share deeply held conservative values and a resolute anti-Communist stance. Yu brings a wealth of knowledge and insight, which provided a solid foundation for this book.

—

In *Mao's America*, I sounded the alarm: The Woke movement is America's Cultural Revolution—a modern echo of Mao's own Marxist Cultural Revolution that ravaged China more than fifty years ago, and a deadly threat from within, aimed at dismantling our freedoms.

In *Made in America*, my goal is to expose how liberals, progressives, gullible conservatives, Communist sympathizers, and fellow travelers in the United States have not only become a threat from within but also played a decisive role in the rise of the Chinese Communist Party—dating back to the early 1900s and culminating in the loss of China to Communism in 1949.

Over time, the influence of these allies of the CCP has only grown—joined by misguided and corrupt politicians of both parties, amoral profiteers, and globalist elites. Together, they empowered the Chinese Communist Party, transforming it into the most powerful and wealthy adversary the United States has ever faced from without—paving the way for the potential loss of America to Communist China and to Communism itself.

In many ways, this book is even more relevant to today's America than my last—because more than a century later, this critical history remains largely unknown to so many Americans, including our political leaders. The same mistakes are repeated again and again, while the CCP's tactics against the United States continue to work—just as they always have.

By learning this history, Americans will not only gain insight into the CCP's tactics but also begin to understand how closely the liberal worldview aligns with that of Communism—making liberals especially vulnerable to Communist deception and propaganda.

History has shown that political liberalism, left unchecked, often drifts toward Communism.

That's why many of today's most prominent conservative voices—such as President Donald Trump, Elon Musk, Robert F. Kennedy Jr., and others—were once liberals themselves. They walked away because they recognized where modern American liberalism was headed. And that is why today's Democratic Party has become in many ways nearly indistinguishable from the Chinese Communist Party.

This is one of the central themes of this book.

In *Made in America*, you will learn:

- How the Chinese Communist Party rose to power with the backing of the Soviet Union—and later, shockingly, the United States.
- How the United States repeatedly rescued the CCP from the brink of collapse, both knowingly and unknowingly.
- How American political leaders, policymakers, journalists, and elites were repeatedly deceived by the CCP, with many willfully choosing to believe blatant lies.
- How the CCP employed its "magic weapon," the United Front strategy, to infiltrate, subvert, and weaken American institutions; and to cultivate an army of allies in the United States known as "the Old Friends of the Chinese People," also referred to as *useful idiots*.
- How the CCP has waged an undeclared, unrestricted, and protracted war against the United States—largely unnoticed by the American public.
- And why defeating the CCP begins with understanding its history, strategies, and ultimate goal.

The past five years have been transformational for me. In 2020, I made the decision to become politically involved for the first time—compelled by the Marxist-inspired Black Lives Matter (BLM) movement and its assault on America's values, institutions, and social fabric. In 2021, I found myself unexpectedly in the spotlight after delivering a one-minute speech at a Loudoun County school board meeting in Virginia. That moment—and the Fox News interview that followed—launched me into public view and turned me into an accidental activist. Since then, I've embraced the role and made it my life's mission to educate the American people about the dangers of Communism and the devastating and immediate threat it poses to our freedom and way of life.

Communism, already a deadly ideology, has become even more lethal in its more deceptive form—Chinese Communism. Trained by their Soviet masters, the Chinese Communist Party has surpassed its teachers in nearly every respect. It has not only modernized its tactics but has also skillfully leveraged the United States to make China the world's second-largest economy in a remarkably short span of time—all the while quietly embedding itself into nearly every aspect of American society.

I believe my story and perspective are critical in helping the American people understand Chinese Communism, classical Communism, and its modern mutation—Neo-Communism, or Woke Communism. It is because those of us who have lived through these regimes possess a hard-won understanding of how they operate, how they deceive, and how they destroy.

For this reason, I proudly call myself an anti-Communist—because Communism remains one of the greatest threats that we, as free people, continue to face.

And it is for that same reason that I wrote this book: to uncover a vital and often hidden history—how the United States became the enabler of the Chinese Communist Party, and in doing so, has come dangerously close to sealing its own fate.

THE FARMER AND THE SNAKE

One cold winter morning, a farmer came across a snake lying nearly lifeless in the snow, frozen stiff. Though he knew the snake was dangerous, he felt sorry for it and tucked it inside his coat to warm it up.

As the snake thawed and regained its strength, it suddenly turned and bit the farmer. The venom quickly spread. As the farmer lay dying, he turned to the bystanders and said: "Let my fate be a warning—never show mercy to the wicked."

—AESOP'S FABLE

CHAPTER 1

THE CCP'S WAR ON AMERICA

On April 2, 2025, President Trump declared the day "Liberation Day" as he introduced sweeping new tariffs: a 10 percent baseline on all imported goods, with higher "reciprocal" rates on countries that imposed tariffs on U.S. exports. The move sparked both celebration and panic. Days later, the dust began to settle, revealing the strategy behind Trump's approach: Countries that refrained from retaliating were granted a ninety-day pause on reciprocal tariffs—all except China. As China responded with counter-tariffs, U.S. tariffs on Chinese goods continued to rise. Now isolated, China stands alone on the world stage, clearly exposed as the true target of the tariff war.

While some continue to debate the pros and cons of tariffs, an increasing number of Americans recognize that what President Trump launched was far more than an economic policy—it was a bold counteroffensive against Communist China, marking a historic turning point. This is not merely a trade war; it is the first real pushback in over a century of U.S. engagement with the Chinese Communist Party. America is finally fighting back.

The trade war ignited a national reckoning: How did America end up here—its industrial base hollowed out, its middle class weakened, and its technological edge ceded to Communist China? Those with long enough memories trace the roots of today's crisis back to President Bill Clinton.

Just as April 2, 2025—Liberation Day—marks the beginning of America's renewal, another date marks the start of its decline: March 8, 2000.

On that day, President Clinton delivered a confident, forward-looking speech at Johns Hopkins University, championing the China Trade Bill that cleared the path for China's entry into the World Trade Organization (WTO), a decision that marked the beginning of America's decline and Communist China's dramatic rise.

In his speech, Clinton delivered the following key promises:

- First, the vast Chinese market would open to American goods and services, creating a tidal wave of opportunities for U.S. exports and significantly boosting domestic employment. "For the first time, our companies will be able to sell and distribute products in China made by workers here in America without being forced to relocate manufacturing to China, sell through the Chinese government, or transfer valuable technology—for the first time. We'll be able to export products without exporting jobs."
- Second, China's WTO membership would bring economic liberalization, paving the way for political reform, empowering Chinese citizens, and fostering democratic development. "The more China liberalizes its economy, the more fully it will liberate the potential of its people...And when individuals have the power, not just to dream but to realize their dreams, they will demand a greater say."
- Third, transformative technologies like the Internet were expected to deliver the triumph of freedom. Clinton confidently stated that the Internet would reshape China's political

landscape, dismissing the Chinese government's efforts to control the web as akin to "that's sort of like trying to nail Jell-O to the wall"—impossible to achieve.

- Last, the rules-based WTO system would be a mechanism for ensuring that China adhered to international norms, with "some of China's most important decisions for the first time being subject to the review of international bodies with rules and binding dispute settlements."

Most Americans were convinced that the agreement was highly promising and that the future looked bright for the United States, which was expected to benefit the most from the deal.

On October 10, 2000, Clinton signed the China Trade Bill into law.

On December 11, 2001, China officially became the 143rd member of the WTO.

With this, Clinton unleashed the "China Shock" that would shake America to its core. Many of us have lived through this historic—and devastating—transformation.

The Hollowing Out of America

Americans were soon to be disillusioned by the promises. If there was any semblance of American prosperity resulting from the new economic trade arrangement with China, it was found in stores like Walmart, where American consumers gained access to inexpensive Chinese-made goods—clothing, toys, Christmas decorations, and even American flags. However, the surge in low-cost Chinese imports triggered a rapid decline in U.S. manufacturing, causing tens of thousands of factories to close and millions of jobs to be outsourced overseas. Industries such as textiles, furniture, and steel were particularly devastated.

Entire regions of the Midwest and Northeast, once vibrant centers of industrial manufacturing—including steel production, automobile manufacturing, and heavy machinery production—became what is now known as the Rust Belt. While the trend had begun earlier, large-scale offshoring to China accelerated and cemented the process. The term "rust" symbolizes the abandoned factories and decaying infrastructure, leaving workers jobless and communities impoverished. "Made in America" all but vanished from store shelves, replaced by "Made in China," as the loss of millions of jobs devastated working- and middle-class families across the nation.

Vice President JD Vance, in his memoir, *Hillbilly Elegy*, vividly depicts the struggles of working-class Americans in the Rust Belt during the era of globalization. He recounts his turbulent upbringing in Ohio and Kentucky, marked by family instability, poverty, and the pervasive impact of addiction and violence. Vance highlights the rise of opioid addiction as a devastating consequence of economic and social decline following the closure of factories and the loss of stable jobs. As traditional industries vanished, many working-class individuals faced unemployment, despair, and hopelessness, often turning to prescription painkillers to cope. While Vance overcame these challenges and rose to success, he acknowledges that many of his peers were unable to break free from this cycle of hardship and decline.

Author Paul Theroux documented similar devastation in southern states in his 2015 book *Deep South: Four Seasons on Back Roads*. The stories echo those of JD Vance: Entire industries—furniture, appliances, roofing materials, textiles, plastics—vanished one after another. In their wake, struggling communities lost not just jobs but the basics of daily life, as grocery stores, fresh produce, and local businesses disappeared—driven out by rising violence, drug abuse, and gang activity. Theroux poignantly remarked, "Though America in its greatness is singular, it resembles the rest of the world in its failures."[1]

Theroux is critical of American philanthropists and charities, accusing them of focusing their "benevolent concern" on poverty abroad while neglecting the struggles of impoverished communities in the American

South. He writes, "They had traveled halfway around the world…to bring teachers to Africa, food to India, and medicine elsewhere; yet they allowed the poor in the South, a growing peasant class, to die for lack of health care, remain uneducated and illiterate, live in poor housing, and, in some cases, starve."[2] In speaking about Bill Clinton, one Arkansan shared this sentiment with Theroux: "He was governor. He was president. His philanthropic charity is worth a couple of billion. I don't see him spending any of it in Arkansas."[3]

With what Elon Musk has uncovered in 2025 thanks to DOGE—the Department of Government Efficiency—one can only wonder how much federal funding, especially through USAID, has been funneled into overseas charities while neglecting our own people at home.

During the COVID pandemic, Americans were shocked to realize the extent to which the United States had outsourced critical manufacturing to Communist China, leaving the nation unable to produce even basic items, like masks, and reliant on China for life-saving medicines.

Over the past three decades, trade with China has made corporations, Wall Street firms, and the elites immensely wealthy by exploiting China's massive market, cheap labor, and favorable policies designed to attract foreign investment. Companies like Apple, Tesla, and Hollywood studios profited greatly, while financiers facilitated China's rise and reaped significant rewards. However, the losers have been the American working class. The United States has experienced massive job loss and deindustrialization, all while becoming dependent on an increasingly assertive and totalitarian Communist China.

To add insult to injury, Americans have watched as iconic brands—names that generations grew up with—have been quietly taken over by Communist China. According to a 2017 CNBC report, Smithfield Foods, GE Appliances, Hoover, and Dirt Devil are just a few among them.[4]

Clinton's catastrophic gamble of admitting China into the WTO inflicted lasting damage on America's middle class and industrial heartland. After countless lives were devastated, manufacturing demolished, and the nation weakened, did he ever formally apologize or explicitly admit his mistake? Not at all.

Threat to the United States and the World

Despite the harsh reality, Americans have been relentlessly fed a false narrative—pushed by policymakers, corporations, and the legacy media—that integrating Communist China into the global economy would lead to its political liberalization, and a prosperous China would be good for America—and good for the world.

Perhaps, as we were led to believe, the loss of American industries and millions of jobs was a price worth paying. As President Clinton convincingly argued in his speech at Johns Hopkins University: "If you believe in a future of peace and security for Asia and the world, you should be for this agreement. This is the right thing to do. It's an historic opportunity and a profound American responsibility."

In becoming the world's second-largest economy, Communist China did the exact opposite of what Clinton promised—and what many had hoped for.

While crushing all calls for political reform at home, the Chinese Communist Party has used its newfound wealth to construct a formidable military machine that now rivals the United States. It no longer hides its true ambition: to replace America as the world's sole superpower—economically, politically, and militarily. Communist China has emerged as a grave threat not just to Asia but to the entire world.

Launched in 2013, the Belt and Road Initiative (BRI) is a global infrastructure and investment strategy personally spearheaded by China's paramount leader, Xi Jinping. While the officially stated goal of the initiative is to enhance global connectivity and economic cooperation through the construction of railways, ports, pipelines, and digital networks across Asia, Africa, Europe, and beyond, its true objective is geopolitical dominance. In effect, the initiative has increasingly taken the form of modern-day colonialism.

The Belt and Road Initiative has also become a vehicle for advancing Xi Jinping's even more ambitious ideological vision: a "Community with a Shared Future for Mankind"—a doctrine now enshrined in China's constitution. As Xi himself describes it, the goal is to "strive to build the planet where we were born and raised into a harmonious big family, turning the hopes of people everywhere for a better life into reality."[5]

Doesn't this sound like a globalist reboot of the New World Order by the World Economic Forum—now rebranded as Communist Utopia 2.0 with Chinese characteristics? The message is clear: Having a seat at the Globalist Club is no longer enough—Xi Jinping wants to build his own and run it.

For a dose of reality, this is what the CCP's global "harmonious big family" truly looks like.

In Asia, China has increasingly acted like a regional bully, with its aggression toward neighboring countries marked by territorial disputes, military intimidation, and economic coercion. It pressures Taiwan through constant military drills, diplomatic isolation, and open threats of a forceful takeover. In the South China Sea, China has constructed and militarized artificial islands, heightening tensions with Vietnam, the Philippines, and other claimants. Along its border with India, repeated standoffs—including deadly clashes—have escalated hostilities. In the East China Sea, it continues to dispute territory with Japan. In February 2025, Chinese naval ships circumnavigated Australia—a feat not even undertaken by the Australian Navy itself. The intent was clear: a show of force and a deliberate act of strategic signaling.[6]

Beyond military actions, Beijing wields trade as a weapon, imposing sanctions or restrictions on countries including Australia and South Korea when they challenge its interests.

In Hong Kong, the CCP has effectively abandoned the Sino-British Joint Declaration—which guaranteed fifty years of self-governance—by dismantling the city's basic law and imposing a police-state-style rule reminiscent of mainland China. The regime has brutally crushed the pro-democracy movement, imprisoning thousands of protesters, including lawmakers, lawyers, and journalists, bringing Hong Kong under the firm grip of Beijing's totalitarian control.

Hong Kong was once the main hub for publishing banned books critical of the CCP. Today the industry has collapsed. All of my co-author Yu Jie's works were removed and destroyed by Hong Kong libraries—while some of his earlier, milder books remain in mainland libraries. This stark contrast shows how Hong Kong has become a police state with less free speech than even mainland China.

Economically, the Chinese Communist Party has expanded its Belt and Road Initiative into numerous developing countries, often leaving behind economic hardship and a troubling erosion of national sovereignty. Nations such as Sri Lanka, Argentina, Kenya, Malaysia, Pakistan, and Tanzania have amassed significant debt tied to BRI projects. In one striking example, Sri Lanka was forced to lease its strategic Hambantota International Port to China for ninety-nine years after failing to repay its loans—an outcome eerily reminiscent of Britain's imperial acquisition of Hong Kong following the Opium War with the Qing Dynasty. Similarly, Kenya's standard gauge railway, financed by Chinese loans, has faced mounting financial difficulties, raising serious concerns that control of the railway could ultimately fall into China's hands as well.

How did China manage to indebt so many countries? One key reason is strategically maintaining "developing country" status—even after becoming the world's second-largest economy—within institutions like the World Bank, International Monetary Fund, and the World Trade Organization. This designation allows China to access low-interest loans and favorable trade terms, which it then redirects to fund its Belt and Road Initiative. The result: Developing nations, lured by infrastructure deals, often find themselves burdened with unsustainable debt—ironically, at the hands of a fellow "developing country" that claimed to be their ally.

In 2019, during his first term, President Trump exposed the CCP's blatant gaming of the WTO system and called for reforms of the rules that allow countries to self-declare as "developing," thereby gaining unfair preferential treatment.[7]

The CCP has also extended its reach into some of the world's most strategically vital locations, posing serious threats to both U.S. national security and global stability. Since Panama severed diplomatic ties with Taiwan in 2017 in favor of Beijing, the CCP has steadily expanded its presence there. Through Belt and Road Initiative projects, China has sought to strengthen its influence by securing footholds along critical global trade routes—most notably the Panama Canal.

In addition, China has sought to expand its influence into the Arctic through BRI. In 2019, a Chinese company withdrew its bid to build two airports in Greenland, a territory with a population of fewer than 60,000.[8] The move attracted international attention due to Greenland's strategic importance, particularly in relation to U.S. military operations and missile defense systems in the region. Although the attempt ultimately failed, it exposed China's ambition to project power even into the world's most remote and geopolitically sensitive frontiers.

Leveraging its economic power, military support, and political influence, China has sought to undermine U.S. interests around the world—standing behind nearly every major terrorist-sponsoring or authoritarian regime, propping up totalitarian governments, and destabilizing entire regions.

Just consider some of Communist China's closest allies: North Korea, Iran, Russia, Venezuela, Syria, even the Taliban in Afghanistan, all openly hostile to the United States. Behind nearly every major international crisis today, one can often trace the hidden hand of the Chinese Communist Party. From supplying arms to Houthi militants in Yemen,[9] to engineering the construction of tunnel networks under Gaza,[10] to providing military aid—including reports of Chinese soldiers fighting for Russia in Ukraine[11]—Beijing is increasingly emerging as a key enabler of global conflicts, determined to reshape the international order on its own terms.

Since 2023, Houthi terrorists have repeatedly attacked U.S. Navy warships and commercial shipping vessels. It has been reported that China's Chang Guang Satellite Technology Company is directly supporting these terrorist operations.[12]

Closer to home, the threat is no less immediate. We've seen CCP spy balloons drift across the American continent and the aggressive purchase of U.S. farmland—much of it alarmingly close to some of the nation's most sensitive military bases. The Chinese military threat is already at our doorstep, yet few are demanding answers from those in power: *How did we let this happen?*

The 2025 Annual Threat Assessment by the Office of the Director of National Intelligence bluntly identifies the Chinese Communist Party as the top national security threat to the United States. The report highlights China's multipronged strategy—military buildup, cyberattacks, economic coercion, and global influence operations—aimed at undermining U.S. power and replacing American dominance both regionally and globally.

Just as the CCP's hand can be found behind nearly every international crisis, financial links to the CCP have also been traced to various instances of social unrest in the United States, including the 2020 BLM riots[13] and recent pro-Hamas protests.[14]

Most alarmingly, the CCP's influence now reaches into nearly every aspect of American society—including our institutions, political parties, and government. It has become disturbingly common to see U.S. political leaders and elites either apologizing for, or openly expressing support for, the Chinese Communist Party.

When President Trump initiated his bold pushback through his tariff war with China, the legacy media responded not with support but with relentless efforts to discredit him and diminish the significance of his actions.

Just consider a few of the headlines soon after Trump's tariff announcement:

- "As Trump Shakes the International Order, China Casts Itself as a Model of Stability"—NBC News
- "There's No Coming Back from Trump's Tariff Disaster"—*The Atlantic*
- "Um, It Turns Out No One at the Ports Is Collecting Trump's Tariffs"—*The New Republic*
- "Trump Is Waiting for Xi to Call. The Chinese See It Differently"—CNN
- "Trump Tariffs on China Will Soon Bring 'Irreversible' Damage to Many American Businesses"—CNBC

Similar narratives are widespread across social media. Influencers like Jackson Hinkle—who boasts 2.9 million followers—frequently post content praising the CCP's pushback against President Trump's tariffs. In one tweet, Hinkle shared a propaganda video featuring Xi Jinping, captioned: "China will never be defeated."

CCP-generated memes have also circulated widely on X, mocking the MAGA movement—including President Trump, Vice President Vance, and Elon Musk—by depicting them working in a sweatshop making shoes for Nike, accompanied by captions like "Make America Work Again." These posts have garnered tens of thousands of likes, amplifying their reach and influence.

Also rooting against President Trump is seemingly the entire Democratic Party and its supporters. Many still view Communist China merely as a trading partner or economic competitor—or worse, regard Communism not as a threat but a noble ideal. These people harbor deep contempt for the America First movement and are determined to do whatever it takes to undermine efforts by President Trump to preserve the nation's strength, security, and sovereignty.

These Americans are either unaware of—or willfully ignoring—the reality that the CCP not only views the United States as its primary enemy but has already waged a multifaceted war against us.

Frontal War Against America

During the Cold War, Americans saw the U.S.S.R. as their primary adversary and existential threat. Few, however, considered that the United States never engaged in direct conflict with the Soviet Union.

Now, consider how many American lives have been lost at the hands of Chinese Communists.

During the Korean War, Mao Zedong sent hundreds of thousands of Chinese soldiers as "volunteers" to fight against American forces, resulting in the deaths of more than 30,000 Americans. Meanwhile, approximately 400,000 Chinese soldiers perished, all to secure the hard-line Communist "Kim Dynasty" in North Korea.[15]

Almost 60,000 Americans died in the Vietnam War, a conflict heavily supported by both the CCP and the U.S.S.R. Over the span of the war, China provided unwavering support, including 320,000 troops and more than $20 billion in aid, even as the Chinese people endured the grinding hardships of extreme poverty. Without this backing, North Vietnam likely would not have been able to sustain the war.[16]

Now consider this: How many Americans die from fentanyl overdoses? Over a quarter of a million since 2018.[17]

According to the House Select Committee on the CCP, China is responsible for producing nearly all illicit fentanyl precursors—the key ingredients driving the global fentanyl trade. The committee further asserts that the CCP government is complicit in facilitating the export of these precursors, fueling this devastating crisis.[18] It is increasingly clear that fentanyl is being weaponized by the CCP to harm and weaken the United States. This is not just a crisis but a deliberate campaign against Americans.

Lawrence Kadish, of the Gatestone Institute, aptly stated that the CCP has "obviously determined that it may be a far more cost-effective way to harm the United States than the trillions of yuan spent to greatly expand their military forces. Without a shot being fired at our nation, the Chinese believe they have found a way of reducing America to a second-rate nation."[19]

One more question: What is the total death toll of Americans in major foreign wars, including World War I, World War II, the Korean War, the Vietnam War, and the wars in Iraq and Afghanistan? Roughly 623,000. Now ask this: How many Americans lost their lives to the virus known as COVID-19—or more precisely, the CCP virus? More than 1 million![20]

The COVID-19 pandemic, allegedly originating from the Wuhan Institute of Virology,[21] has been the CCP's most devastating export.

Both the "leak" and its cover-up were extraordinary. In 2020, I made my annual visit to China for Chinese New Year to visit family. Before leaving, I had heard news reports of a new virus concentrated around Wuhan. At the Beijing Airport, I noticed that the gate designated for Wuhan flights was closed, while all other gates, including those for international flights, remained wide open.

Meanwhile, New Year's Eve celebrations carried on across China as normal, with gatherings large and small marking the occasion and watching the Chinese Central Television's (CCTV) *The Chinese New Year Gala*. This CCP tradition, dating back to 1983, when TV sets became widely available, has evolved into one of the most significant media events for CCP propaganda. The atmosphere was festive, and few gave much thought to the rumors of a virus. But just after midnight—immediately following the party's triumphant messaging—CCTV abruptly announced that a coronavirus outbreak was spreading like an epidemic. Panic set in. When I went to buy masks the next morning, they were already sold out.

I spent another terrifying week in China before managing to catch literally the last flight back to America—just before Trump's ban on incoming flights from China took effect.

Although the world has yet to determine how the virus escaped the Wuhan lab, I can personally attest that the Chinese government knowingly allowed potentially infected citizens to travel to the U.S. and other countries, accelerating its global spread. Meanwhile, the CCP banned all flights from Wuhan to Beijing, in an apparent effort to prevent the virus from reaching China's political center.

The CCP also worked to silence those who tried to warn the public, including Dr. Li Wenliang, the Wuhan doctor who was the first one to raise concerns about a SARS-like virus on the Chinese social media app WeChat.

In just a few months, COVID-19 spread across the globe, claiming millions of lives, causing widespread suffering, and inflicting immense economic damage—exacerbated by ineffectual, totalitarian lockdowns modeled after the CCP's response.

A report released July 8, 2024, by the Heritage Foundation, a conservative think tank, revealed that the total economic damages to the United States from COVID-19 are more than $18 trillion, and COVID-19 resulted in more than 38 million excess deaths globally and over 1 million in the United States alone.[22]

In addition to the human and economic toll, COVID-19 significantly impacted the 2020 election, leading to an unprecedented expansion of mail-in voting. This shift raised concerns about election integrity, as it created opportunities for irregularities, casting doubt on the legitimacy of the results.

COVID also brought draconian lockdowns, mask mandates, vaccine requirements, and widespread censorship, giving many Americans their first experience with a level of totalitarianism reminiscent of the CCP's control tactics.

Five years after COVID-19 swept through the United States, we still have no answers about how the virus leaked from the Wuhan lab—and no one has held the CCP accountable. How is that even possible? Why did the Biden administration show such little interest in uncovering the truth?

This is the hard reality—the CCP has been waging an undeclared cold war against the United States for a long time, warming it up gradually by using chemical and biological weapons like opioids and viruses.

Future War with the United States

While many Americans are still grappling with the question of whether the CCP released the COVID virus accidentally or intentionally, a far more sobering reality confronts us: The Chinese Communist Party—and its military arm, the People's Liberation Army (PLA)—has long viewed war with the United States as inevitable and is actively preparing for such a conflict.

CCP General Chi Haotian, China's Minister of National Defense from 1993 to 2003, openly stated as early as 1999 that China must seize the initiative in any future war with the United States. The PLA's strategy centers on surprise, speed, and overwhelming force—drawing clear parallels to Germany's blitzkrieg tactics in World War II. This warning revealed by Representative Bob Schaffer was officially recorded in the 2002 U.S. Congressional Record.[23]

After his retirement, General Chi reportedly stated in a 2005 internal speech that the most effective way to win a war—and fully capitalize on the victory—would be to use biological weapons to "clear out" the United States: to keep the land, but not the people.[24]

The speech was widely circulated online. While its authenticity cannot be independently verified under the CCP's tight information control, its rhetoric and intent are all too familiar to those of us who grew up under the party's relentless vilification of perceived enemies—both foreign and domestic—and seeing that hostility put into practice.

Meanwhile, the rapid advancement of gene technology has raised real concerns about the development of genetic weapons capable of targeting specific racial groups[25]—making such threats more plausible and increasingly urgent.

The CCP targets not just the population, but the very systems that sustain the nation. Just as I was about to finalize this manuscript, news broke that federal authorities had charged several Chinese nationals with conspiracy and smuggling biological pathogens into the United States for use in university laboratories and research institutions. These pathogens pose a potential agroterrorism threat, capable of infecting vital crops and undermining America's food security.[26]

—

To understand why the American people were never warned about any of this is to recognize that President Trump's tariffs were never merely about trade—but about confronting a much deeper existential threat posed by the CCP.

To truly grasp how the Chinese Communist Party has become such a monstrous threat to the United States and the entire world, we must return to the beginning—over a century ago, to China.

Surprisingly, it all began with America.

CHAPTER 2

ABANDONING AMERICA FOR RUSSIA

The Chinese term for America, Mei Guo (美国), translates to "beautiful country." In the last years of the Qing Dynasty (1644–1911), many Chinese were already very familiar with America and viewed it as unique among Western nations.

Unsurprisingly, the U.S.–China relationship began with trade—a relationship that has evolved over centuries into perhaps the most consequential in the world today.

In March 1783, the American merchant ship *Empress of China* set sail carrying American ginseng and a trade delegation bound for China. Aware of the importance of the mission, the owners wrote formal instructions to its captain, John Green: "It is earnestly recommended to you as well on board as on Shore to cultivate the good will & friendship of all those with whom you may have dealing or Connections. You will probably be the first who shall display the American Flag in those distant regions, and a regard to your own personal honor will induce you to render it respectable by integrity and benevolence in all your conduct and dealings." The ship arrived back in New York on May 11, 1785, filled with tea, silks, fine china, and gunpowder, returning a 25 percent profit. The U.S. government was pleased by the success of the voyage. In 1786, the United States sent its first diplomatic representative to China.[1]

From the outset, the United States set itself apart from imperial powers like Britain, France, Russia, and Japan, which waged wars against China and seized its territory. To offset its trade deficit, Britain flooded China with opium, triggering the Opium Wars and resulting in unequal treaties that ceded Hong Kong and opened treaty ports. France later joined Britain in the Second Opium War, further eroding China's sovereignty.

Russia and Japan inflicted the greatest harm on China through repeated acts of aggression. Between 1858 and 1860, the Qing court was forced to cede more than a million square kilometers of land to Tsarist Russia. In 1904, Russia and Japan fought a war on Chinese soil, ending in Russia's defeat. Japan later occupied Manchuria in 1931 and launched a full-scale invasion of China in 1937.

These foreign aggressions fueled a surge of anti-foreign imperialist sentiment, which was manipulated by the Qing rulers. In 1900, that hostility culminated in the Boxer Rebellion, a violent uprising that targeted foreigners—including businessmen and missionaries. After the rebellion was crushed by the Eight-Nation Alliance, which included the United States, the Qing government was forced to pay heavy indemnities.

The United States, however, stood apart by not keeping the indemnity. Instead, it reinvested the funds into initiatives aimed at helping China modernize. These efforts included the establishment of educational and medical institutions, such as Tsinghua University—now one of China's premier institutions. Additionally, the United States used part of the indemnity to fund scholarships for Chinese students to study in America. From 1909 to 1937, the Boxer Indemnity Scholarship Program supported approximately 1,300 Chinese students for study in the United States,[2] many of whom later played a crucial role in modernizing China.

This goodwill earned the gratitude and admiration of the Chinese people, who came to view the United States as a model to emulate and a symbol of progress and modernization.

No one, however, anticipated that, within a few short years, America's respected standing would be shattered by the actions of one of its own leaders.

A New Republic

Starting in the mid-1800s, American missionaries began pouring into China, and by the early 1900s they had established a substantial presence. While focusing on spreading the Gospel, they also sought to promote democratic ideals.

Among the prominent figures was Young John Allen (1836–1907), a missionary and journalist who arrived in China in 1859. In addition to his religious work, he founded *The Globe Magazine* and *Review of Times*, using them to introduce Western culture, political thought, and liberal values to Chinese readers. Allen also translated numerous Western books into Chinese, which were widely read by scholars and Qing officials, sparking reform debates. Influential figures, including Kang Youwei, credited his work as a key source of inspiration.[3] In 1875, Allen wrote an essay explaining concepts such as "democracy," "constitution," and "legislature" to help Chinese audiences grasp unfamiliar political ideas—while emphasizing he did not claim Western superiority.[4]

Through the works of Allen and others, Chinese intellectuals of the late Qing Dynasty greatly admired America and were familiar with its unique form of government and its standing among nations.

In 1902, the Shanghai Civilization Book Company published *Summary of the U.S. Constitution*, the first complete Chinese translation of the document as a standalone text. It was translated by Zhang Zongyuan (1877–unknown), a jurist and economist educated at the University of

California, who called the Constitution "the progenitor (or forefather) of constitutional law in all nations."[5]

In 1903, Zou Rong (1885–1905), a young revolutionary, published *The Revolutionary Army*, the most widely circulated revolutionary text of its time. It inspired future leaders such as Chiang Kai-shek. Zou envisioned a Chinese republic modeled on the U.S. Constitution and the spirit of the American Revolution, free from Manchu* rule and founded on American-style self-governance.

American-inspired ideas of representative democracy helped fuel the 1911 Revolution, also known as the Xinhai Revolution. On February 12, 1912, the Qing Dynasty was overthrown and the last emperor, Puyi—later portrayed in the Oscar-winning film *The Last Emperor*—was dethroned, ending China's dynastic rule and ushering in a new republic.

One should take note that within the new republic lay the seeds of American ideals and the seeds of Christianity, sown through decades of tireless work by devoted missionaries.

However, the republic's fragile beginning was quickly undermined. Sun Yat-sen (1866–1925), the revolutionary leader and first provisional president, was soon pressured to relinquish power to Yuan Shikai (1859–1916), a dominant warlord with control over the Beiyang Army. By securing the Qing emperor's abdication, Yuan positioned himself to claim the presidency—an act that sowed the divisions that would ultimately fracture the young republic.

Despite internal tensions, on May 2, 1913, the United States officially recognized the new Chinese republic—becoming one of the first major powers to do so. President Woodrow Wilson extended diplomatic recognition to the Republic of China (ROC), offering "a greeting of welcome to the new China thus entering into the family of nations."[6]

The newly formed republic, Asia's first, embarked on an ambitious

* An ethnic tribe from the northeastern region known as Manchuria that conquered China and established the Qing Dynasty, which lasted from 1616 to 1911.

experiment to transform the nation, modeled after the United States, based on the principle of separation of powers among the executive, legislative, and judicial branches.[7]

Although it lasted only until 1928, a total span of sixteen years, it displayed several key features of a republic despite significant shortcomings:

- Relatively fair and transparent elections (in 1918, more than 40 million participated in the election among a population of roughly 400 million)
- Multi-party system (within a short period, thirty-five active political parties emerged)
- A relatively independent judicial system
- Federal model of power distribution between central and local governments.[8]

Considering that China had been under dynastic rule for thousands of years, these achievements were anything but trivial. Indeed, they were monumental.

The vision of a genuine Republic of China, however, was quickly derailed. With less than four years as the president, Yuan betrayed the republic's democratic ideals by proclaiming himself emperor. Facing widespread opposition, Yuan was forced to abandon his imperial ambitions after just eighty-three days. But the damage was done: Yuan's actions severely undermined the legitimacy of the new government, known as the "Beiyang government," or "Beijing government." His death in 1916 further destabilized the regime.

Meanwhile, Sun Yat-sen, disillusioned and marginalized, retreated to the south in Guangzhou, where he eventually founded the Chinese Nationalist Party (Kuomintang or KMT) and began strategizing for the next revolution to overthrow the Beijing government and reclaim power.

Thus, the 1911 Revolution, which ended imperial rule and established the Republic of China, inadvertently set in motion a new revolution that would ultimately lead to its own demise.

Shattered Dreams

After World War I, the United States emerged as the world's leading power. At the Paris Peace Conference, where the postwar international order was being shaped, U.S. President Woodrow Wilson was held in high regard and captured global attention. "For a brief interval, Wilson stood alone for mankind...He was transfigured in the eyes of men. He ceased to be a common statesman; he became a Messiah."[9]

On January 8, 1918, President Wilson delivered his "Fourteen Points" speech to Congress, emphasizing self-determination, national sovereignty, and collective security. It was partly a response to Lenin's "Decree on Peace," issued two months earlier on November 8, 1917, which also called for peace based on self-determination and national sovereignty. Though both aimed to reshape the global order, their visions were rooted in opposing ideologies.

Wilson's advocacy for "self-determination" inspired many weaker and smaller nations around the world, including China. Many Chinese viewed Wilson as a champion of oppressed nations and peoples, and the Chinese media widely hailed his peace ideals as a beacon of light for the world.

On the eve of the 1919 Paris Peace Conference, the Chinese had high hopes. They expected President Wilson to support their bid to reclaim the Shandong Province and help secure China's equal standing among nations. The territory had been under German colonial control. With Germany defeated, China rightfully wanted it returned.

China's expectation was further validated by its wartime contribution. Between 1916 and 1918, China had contributed about 140,000 laborers—the largest non-European workforce—to the Allied war effort, performing vital tasks such as trench digging, repairs, and artillery assembly.[10]

On March 1, the Chinese Students' Alliance, representing about 1,400 Chinese students in the United States, presented a petition to President Wilson. They called him the "only great champion China has" and urged him to oppose Japan's claim over Chinese territory.[11]

On April 25, a petition from Sun Yat-sen's opposition government was forwarded to President Wilson, pressing him to denounce Japan's Twenty-One Demands on China. The petition emphasized that these demands were contrary to the spirit of Wilson's Fourteen Points, particularly the principle of self-determination.[12]

Wilson indeed tried to secure Shandong for China by making the case for China during the peace conference:

> For China, it is not only for economic reasons that they want to get rid of all foreign concession in Shandong. It is because the area evokes the most sacred and historic memories [as the birthplace of Confucius] that she is particularly keen to remove foreign influence...My sympathy is with China, and we should not forget that in the future, the greatest danger to the world could well arise in the Pacific region.[13]

However, Wilson ultimately succumbed to pressure from Allied Powers, which had prewar agreements with Japan and looked after their own colonial interests, agreeing to grant Shandong to Japan. His decision was largely driven by his desire to secure support from these influential powers for the League of Nations, which he considered his crowning diplomatic achievement. Wilson rationalized that the league would serve as a mechanism for global peace and enable the United States and other major powers to monitor, critique, and potentially regulate Sino-Japanese relations.[14] However, his vision inevitably proved to be mere wishful thinking.

Robert Lansing (1864–1928), Woodrow Wilson's secretary of state, foresaw the potential dangers of the principle of self-determination.

He argued that its indiscriminate application could incite unrest and rebellion among colonized and minority populations, potentially destabilizing established governments. Lansing famously warned, "The phrase is simply loaded with dynamite. It will raise hopes which can never be realized."[15]

After Wilson yielded to his own lofty idealism, Lansing wrote in his diary: "China has been abandoned to Japanese rapacity...I am heartsick over it, because I see how much good-will and regard the President is bound to lose. I can offer no adequate explanation to the critics. There seems to be none." Lansing pledged to the Chinese delegates that he would do everything in his power to rectify the "great wrong" that had been committed. However, he was ultimately powerless to act.[16]

Paul Samuel Reinsch (1869–1923), a U.S. minister to China appointed by Wilson, reported from Beijing that people were "deeply depressed" and felt "utterly helpless." Chinese officials, expressing disbelief, told him that they did not see how China could affix its signature to a treaty that sanctioned such an outrage. Reinsch, who had worked hard to build Chinese goodwill toward the United States during his tenure in Beijing, now saw his efforts collapse. Disheartened, he resigned soon after, in the form of a long, bitter letter to the president.[17]

The Chinese response was even more fervent and impassioned. As a victorious nation, they felt China was treated like a defeated country at the Paris Peace Conference. When this devastating news reached China, the goodwill that the Chinese had had toward the United States since the late Qing Dynasty instantly vanished. This goodwill had been built through the efforts of thousands of American missionaries over several generations and by the U.S. government itself. Wilson's actions quickly transformed the Chinese people's admiration for him and the America he represented into deep resentment.

Chinese youth, students, and intellectuals, who had long been immersed in American progress and optimism, developed an unprecedented despair and outrage toward the West as represented by the United States.

The disillusionment of American-educated Chinese intellectuals was clear at the Paris Peace Conference. Wellington Koo, a Columbia-trained lawyer and China's chief negotiator, was disappointed that Wilson's Fourteen Points were barely discussed. Wang Zhengting, a Yale-educated expert in international law and fellow delegate, saw only one path forward: "No hope now for China, save in revolution."[18]

On July 25, immediately after the Paris Peace Conference concluded, Moscow issued the "Karakhan Manifesto," authored by the Soviet deputy commissioner for foreign affairs Lev Karakhan. As a direct response to the Shandong Resolution, the manifesto declared the Soviet government's intent to relinquish all unequal treaties previously signed by the tsarist regime.[19]

This action underscored the warning issued by Joseph P. Tumulty, President Wilson's private secretary: "If the statesmanship at Versailles cannot settle these things [disputes between nations] in the spirit of justice, Bolshevism will settle them in a spirit of injustice."[20]

As Wilson became the rapidly setting sun, Lenin emerged as the rising dawn. The failure of the Paris Peace Conference marked a turning point for China, shifting it from looking to the United States as a model to embracing Soviet Russia as the alternative.

From 1917 to 1919, most Chinese intellectuals were more familiar with Wilson than Lenin, and Wilson's rhetoric had a far greater influence on them than the revolutionary discourse in Russia. When Wilson's promises unraveled in the summer of 1919, Chinese nationalists began to seriously consider Bolshevism as an alternative solution for resisting imperialism and achieving China's rise.

In short, Wilson lost China to Lenin.

The May Fourth Movement

After the Paris Peace Conference, Wilson returned to the United States in triumph, unaware that a disaster had been set in motion—he had opened

Pandora's box. China shifted from being pro-America to anti-America, allowing Soviet Russia to take advantage of the situation. A red tide was poised to sweep across China.

China's humiliation at the Paris Peace Conference quickly triggered large-scale protests. On May 4, 1919, thousands of enraged students from thirteen universities, led by those from Beijing University, gathered at Tiananmen Square to protest the Shandong Resolution. That afternoon, protesters sent their representative to march to the American embassy to deliver their condemnation letter. They then marched north to the residence of Cao Rulin, a senior Beijing government official responsible for handling foreign affairs. After a rampage, they set his house on fire. The police exercised considerable restraint, arresting thirty-two students, who were released shortly after.[21]

The protest rapidly escalated into a nationwide movement, spreading like wildfire across the country and becoming known as the May Fourth Movement.

Many future Communist leaders were key figures in the movement. Chen Duxiu (1879–1942), a professor at Beijing University, dean of the faculty of arts, and the future CCP's founder and first general secretary, was briefly arrested for distributing pamphlets on the streets. Mao Zedong (1893–1976), the future leader of Communist China, condemned Wilson and other Western leaders as liars in an article published in *Xiangjiang Review*, a small magazine he founded following the May Fourth Movement. In the same piece, he expressed his interest in the theories of the Russian Bolsheviks. In Tianjin, Zhou Enlai (1898–1976), the future premier of China, led student activism in Tianjin where he established the progressive youth organization Awakening Society and founded the magazine *Awakening* to promote anti-imperialist and anti-regime ideas. As a student leader, he was arrested and spent 180 days in prison.[22] Liu Shaoqi (1898–1969), future president of China, participated in demonstrations and petition activities at Tiananmen Square.[23]

The May Fourth Movement of 1919 holds a unique place in modern Chinese history, marking the beginning of new social and political developments. This movement did not arise in a vacuum—it was preceded by the New Culture Movement, which began in 1915 as a campaign akin to the European Enlightenment, aimed at introducing science and democracy into China.

In the aftermath of the May Fourth Movement, the surge of nationalism soon gave way to Marxism and Leninism, as intellectual leaders concluded that saving the nation required mass mobilization, propaganda, organization, and revolutionary discipline. This shift gave rise to anti-liberal and anti-individualist currents, laying the groundwork for the totalitarian regime that would emerge in the decades to follow.

Chinese historian Li Zehou insightfully summarized this transformation, noting that the pursuit of national salvation ultimately overshadowed the quest for enlightenment.[24]

The Chinese Communist Party has since memorialized the May Fourth Movement as Youth Day, making it the only student protest movement it celebrates—and it's easy to see why.

The Beijing Government's Struggle for Legitimacy

Another consequence of the Paris Peace Conference was the breakdown of peace talks between the Beijing government and the insurgent government in Guangzhou. A better outcome for China might have strengthened Beijing's position and forced Sun Yat-sen to compromise. Instead, the Shandong Resolution badly damaged Beijing's legitimacy, despite it being the only Chinese government recognized by the United States and other Western powers. Although Beijing refused to sign the treaty amid public outrage, it was still widely viewed as corrupt and ineffective—accused of betraying the nation and giving Guangzhou further reason to resist.

In 1921, the Beijing government sent a delegation to the Washington Naval Conference, where major powers met to discuss naval disarmament and tensions in East Asia. To show unity, Beijing invited the Guangzhou government to join, but Guangzhou refused, citing Beijing's lack of legitimacy in the eyes of the Chinese people.[25]

Although the conference secured the return of Qingdao City in Shandong Province to China on more favorable terms, the gesture came too late. Anti-American sentiment—ignited by the May Fourth Movement—had already taken hold. Communist groups, the precursors to the Chinese Communist Party, actively fueled this resentment to sustain and deepen public hostility.

After 1919, political mobilization and mass protests became increasingly common, further weakening the already fragile Beijing government. It lost public support and faced criticism no matter its actions—a classic case of "damned if you do, damned if you don't." This unrest foreshadowed the internal conflicts that would engulf China through the 1920s to the 1940s.

This historical fact is seldom acknowledged by either the Nationalists or the Communists. In reality, the Beijing government at the time was one of the most democratic, tolerant, moderate, and free systems of governance in Chinese history—more so than Chiang Kai-shek's authoritarian regime (excluding modern democratic Taiwan) and unquestionably more so than the Communist regime that followed.

However, the Beijing government's future was now severely dimmed. It would manage to survive for just over eight more years until 1928, when it was overthrown.

One could say that Wilson singlehandedly crushed China's hope for a republic.

Founding of the Chinese Communist Party

In modern Chinese history, Tsarist Russia stands out among imperial powers as the one that seized the most Chinese territory, inflicting immense suffering through its military aggressions. However, the Karakhan Manifesto, which pledged to abolish all Russian privileges acquired under the tsarist regime, positioned Soviet Russia as a champion against Western imperialist powers in the minds of the Chinese people.

This was the first Big Lie the Chinese people heard from the Communists. Tragically, it was only the beginning. More lies would follow, each one drawing the Chinese people deeper into the trap laid for them.

The lie worked. Admiration and gratitude toward Soviet Russia grew, prompting many Chinese to call for the Beijing government to establish diplomatic ties with the Soviet regime, envisioning future cooperation against imperialist oppression.[26]

Unbeknownst to most hopeful Chinese, this path would prove perilous. At the Second Congress of the Communist International, known as Comintern, in 1920, Lenin outlined a global strategy for poor nations like China: use anti-imperialism and nationalism as tools to ignite Communist revolutions, while subordinating local struggles to the broader Soviet agenda. Behind its talk of liberation, Lenin's vision turned these nations into tools of Soviet imperialism to serve Moscow's goals and agendas.

Just a few years earlier, most Chinese had never even heard of Marxism. It entered China alongside a wide array of Western ideas, philosophies, and ideologies during the New Culture Movement. Initially, Marxism struggled to gain traction, as the ideals of democracy and science—affectionately called "Mr. De" and "Mr. Sci"—dominated the intellectual discourse of the time.

Mao later succinctly put it as follows:

> It was through the Russians that the Chinese found Marxism. Before the October Revolution, the Chinese were not only ignorant of Lenin and Stalin, they did not even know of Marx and Engels. The salvoes of the October Revolution brought us Marxism-Leninism. The October Revolution helped progressives in China, as throughout the world, to adopt the proletarian world outlook as the instrument for studying a nation's destiny and considering anew their own problems. Follow the path of the Russians—that

> was their conclusion. In 1919, the May 4th Movement took place in China. In 1921, the Communist Party of China was founded.[27]

This is something I've been trying to warn the American people about: Communism is globalism, or, perhaps better phrased for today's reader, globalism is Communism. At its core, Soviet imperialism was simply Communist globalism by another name—an ideology engineered to spread, dominate, and remake the world on its own terms.

In the spring of 1920, the Comintern sent Grigori Voitinsky (1893–1953) to China to connect with key leftist intellectuals like Chen Duxiu and Li Dazhao (1889–1927). His mission was to establish the Comintern China Branch and lay the groundwork for the Chinese Communist Party. Under his guidance, the Shanghai Communist Group was formed, with other groups soon emerging in Beijing and major cities. Voitinsky is widely regarded as the "architect of the party" for his pivotal role in organizing the CCP's founding structure.[28]

In June 1921, another Comintern agent, Henk Sneevliet, also known by his pseudonym Maring, arrived in Shanghai under the guise of being a journalist to help expedite the formal establishment of the Chinese Communist Party.

On July 23, the First National Congress was held secretly in Shanghai, formally declaring the founding of the Chinese Communist Party, with Chen Duxiu as the party's general secretary.

The congress was convened so hastily that only thirteen participants could attend, including Mao Zedong, while key leaders Chen Duxiu and Li Dazhao were absent. Bao Huiseng, who represented Chen, later wrote that the congress's planning and funding were entirely orchestrated by Maring.[29] Travel expenses were fully covered: Delegates from Shanghai received 100 yuan, while those from outside were given 1,000 yuan.[30] For context, just three years earlier, Mao had earned only 8 yuan a month as a library assistant at Beijing University—making these subsidies remarkably generous.

In addition to outlining revolutionary principles and goals, the congress passed a resolution requiring the Party Central Committee to report to the Comintern on a daily basis. In its first year, the Chinese Communist Party operated on a budget of 17,000 silver dollars—an astonishing 94 percent of which was funded by the Comintern.[31]

This is the origin of the Chinese Communist Party: created, funded, and controlled by Soviet Russia, with the mission of seizing China through a Communist revolution.

What was the American response to this significant development? My research reveals no documented reaction from the United States, indicating that Americans were likely oblivious to this event unfolding in China.

At its founding, the CCP had only fifty members—all educated elites and leaders of the May Fourth Movement—confirming the pattern that radical mass movements often begin with a small group of radicalized intellectuals.

From its humble beginnings, the CCP would rapidly grow. In just twenty-eight years, it would seize power and establish a totalitarian state that continues to rule over China to this day, and rose to become a global power—ultimately becoming the foremost threat to the United States. As the ancient Chinese sage Zhuangzi once said, "The beginning is simple, but the end is immense."

The Anti-Christian Movement (1922–1927)

Immediately after its founding, the CCP, under the direction of the Soviet Comintern, launched its first major campaign: the Anti-Christian Movement. The reason was simple: They feared the seeds of American ideals and Christianity that had been sown in the republic might take root. Their goal was to stamp them out before they could grow—and replace them with Marxism.

Under the guise of nationalism, the CCP targeted Christian missionaries and organizations, with the goal to weaken Christianity in China, undermine American and Western influence, mobilize nationalist sentiment, and advance the Communist agendas.

The campaign began with large-scale campus protests opposing a major Christian event at Tsinghua University—the Eleventh Conference of the World Student Christian Federation of 1922, a high-profile gathering of the global Christian community.

Another major goal of the Anti-Christian Movement was to infiltrate and weaken influential Christian organizations like the YMCA and the YWCA, founded in China in 1870 and 1899, respectively. While publicly denouncing these groups, the CCP privately recruited their members. By the early 1930s, YMCA leaders admitted to losing idealistic youth to the Communists, attributing it to the powerful appeal of Communism's clear and radical promises.

A key component of the Anti-Christian Movement was the Educational Rights Movement. At the time, Christian missionaries operated an extensive network of schools in China, including 265 secondary schools across nineteen provinces and sixteen prominent universities, far surpassing the number of China's public universities.[32] The movement demanded these institutions be secularized and aligned with Chinese national education objectives. In plain terms, they set out to drive God out of Christian education—a tactic mirrored by American Marxists, who have worked to purge public education of faith and morality under the banner of "separation of church and state."

The Educational Rights Movement led to the 1927 Organization Law of the Academia Sinica, requiring Chinese management of church-affiliated schools and prohibiting religious activities, enforcing conformity to state-defined educational standards.

The Anti-Christian Movement, widely perceived by ordinary Chinese as a continuation of the patriotic May Fourth Movement, gained broad popular support. It soon expanded to include workers and urban residents targeting foreign businesses, further fueling anti-foreign sentiment and accelerating the campaign.

The movement clearly demonstrated the CCP's particular hostility toward Christianity above all other religions. From its inception, the CCP has consistently viewed Christianity, capitalism, and the United States as a unified "trinity" of enemies.

Once again, the United States seemed unaware that these seemingly organic nationalist student movements were in fact orchestrated by the Communists as part of a broader ideological and revolutionary strategy. The tactic—learned from the party's Russian masters—of mobilizing students and youth for political purposes would be used repeatedly by the CCP in its quest for power. It remains a favored tool of Communists everywhere, including in the United States today.

Turning to Russia

By 1921, three major political forces had emerged in China: the Beijing government, the Chinese Nationalist Party and its Guangzhou government, and an emerging newcomer, the Chinese Communist Party, although still in its infancy.

It is important to note that the Guangzhou KMT government was not much more popular than the Beijing government. The Beijing government was entangled in internal conflicts among northern warlord factions, while Sun Yat-sen's KMT government in the South depended on the backing of southwestern regional warlords. This lack of popular and stable governance created an opportunity for the Chinese Communist Party to expand its mass base by rallying support under the guise of nationalism.

The CCP and the KMT were rivals from the outset. Although both called themselves revolutionaries, they drew support from distinct social bases.

The Communists, though led by progressive elites, primarily recruited poor peasants and radicalized intellectuals. In contrast, the Nationalists drew support from the middle and upper classes in both urban and rural areas, as well as from intellectuals who favored gradual, evolutionary reforms to address China's challenges. While the Communists embraced a Bolshevik-style violent revolution, the Nationalists pursued a path of more moderate, incremental change.

The parallels should be obvious to American readers. The Communist Party's base was made up of ideologically driven intellectuals and the so-called oppressed classes—the equivalent of well-educated white liberals and marginalized groups in today's America. While these divisions were unfolding within China, American policymakers faced a critical choice: whether to support the North, represented by the Beijing government, or the South, led by Sun Yat-sen's Guangzhou government. At this stage, the infant CCP was not yet part of the equation.

The Beijing government held control over several provinces, and other semi-autonomous provinces recognized it as the legitimate central authority. Centered in Beijing, where the national parliament resided, it garnered recognition from most Western countries. In contrast, Sun Yat-sen's Guangzhou regime controlled only portions of Guangdong Province, maintained an alliance with Guangxi warlords, and lacked sufficient foreign recognition as a legitimate government. In truth, it is a stretch to even call it a government.

Believing himself the rightful heir to the 1911 Revolution and legitimate president of the republic, Sun Yat-sen and his Nationalist Party vowed to overthrow the Beijing government through a military campaign known as the Northern Expedition. Sun aimed to unify China by defeating what he termed "a group of warlords."

But Sun faced a critical obstacle: He had neither the funds nor the troops to carry out his plan, making foreign backing essential.

Faced with the choice between Beijing and Guangzhou, the United States rejected Sun Yat-sen and refused to recognize his southern government, repeatedly turning down his attempts to establish diplomatic relations. Most U.S. officials involved in Chinese affairs viewed Sun unfavorably, dismissing his Guangzhou regime as a "red regime,"[33] aligned too closely with revolutionary elements.

Sun Yat-sen was not a strict Communist; he would best be described as a chameleon-like realist who could continuously shift his ideology in order to maintain power. His "Three Principles of the People"—summarized as nationalism, democracy, and the people's livelihood—reflected a blend of ideals. The third principle, emphasizing social welfare, had socialist undertones, particularly in his land policy of "land to the tillers." This policy, which aimed to redistribute land to those who worked it, was later adapted by the CCP as a key slogan for its bloody land reform.

It was understandable for American policymakers to withhold recognition of Sun Yat-sen and his separatist "red government." Their true misstep, however, lay in failing to actively support the Beijing government and recognize the profound threat posed by Communism and Soviet Russia. Although the Beijing government was controlled by increasingly weaker warlords, making them far from ideal allies for the United States, these warlords had one important positive: They were generally anti-Soviet Russia and anti-Communism.

Later U.S. presidents would face similar choices. Tragically, most chose poorly—failing to grasp the true nature and threat of Communism. In 1922, after being rebuffed by the United States, Britain, and Japan, Sun Yat-sen turned to Soviet Russia for support, formally forging an alliance and increasingly incorporating elements of its ideology. Just as Wilson's betrayal contributed to the founding of the Chinese Communist Party, it also drove Sun into the arms of the Soviets. "We no longer look to the Western Powers. Our faces are turned toward Russia," Sun told a YMCA audience in 1923.[34]

The alliance enabled Sun Yat-sen to secure a steady flow of funds, weapons, and advisors. From the outset, Soviet Russia was steadfast in its efforts to bring China under its influence, supplying money, personnel, and arms to forces intent on overthrowing the Beijing government. The first Soviet envoys to China, lacking cash, arrived with large bags of gold and jewelry looted from the Russian royal family and nobility, which they exchanged for silver dollars in Shanghai to finance anti-government efforts.[35]

In stark contrast, the Beijing government received no support—not even a token statement—from the United States or other Western nations.

Had the United States invested as much in supporting the Beijing government as the Soviets did in backing Sun's Guangzhou regime—especially considering America's vastly superior economic strength compared to the war-ravaged Soviet Union at the time—the Beijing government might have stood a chance of survival.

This pivotal development in China unfolded during a period of U.S. isolationism. American indifference toward both the Beijing government and Sun Yat-sen enabled Soviet Russia to shape and control the trajectory of China's future. Isolationism—now reemerging in today's America—can come at great cost, especially when it means overlooking the threat of Communism. This critical historical lesson must not be ignored.

The First United Front

Sun's alliance with Soviet Russia came with conditions: He was required to adopt the guiding principle of "allying with Russia and accommodating the Communists," or *lian e rong gong* (联俄容共). This allowed the small and weak Chinese Communist Party to infiltrate the KMT, leveraging its resources and political influence to gain strength—a parasitic arrangement that almost proved fatal to the host.

By late 1922, under the directives of the Comintern, top CCP leaders such as Chen Duxiu and Li Dazhao joined the KMT as individuals. Mao Zedong did the same, eventually holding various leadership positions, including Acting Minister of the KMT Central Propaganda Department.[36]

The following year, the CCP officially required all its members to integrate into the KMT. While the CCP maintained full awareness of its members' identities, the KMT was largely kept in the dark, aside from recognizing a few prominent CCP figures. This lack of transparency made it challenging for the KMT to identify and address potential internal threats.

The United Front alliance between the CCP and the KMT marked the inception of the CCP's United Front strategy. This approach—forming coalitions even with ideological adversaries—has proven extraordinarily effective. By infiltrating organizations and exerting influence from within, the CCP aimed to gradually reshape institutions, political parties, and public narratives to align with its goals, all while maintaining an outward appearance of cooperation. Over the years, the CCP has skillfully refined these tactics which remain highly relevant today, especially for America, as this book will reveal.

In 1923, the Comintern dispatched Mikhail Borodin (1884–1951) as the permanent representative to Guangzhou to oversee KMT affairs. Borodin became Sun Yat-sen's political advisor and gradually earned his trust. From the outset of his time in Guangzhou, Borodin repeatedly proved that the Russians could deliver. Consequently, Sun grew to trust Borodin more than he did the Bolsheviks as a whole.[37] This close relationship afforded Borodin significant access to and influence over the internal operations of the KMT, with the ultimate goal of transforming it into a Leninist-style party.

In the same year, Sun Yat-sen sent his most trusted disciple, Chiang Kai-shek, to lead a delegation to the Soviet Union to study military, political, and party affairs and to negotiate Soviet aid. Chiang's time in Russia had a profound impact on him. For more than three months, he was welcomed by prominent leaders like Stalin and Trotsky, and toured Soviet factories, farms, military units, and schools. Although initially impressed, Chiang's perspective shifted as he came to better understand Soviet "internationalism" and that the Communist call for world revolution was simply Soviet imperialism under a different name.[38] He began to question Communist ideology and view Soviet Russia as a new imperialist force that posed a threat to China's independence and stability, marking the start of his lifelong journey as an anti-Communist. This demonstrated his remarkable ability to see beyond the propaganda that deceived so many others, including Americans, and to grasp the true nature of Communism.

In 1924, the Whampoa (or Huangpu) Military Academy was established with Russian assistance to train KMT military officers in preparation for the Northern Expedition. Its funding, weapons, teaching materials, and military advisors all came from the Soviet Union.[39]

Modeled after Soviet institutions, the academy included both military and political instructors. Unsurprisingly, most of the political instructors were Communists, with Zhou Enlai as their director, while Chiang Kai-shek served as the academy's superintendent. The Whampoa Military Academy played a pivotal role in training future military leaders for both the KMT and the CCP. Notably, five of the CCP's future ten marshals were graduates of the academy.

Some KMT members opposed the policy of accommodating the Communists, submitting a report to Sun Yat-sen that recommended impeaching Communist leaders. The report stated: "Chen Duxiu and others have joined the CCP in a systematic and organized manner... Their primary goal is to inject the spirit of the CCP into the body of the KMT."[40] Sun dismissed this suggestion and expelled the dissenting members from the party.[41]

On March 25, 1925, Sun Yat-sen passed away. Over the next year, Chiang Kai-shek, who held military power, defeated other rivals and became Sun Yat-sen's successor and the leader of the Kuomintang. Initially, both the Soviets and the CCP viewed Chiang as a cooperative leftist KMT member. They soon realized they were mistaken.

Resistance grew among conservative factions within the KMT, who became increasingly alarmed by CCP infiltration and the perceived threat it posed. Opposed to the Soviets and the KMT-CCP alliance, these conservatives convened in 1925 and passed resolutions proposing to revoke the party membership of Communist members within the KMT, expel them, and dismiss Borodin from his advisory role.[42] However, they would have to wait another two years before they could put these measures into action.

Collapse of the First United Front

In 1926, the KMT, under Chiang Kai-shek's leadership, launched the Northern Expedition from Guangzhou, aiming to dismantle the Beijing government, defeat regional warlords, and unify China. Backed by Soviet funding, arms, and military advisors, the campaign advanced steadily northward.

During the Northern Expedition, the CCP, operating under the umbrella of the KMT-led campaign, orchestrated strikes and uprisings in cities, attacks on foreign interests and missionaries, and agrarian revolutions in rural areas. These actions triggered widespread discontent within the Northern Expedition army. Many soldiers and officers, who came from landlord families, were deeply demoralized as they saw their own families being attacked, their lands and properties confiscated, and their loved ones killed—all while they were fighting to unify China against the warlords.

In March 1927, the Northern Expedition army captured the city of Nanjing. During the takeover, some soldiers attacked the British, American, and Japanese consulates; looted; and assaulted Western missionaries, killing six—including John Elias Williams, an American serving as vice president of Nanjing University. The KMT accused CCP members within the army of deliberately inciting violence to damage the Nationalist government's relations with Western powers.

All these marked CCP's earliest strikes as the parasite to weaken its host, the KMT, by eroding its reputation and sowing division within its ranks and among its supporters.

By early 1927, the KMT had been nearly hollowed out. Approximately one-third of its leadership were Communists, while another one-third consisted of left-leaning KMT members, often referred to as "Communist-lite."[43] By this stage, the Nationalist government had effectively fallen under the full control of Soviet advisors and the CCP, making a Communist takeover of the KMT appear imminent.

At the same time, Communist-backed peasant violence against the landowning class and endless factory workers' strikes in urban areas foreshadowed a nationwide Communist revolution.

By now, many Americans should be able to recognize the same tactics playing out within legitimate movements in the United States today.

Finally, enough was enough. As Communist subversion escalated, Chiang Kai-shek decided to act. On April 12, 1927, he launched a sweeping purge—arresting and executing thousands of suspected CCP members, expelling Soviet advisor Mikhail Borodin, and severing ties with Soviet Russia.

This crackdown abruptly halted the radical workers' and peasants' movements, as well as the anti-Christian movement—exposing the true agitators behind these upheavals.

The First United Front between the KMT and CCP was officially dismantled, marking a definitive break in their alliance.

In 1928, the Northern Expedition forces entered Beijing, effectively dissolving the Beijing government, reuniting the Republic of China, and establishing Nanjing as the new capital.

Despite the Nanjing government's claim to represent the legitimate Republic of China founded in 1912, the republic soon became a diminished version of its former self. Under KMT rule, parliament and the constitution were abolished, and the separation of powers that had defined the early republic was dismantled. In their place, the regime adopted authoritarian characteristics typical of a one-party state system.

Though unification was nominally achieved, the reality was far more complex. With the Beijing government eliminated, the battle for

China's future shifted to a contest between the Nationalists and the Communists—who, having gained strength and confidence through the First United Front, were now a far more formidable force.

This chapter may feel dense with historical events—but that is inevitable, as it spans over a century of pivotal moments. It begins in 1783 with the voyage of the American merchant ship *Empress of China*, moves through the founding of the Republic of China and the rise of the Chinese Communist Party, and culminates in 1927, when Chiang Kai-shek launched his purge and reclaimed the republic—marking the beginning of a long and bitter struggle between the Nationalists and the Communists for China's future.

These historic threads reveal how the promising seeds of a democratic republic—sown by generations of American missionaries—were strangled by the false promises of Communism. This outcome was not inevitable; it was shaped, in part, by a series of disastrous choices made by the United States. While the missionaries believed China was worth saving, U.S. policymakers showed far less concern for its fate. That indifference contributed to America's failure to grasp the threat posed by the Soviet Union and the expansionist nature of Communism.

If the United States truly made a mistake in "losing China," these were the first steps taken toward that error.

CHAPTER 3

"OLD FRIENDS OF THE CHINESE PEOPLE"

In the years following the purge, Chiang Kai-shek launched a series of successful military campaigns to root out the CCP, ultimately reducing it to a scattered band of insurgents hiding in remote mountainous regions. By then, most Chinese believed the Communists had been effectively eliminated—and to the outside world, they had all but disappeared.

That was about to change—thanks to progressive American writers and journalists. Their work thrust the Chinese Communists into the spotlight, capturing the attention of both the Western world and Chinese society. Through sympathetic portrayals, they cast the CCP in a favorable light and helped raise the "Red Star over China."

These Americans played a crucial role in advancing the CCP's cause. The party honored them as "Old Friends of the Chinese People"—a term often used as code for "useful idiots."

This chapter highlights notable Americans from the CCP's early pantheon of "Old Friends," whose contributions were instrumental in propagating the party's narrative.

But first, let's rewind to late 1928 and the years that followed to understand the events that set the stage for these Americans to become involved.

Republic Not Restored

After overthrowing the Beijing government, Chiang Kai-shek consolidated power and declared Nanjing the new capital. With the republic seemingly restored, China appeared to be on a hopeful path. The new regime looked to the West—especially the United States—for recognition and support, but its hope was soon dampened.

Politically, Washington showed little interest. It wasn't until 1935—seven years later—that the United States upgraded its legation in China to an embassy. Without meaningful diplomatic presence, there was little pressure on Chiang to stay the course set by the Republic. U.S. officials underestimated China's strategic importance and overlooked Soviet expansion in the region. Even George Kennan, an American diplomat and historian who later shaped Cold War policy, believed that China was too poor and too weak to warrant significant U.S. attention.[1]

Militarily, the United States was even less inclined to help modernize China's army against Communists, warlords, and Japan. Desperate for support, Chiang turned to Weimar Germany. From 1928 to 1936, before Germany allied with Japan, Chiang built his closest foreign ties with Berlin. German advisors helped reorganize his army and served as key political and military consultants.

During this critical window, the United States missed a historic opportunity to support a fledgling republic in East Asia.

Furthermore, Chiang's government became increasingly influenced by militarism starting in late 1928, originating with the German military advisory mission. Colonel Max Bauer, who headed the mission from 1928 to 1929, had strong connections with Hitler and the Nazi movement in Germany. Many of the mission's members were chosen in part because they shared Bauer's political leanings. This influence pushed the Nanjing government toward a military dictatorship, steering it away from democracy.[2]

The Long March

Although the Communists had been temporarily defeated after their failed uprisings in the wake of Chiang's purge, they were far from being eradicated. Out of sight but never out of mind, they continued to be a constant source of concern for Chiang Kai-shek.

Meanwhile, things looked even grimmer for the Communists—purged, defeated, driven to remote mountains, and tightly blockaded. Yet they remained determined to recover and rebuild. After retreating to the Jinggang Mountains on the border of Jiangxi and Hunan Provinces in the south, they began reconstructing their movement by creating and expanding their base, establishing the so-called Central Soviet Area, which they declared as the Chinese Soviet Republic as an oppositional government, and forming the Red Army, the precursor to the People's Liberation Army.

In Communist mythology, the Jinggang Mountains are revered as the sacred birthplace of the Chinese Communist Revolution. In reality, however, the Red Army was poorly trained and equipped, branded by the KMT as mere "red bandits." Despite these challenges, Mao remained steadfast, famously declaring, "A single spark can start a prairie fire."

Chiang Kai-shek was resolute in his vow to extinguish that "prairie fire" before it could spread further. Beginning in 1933, the Nanjing government initiated several encirclement campaigns against the Central Soviet Area.*

The first four campaigns failed as a result of various factors, including poor military performance against the CCP's guerrilla tactics and

*An encirclement campaign is a military operation designed to isolate and surround the enemy forces, restricting their mobility and cutting off their access to resources or reinforcements.

the rebellions of other regional warlords. In response, Chiang Kai-shek turned to his German advisors and officers, who proposed a strategy of surrounding the Soviet areas, involving the construction of blockhouses to gradually strangle and then crush the opposition with a massive offensive.[3] This strategy worked successfully in the fifth encirclement campaign.

By 1934, Chiang had captured Ruijin, the capital of the Chinese Soviet Republic, forcing the Red Army to retreat toward the remote, impoverished regions of the southwest. Chiang Kai-shek deliberately allowed the Red Army to continue fleeing into the southwest, with his loyal Central Army trailing them. His strategy was to let the Red Army and the regional warlords weaken each other through mutual conflict, positioning himself to seize control once both sides were exhausted. However, this tactic ultimately failed, inadvertently providing the Communist Party with a crucial lifeline.

The retreat is known as the "Westward Flight" by the KMT and the "Long March" by the CCP. The Long March covered approximately 6,000 miles across some of the most treacherous terrain in China—snowcapped mountains, swollen rivers, and marshlands. Along the way, strategic errors in command by the Comintern advisor Otto Braun, known in China as Li De, led to heavy losses for the Red Army.

In response, the Chinese Communist Party convened a high-level military conference in Zunyi, Guizhou—a province in southwest China—where military leadership was transferred to Mao Zedong, and the decision was made to head northwest to a remote town called Yan'an. Yan'an was chosen because it was home to an existing Communist base and lay closer to the Soviet border, facilitating potential support from Moscow.

The Zunyi Conference was a pivotal event in CCP history, which marked Mao's victory over the Comintern faction. While the Comintern prioritized urban proletarian revolution, Mao advocated a rural-focused strategy centered on peasants and guerrilla warfare, leading to a shift toward a uniquely Chinese Communist ideology and solidifying his leadership.

In 1935, after a year-long journey, the Red Army eventually reached the remote and desolate town of Yan'an in northern Shaanxi, and there made its new stronghold. Of the roughly 85,000 troops who began the march, no more than 15,000 survived the journey.[4]

The Second United Front

By the time the Communists arrived in Yan'an, China had already endured five years of Japanese aggression. In 1931, Japan launched a swift invasion, capturing the entire northeastern region of Manchuria and establishing the puppet state of Manchukuo, with the former Qing emperor Puyi installed as its figurehead ruler. This event later inspired the term "Manchurian candidate," symbolizing a politician controlled by a foreign adversary. At the time, it was generally perceived that Japan's further expansion into mainland China was imminent.

Anti-Japanese sentiment surged across China, along with growing public discontent and demands for the Chiang government to take decisive action against Japan. This provided the CCP with a perfect opportunity to rebrand itself as the champion of resistance against Japan.

Chiang Kai-shek faced immense challenges on both external and internal fronts. Externally, the Japanese military posed a devastating threat, wielding overwhelming power that made direct confrontation suicidal—any full-scale engagement risked the total destruction of his forces. Internally, the Chinese Communists—though weaker than the KMT—remained a determined force intent on undermining his rule. Together, these dual pressures placed enormous strain on Chiang's government and military resources.

Chiang came to believe that the top priority was eliminating the Communist insurgency and restoring national strength. Without achieving these goals, he argued, China could neither effectively resist foreign invasion nor achieve national unification.

Had the Nationalist army continued its pursuit, the remaining Communist forces in Yan'an might have been completely destroyed.

However, one incident completely altered the course of history.

In 1936, Chiang Kai-shek traveled to Xi'an—an ancient city just south of Yan'an, and my birthplace, from which my name Xi is derived. Chiang went there to oversee anti-Communist operations and pressured his general, Zhang Xueliang (1901–2001), to intensify the campaign against the Communists. In response, Zhang, along with another general, staged a military coup by detaining Chiang, known in history as the Xi'an Incident.

There has always been some mystery surrounding the Xi'an Incident, although the most common explanation is that General Zhang was resentful about being tasked with fighting the Communists while his ancestral homeland of Manchuria remained under Japanese occupation. Others believed that Zhang had been subverted by the CCP and the Soviet Union. Regardless of his motivations, Zhang's actions against Chiang resonated with the growing dissatisfaction among the public toward Chiang Kai-shek's failure to address the Japanese threat.

As a hostage during the Xi'an Incident, Chiang Kai-shek was forced to halt his military campaign against the Communists and instead redirect his focus toward resisting the Japanese invasion. Under intense pressure, he was compelled to agree to an alliance with the Chinese Communist Party once again—an arrangement known as the Second United Front—to unite against their common enemy: imperial Japan.

This so-called common enemy turned out to be a gift to the CCP. After taking over China, Mao—on more than one occasion—expressed gratitude to Japanese visitors for the Japanese invasion of China. On January 24, 1961, during a meeting with Japanese Socialist Party member Kuroda Hisao and others, Mao made the following remarks:

> If Japan hadn't invaded, we might still be hiding in the mountains—we wouldn't have made it to Beijing to watch Beijing Opera. It was precisely because the Japanese army occupied so much of China that we were able to establish numerous anti-Japanese base areas, which created favorable conditions for the later War of Liberation [the Chinese Civil War]. Japanese monopoly capital and militarists actually did us a "favor." If thanks are in order, I would like to thank the Imperial Japanese Army for invading China.[5]

The Second United Front granted the CCP newfound legitimacy, recognizing it as a political force rather than a mere rebel faction. It also allowed the Party to establish a formal office in Chongqing, the wartime capital of the KMT government in remote mountainous southwest China. The CCP utilized this office as a hub to communicate with international allies, forge relationships with influential figures, and promote their revolutionary ideals under the guise of national unity against Japanese invasion.

Much like the First United Front, the Second United Front proved highly advantageous for the CCP's long-term strategy.

In 1937, Japan launched a full-scale invasion of China, marking the beginning of the Second Sino-Japanese War.*

The war with Japan and the subsequential formation of the Second United Front provided the CCP with a golden opportunity to reestablish itself, expand its influence and ultimately secure victory over the KMT. However, to reclaim its legitimacy as a political force—shedding the image of "red bandits" held by the Chinese public and the international community, especially the Untied States—the CCP needed to break through what they called the KMT's media blackout. To achieve this goal, they needed substantial help.

* The First Sino-Japanese War, fought between 1894 and 1895, was a conflict between the Qing government and Japan over control of Korea, ending with Qing's defeat.

Fortunately for them, that assistance was soon on its way.

Edgar Snow (1905–1972)

Snow, a Missouri native and journalism graduate, began a world journey in 1928 that led him to China, where he became a prominent reporter for major U.S. news outlets.

He arrived amid political chaos—the collapse of the First United Front, the Nationalists' purge of Communists, and rising Japanese aggression that escalated into full-scale invasion in 1937. When he left in 1941, China was still locked in its struggle against Japan.

Deeply troubled by China's plight, Snow soon became disillusioned with Chiang Kai-shek's authoritarian rule and ineffective response to the Japanese invasion. Searching for an alternative that could lead to China's salvation, Snow connected with numerous progressive intellectuals and journalists who were sympathetic to or supportive of the Communist cause. Among them were Madame Sun Yat-sen, the widow of the KMT founder and a close ally of the Communists; Agnes Smedley, a radical leftist and feminist (more on her shortly); and Lu Xun, a leading Chinese progressive literary figure. These individuals profoundly shaped Snow's worldview, with some playing key roles in facilitating his historic journey to Yan'an.

After settling in Yan'an, Mao was eager to reach out to the outside world to garner sympathy and support for the Communist cause. Understanding the power of propaganda, Mao believed that inviting Western journalists to visit Yan'an and report on the CCP would be an ideal strategy. To facilitate this, he enlisted the help of Madame Sun Yat-sen, who had strong connections with Western intellectuals and journalists. Among the candidates she recommended was Edgar Snow, who had originally approached her to write a profile for the *Herald-Tribune*.[6]

Snow was selected not only because of his previously sympathetic reporting on leftist movements but also due to his status as a columnist and contributor to prominent American publications, which Mao believed could amplify the Communist perspective to an international audience. Another crucial factor in his selection was that Snow was not a member of the Communist Party, lending him an appearance of impartiality that would make his reporting more credible to Western readers.

In July 1936, Edgar Snow arrived in Yan'an, becoming the first Western journalist to visit the red capital. His book based on this visit, *Red Star over China*, would ultimately become one of the most influential works ever produced about Mao Zedong and the Chinese Communist Revolution—the "origin story" of the CCP. It is still in print today.

Mao meticulously prepared for Snow's visit (similar tactics were later used to impress many Western journalists, diplomats, and military officers visiting Yan'an), insisting on fanfare and ceremony. Snow was received with all the honors of a state guest in Yan'an.

Everything was carefully orchestrated, and the Politburo prepared standardized answers to the questions he submitted—a blend of truths and fabrications. Snow appeared genuinely impressed, which was evident in his portrayal of Yan'an's "Soviet society" as vibrant, well-organized, and committed to the well-being of ordinary people. He highlighted the redistribution of land to peasants, the promotion of women's rights, and the efforts to improve literacy and healthcare.

Snow's most outlandish portrayal was of Mao himself. He wrote: "Mao Zedong's life story represents a rich cross-section of an entire generation and serves as a vital guide to understanding the trends within China." In Snow's eyes, Mao was a "Lincolnesque figure." "There would never be any one 'savior' of China, yet undeniably one felt a certain force of destiny in Mao. It was nothing quick or flashy, but a kind of solid elemental vitality."[7]

The admiration continued, with Snow portraying Mao almost as a Christ-like figure: "Mao's chief luxury...was a mosquito net. Otherwise, Mao lived very much like the rank and file of the Red Army. After ten years of leadership of the Reds, after hundreds of confiscations of property of landlords, officials, and tax collectors, he owned only his blankets and a few personal belongings, including two cotton uniforms. Although he was a Red Army commander as well as chairman, he wore on his coat collar only the two red bars that are the insignia of the ordinary Red soldier."[8] Snow reported that Mao's food was the same as everybody's with the only exception that his food was prepared with hot chili pepper. Except for this passion, Mao scarcely seemed to notice what he ate.[9]

Unbeknownst to Snow, Yan'an operated under a strict hierarchy, with food allowances meticulously allocated by rank. Ordinary soldiers received only the most basic meals. Regimental-level officers were provided with one dish and one soup, division-level officers and central party department cadres received two dishes and one soup, and Politburo members were entitled to four dishes and one soup.[10]

The party justified these privileges as a necessity for the revolution, stating: "It is not the leading comrades who seek privilege themselves… It is the order of the Party. Take Chairman Mao, for example: the Party can order him to eat a chicken a day."[11] Doesn't this justification mirror Bernie Sanders's defense of flying private jets to attend events aimed at fighting oligarchy and the climate crisis—arguing that he can't afford to waste time standing in line for commercial flights like ordinary people?[12] But what if someone dared to challenge that justification? Not long after Snow's visit, Wang Shiwei, a writer and translator who had joined the CCP in Yan'an, was persecuted and ultimately executed—hacked to death with a large machete, to save bullets—for daring to criticize the glaring inequalities that contradicted the very Communist principles the CCP preached. The catalyst for Mao's wrath was Wang's widely read essay "Wild Lilies,"[13] in which he wrote, "I am not an egalitarian, but the division of clothing into three grades and canteens into five tiers seems neither necessary nor reasonable." Wang's tragic fate underscored the deep-seated tensions and contradictions within the CCP's structure—realities carefully concealed from foreign observers like Snow during his visit.

Snow's *Red Star over China* portrayed the CCP in an overwhelmingly positive light. It also introduced the Long March to Western readers as a mythical tale of heroism and perseverance. The term quickly took on symbolic meaning beyond China. In 1967, German Marxist Rudi Dutschke coined the phrase "the Long March through the institutions," referring to a strategy of gradual, internal transformation of Western institutions from within—a phrase that has since entered the American political lexicon.

However, few—including Snow himself—knew the real story behind the Long March.

After settling in Yan'an, the CCP quickly recognized the symbolic power and propaganda potential of its epic journey. In 1936, Mao called for submissions from participants of the Long March to document their personal experiences for international publicity and fundraising efforts. Within three months, more than two hundred submissions were collected. A careful selection process was undertaken to compile these accounts into a finished work titled *The Record of the Red Army's Long March*. Many of the materials Edgar Snow used in his influential book *Red Star over China* were drawn from these submissions.[14]

When *Red Star over China* was published in 1938, the foreign public knew almost nothing about the CCP. The book became an instant sensation, selling millions of copies and profoundly shaping Western perceptions of Mao and the Communists. Despite Snow's emphasis on their Marxist-Leninist credentials, many readers viewed the CCP as agrarian reformers with distinctly Chinese characteristics. Literary critic Henry Seidel Canby described the movement as "an agrarian revolution" so uniquely Chinese that the label "Communist" seemed misleading. The *New York Times* concurred, writing that "the significance of Red China lies not in its being red, but in its being Chinese," and observed that the so-called red bandits resembled what Americans might consider patriots—driven less by Marx, Lenin, or Stalin than by China's own realities.[15]

Astoundingly, these misconceptions have persisted to this day.

The Chinese translation of *Red Star over China* was later published under the alternative title *Journey to the West*, evoking the very popular and classic Chinese novel of a similar title about a Buddhist monk's adventurous pilgrimage to India. This clever choice was intended to bypass KMT censorship. It also became a bestseller in China.

In many ways, Snow's book marked the beginning of the CCP's resurgence within China. It had enormous influence among radical youth, drawing thousands of passionate educated young people to the "red capital" of Yan'an, much like moths drawn to a flame. Among them were two of my uncles, who turned their backs on their "oppressive" landowning family and were swept into the Communist cause—and into the flame. Snow's portrayal elevated Yan'an to the status of a "New Jerusalem," and propagated the misconception that the CCP were reformers rather than radicals—a myth that would persist long after his time. Most significantly, Snow crafted a larger-than-life image of Mao as a symbol of hope for China's future, epitomized by the iconic photo he captured of Mao wearing a red star hat—young, determined, and self-assured.

Snow and his book inspired a stream of American and Western visitors to journey to Yan'an and witness the revolutionary movement firsthand, eventually attracting high-level U.S. officials as well.

Edgar Snow's monumental contribution cemented his status as one of the most celebrated "Old Friends of the Chinese People"—a title the CCP bestows on loyal foreign allies who serve its interests.

Renowned as one of the few Westerners who truly understood the Chinese Communists, Snow became a trusted source of information and insight for Presidents Roosevelt, Truman, and Nixon. His work influenced nearly all of the so-called China hands—American experts on China in the 1940s—who regarded *Red Star over China* as essential reading. Snow's influence on U.S. policy toward China cannot be overstated.

Snow remained a propagandist for the CCP for years after it rose to power. During the Great Famine (1959–1962), which killed tens of millions of Chinese, Snow was invited by the CCP to visit China. He reported that "Considerable malnutrition undoubtedly existed. Mass starvation? No."[16] At this point, Snow's role mirrored that of the *New York Times* correspondent Walter Duranty, who, two decades earlier, had covered up the truth about the Ukrainian famine and Stalin's purges, presenting a fictional socialist utopia that catered to the fantasies of American leftists.

Snow's first wife, Helen Foster Snow, also a writer, shared her husband's views. She made her own journey to Yan'an to document the Chinese Communists. Her book *Inside Red China*—also known as *China Builds for Democracy*—is widely regarded as a sequel to *Red Star over China*.

Like her husband, Helen Snow was sincere in her beliefs, genuinely convinced that both she and Edgar were reporting honestly and without bias. "Had Ed been a Communist, his story would have had little value. He actually was a reporter telling it like it was. He disliked propaganda intensely. He liked his readers and thought of them first..."

The challenge for readers arises when reporting becomes biased—not from deliberate deception, but because journalists themselves fall victim to propaganda, knowingly or not, as appears to have been the case with the Snows.

From 1970 to 1971, during the height of the Chinese Cultural Revolution, Snow made his final visit to China. During this visit, Snow also took on an important mission: conveying China's willingness to change its adversarial policy toward the United States. Mao asked him to deliver a message to US President Richard Nixon, inviting him to visit China.[17]

The scenes he observed during the Cultural Revolution, however, left Snow disheartened. After attending countless meetings steeped in Maoist ideology, he noted in his diary that "China is a country with a single scenario," with a tedious and long-winded ritualistic sameness; that the largest bookstore in Beijing now offered "nothing but Mao" and a few shelves of Marxist-Leninist works; and that "All rival or complementary thought or doctrine being heresy as interpreted in the eyes of a rising new priestcraft..."[18]

In 1972, Edgar Snow, disillusioned with his ideals, died in Switzerland.

His second wife and widow, Lois Snow, in her later years transformed from a passionate supporter of the CCP to a sharp critic, with the 1989 Tiananmen Square Massacre being a turning point. "It woke me up," she said in an interview. "I saw people being dragged away with blood on their faces...It was right there on TV, in the living room, in front of you. The children, my own kids, were around me. We screamed. It felt like we were right there." She publicly condemned the massacre and wrote numerous letters to Chinese leaders, including Deng Xiaoping, urging the CCP to stop persecuting the "Tiananmen Mothers" who had lost children to the massacre.[19]

In 2000, at the age of seventy-nine, Lois made her final visit to Beijing. She hoped to deliver a donation to one of the Tiananmen Mothers, Ding Zilin, whose teenage son was killed during the massacre, but their meeting was forcefully blocked by more than twenty secret police officers.[20]

In contrast, Helen Snow never reflected on or wavered in the face of Mao and the CCP's repeated atrocities after they seized power. She remained ideologically frozen in her romanticized vision of Yan'an in 1937, maintaining her support until the end of her life. For her, as for many others, denouncing the CCP may have felt like betraying the ideals of her youth and the cause to which she had devoted her life—a reckoning so profound it bordered on psychological self-destruction.

Agnes Smedley (1892–1950)

In her 1928 autobiographical novel, *Daughter of Earth*, Agnes Smedley traces her path to becoming a committed Communist. She was born into poverty in Missouri, and her difficult upbringing shaped a lifelong dedication to social justice. After moving to New York in the 1910s, she became active in the socialist and Indian independence movements, building ties with Soviet Russia and the Comintern. Her unconventional personal life reflected her rejection of societal norms. In 1928, Smedley went to China, where she spent much of the next decade reporting on and embracing the Communist revolution.

At the end of 1936, Smedley arrived in Xi'an, seemingly by fate, just as the infamous Xi'an Incident began to unfold, during which Chiang Kai-shek was detained by his own generals. Smedley seized the moment, becoming the first foreign journalist to report on the event. She delivered forty-minute radio broadcasts in English each evening, providing the only daily news emerging from Xi'an.[21]

By January 1937, Smedley's reporting gained significant attention in the American press. Stories about her featured prominently in newspapers. The Associated Press published an article that described her as "the former American farm girl who may become a virtual 'white empress' over yellow-skinned millions."[22]

In early 1937, Agnes Smedley traveled to Yan'an, becoming the first Western woman to visit the Communist stronghold. She had seen the draft of Snow's *Red Star over China* in Xi'an and firmly believed that she was more revolutionary than Snow and could better connect with the revolutionary spirit in Yan'an.[23]

Upon her arrival, she was warmly received by Mao and General Zhu De. During the welcome rally Smedley delivered an impassioned speech, speaking for more than an hour about her experiences and dedication to the anti-imperialist struggle.[24]

In Yan'an, Agnes Smedley quickly developed a strong rapport with Zhu De, the commander-in-chief of the Red Army, in stark contrast to her dislike of Mao, whom she described as "sinister and feminine."[25] Her biography of him, *The Great Road: The Life and Times of Chu Teh,* remains a classic work on Zhu's pivotal role in Chinese Communist history.

Smedley could be seen as an early prototype of today's "Karen"—an entitled, self-righteous white woman who insists on imposing her views on everyone else. She did more than just interview and write, as Edgar Snow had done; she took on the role of social reformer and activist, striving to leave a significant mark on Yan'an.

As a staunch feminist, Agnes Smedley sought to reform what she perceived as the Chinese Communist Party's "outdated" views on sex, arguing that the "undisciplined guerrilla warfare" in Yan'an highlighted the need for a more progressive attitude to sexuality. She enlisted the help of Margaret Sanger, the American eugenicist and founder of Planned Parenthood, to send her medical examination tools and contraceptive devices for the CCP troops.[26]

Smedley often teased CCP leaders for being intimidated by their wives, half jokingly suggesting that if they couldn't free themselves from their wives' "oppression," they wouldn't be able to liberate China.[27] She also took on the role of social dance instructor, teaching senior CCP leaders how to dance. This newfound activity made both Smedley and her attractive interpreter, Lili Wu, immensely popular. However, their popularity provoked unease and resentment among women cadres, who were displeased with the attention their husbands lavished on the two women.

Smedley openly expressed her view on the female cadres and wives in Yan'an as "backward" and "feudal-minded." The feeling was mutual. Among the women in Yan'an, Mao's wife, He Zizhen, held the strongest aversion to Smedley. As their dislike of each other escalated, Smedley found herself entangled in a series of events that contributed to Mao's decision to divorce He.[28] This opened the door for Jiang Qing, a leftist movie star from Shanghai who would soon arrive in Yan'an to join the Communist Revolution, to become Mao's new wife—and later infamous as Madame Mao, the name by which she would become known in the West.

Facing organized opposition from the wives, Smedley ultimately was compelled to leave Yan'an.

While in Yan'an, Smedley applied to join the Chinese Communist Party, but her request was denied. Leaders, including Mao Zedong and

Zhu De, knew that it would not be a good fit. Membership in the CCP demanded absolute loyalty and complete subordination to the party, leaving no room for individuality. Smedley's strong-willed and independent nature made her unsuitable for party membership. They explained to her that she could contribute more effectively as an independent journalist.[29]

After leaving Yan'an, Agnes Smedley devoted herself to securing medical supplies and raising funds for the CCP. Between 1938 and 1940, she traveled extensively across regions north and south of the Yangzi River, visiting frontline units fighting the Japanese, all while reporting on the war.

One of her photo essays, "China's Guerrilla Armies Stab Japan in the Back," which focuses on the New Fourth Army, a newly rebranded CCP force under the banner of the Second United Front, was published in the July 1939 issue of *Life* magazine. She later compiled her extensive reports on the New Fourth Army into the book *China Fights Back*. Her journey became the longest sustained tour of a Chinese war zone by any foreign correspondent.[30]

During her time in China, Smedley established connections with and influenced many American journalists, diplomats, and military leaders, including General Joseph Stilwell, who met with her often to discuss the Chinese Communists.[31] A more detailed account of Stilwell's story will follow in the next chapter.

In May 1941, Smedley returned to the United States and published a series of works lauding the Chinese Communist Party. However, by 1949, during the height of the anti-Communist "Red Scare," she faced accusations of being a Soviet spy. To evade further investigation, she relocated to the United Kingdom, where she died in 1950.

On May 6, 1951, her ashes were interred at the Revolutionary Cemetery of Babaoshan in Beijing, which is where the highest-ranking revolutionary martyrs are buried, with a tombstone inscribed by Marshal Zhu De: "In Memory of Agnes Smedley, American revolutionary writer and *friend of the Chinese people*."

Anna Louise Strong (1885–1970)

Born into a middle-class family in Nebraska, Anna Louise Strong developed a strong sense of social justice early in life, influenced by her father, a social gospel* minister. At just twenty-three years old, she earned a PhD in philosophy from the University of Chicago, making her academically more accomplished than either Edgar Snow or Agnes Smedley.

In her 1935 autobiography, *I Change Worlds: The Remaking of an American*, Anna Louise Strong recounts her path to radical Communism. Her 1921 visit to Moscow proved pivotal, cementing her belief in the Communist vision of a classless society as a superior alternative to capitalism. Strong became a devoted supporter of Stalinism and a vocal advocate for global Communist revolution, uncritically endorsing the Soviet regime's ideals and methods. She spent nearly three decades in the U.S.S.R., reporting and writing extensively in support of its policies.

Anna Louise Strong first visited China in 1925 and returned repeatedly, producing extensive writings on the Chinese Communist revolution. The CCP hails her as a chronicler of China's revolution.

During her 1938 trip, she traveled to the CCP's Eighth Route Army, newly rebranded under the Second United Front, headquartered in Shanxi's Wutai Mountains, where she interviewed senior CCP leaders including Commander-in-Chief Zhu De, whom she described as kind, unassuming, and dressed plainly like a farmer. Strong shared in the hardships of local villagers and soldiers, subsisting on two simple meals a day in a freezing, roofless shelter.[32]

In 1946, amid the civil war between the CCP and the KMT for control of China's future, Strong traveled to Yan'an, where she met with Mao and other Communist leaders. During her interview with Mao, he famously declared, "All reactionaries are paper tigers." The phrase became

*The social gospel was a Christian social reform movement in the U.S. from 1870 to 1920 that emphasized social justice through the application of Christian ethics to societal issues.

a favorite CCP slogan to characterize the United States and the West as ultimately weak despite their apparent strength. During the trade war with President Trump, the CCP frequently revived the term to project confidence in defeating the "paper tiger" they saw in him.

In the same interview, Mao also expressed confidence that "history will finally prove that our millet plus rifles is more powerful than Chiang Kai-shek's aeroplanes plus tanks." However, as we will see in the next chapter, Mao's assertion does not hold up. It is, in fact, a complete lie.

In 1958, after falling out of favor with the Soviet regime, Strong moved to Beijing at the age of seventy-two. The Chinese Communist Party appointed her as the editor-in-chief of *China Reconstructs*, a publication used for external propaganda.

In her 1959 book, *The Rise of the Chinese People's Communes*, Anna Louise Strong praised the agricultural collectivization campaigns known as the People's Commune and the Great Leap Forward. Despite the catastrophic outcomes of these policies, including the Great Famine that claimed tens of millions of lives, she never retracted her propaganda supporting these disastrous campaigns.

In 1959, Strong organized a group of nineteen journalists from eleven Western news agencies and newspapers to visit Tibet under Communist control.[33] She later wrote the book *When Serfs Stood Up in Tibet*, in which she defended the CCP's policies and echoed propaganda slogans like "Building Paradise on the Roof of the World." Completely disregarding the brutal reality of the CCP's takeover of Tibet, she portrayed the violent invasion as a liberation, stating: "The awakening of human beings from bondage to freedom has happened often before in human society. Usually, it has been in bloody uprisings at heavy human cost. Seldom has it been done with such careful social reengineering as today in Tibet."

Strong spent the remainder of her life in China, steadfastly supporting and defending Mao's actions, including the Cultural Revolution. In 1966, at the age of eighty, she was honored with the title of an honorary

Red Guard.* A famous photo captures her with Mao, proudly wearing the Red Guard armband.

She died in Beijing on March 29, 1970, and was also laid to rest at the Babaoshan Revolutionary Cemetery in Beijing. Inscribed on her tombstone were the words: "In memory of Anna Louise Strong—Progressive American writer and friend of the Chinese people."

Edgar Snow, Agnes Smedley, and Anna Louise Strong—three Americans from the Midwest—were collectively known in China as the "Three S's," the leading Western journalists who made an immeasurable contribution to the Chinese Communist cause, with Snow regarded as the most influential of the trio.

In 1984, the Smedley-Strong-Snow Society of China was established under the Chinese Academy of Social Sciences to honor their contributions. The society organizes commemorative events, preserves archives, and promotes research on their roles in advancing the Chinese Communist movement. And all three of the S's were individually featured on postage stamps issued in China.

While Smedley and Strong were openly Communist and connected to the Comintern, their work was often dismissed in the West due to its overt ideological slant. Snow, by contrast, was seen as an independent voice. This perceived neutrality gave his work greater credibility in the West—making it arguably more deceptive and dangerous.

Today, the CCP is actively seeking new "Snows" for Xi Jinping's "new era," those who can fulfill a similar role as Edgar Snow in promoting China's narrative on the global stage. In 2021, the CCP media outlet *China Daily* launched the Edgar Snow Newsroom, aimed at recruiting foreign reporters to engage in propaganda work for the

*The Red Guards were militant student groups mobilized by Mao Zedong during the Cultural Revolution (1966–1976) to enforce Maoist ideology by attacking perceived enemies of the revolution and dismantling traditional cultural and social structures.

CCP. Evidently, there is no shortage of candidates for the CCP to choose from.

The widespread popularity of the work of the Three S's can be attributed to the historical context of the 1930s. During this time, the United States was still recovering from the Great Depression, which had deeply shaken confidence in capitalism. President Franklin D. Roosevelt's New Deal introduced socialist policies, reflecting a broader leftward shift in American society.

Interestingly, Edgar Snow noted in *Red Star over China* that Mao Zedong held a favorable view of President Roosevelt, even expressing interest in learning about FDR's New Deal. Mao was likely inspired by FDR's large-scale government initiatives aimed at rapid economic transformation.

In this historic environment, writings that glorified and promoted Chinese Communism unsurprisingly found a receptive audience among American readers, who were increasingly exploring alternative economic and political ideologies.

In the Footsteps of Edgar Snow

Sadly, the Three S's were not the only American journalists drawn to Chinese Communism who made their way to Yan'an. Here are a few others.

Theodore H. White, a war correspondent, published a series of compelling reports in *Time* magazine about war-torn China. His coverage of the catastrophic Henan Famine (1942–1944), which claimed over a million lives, helped to expose the KMT regime's corruption and prompt increased relief efforts.

White's experiences in Henan profoundly altered his perception of Chiang Kai-shek, turning his initial admiration into outright disgust. Over time, his distrust intensified to the point where he likened Chiang and his regime to Hitler and the Nazis.[34] Now you can see—calling right-wing political leaders "Hitler" didn't begin with Trump.

This growing disenchantment led White to shift his focus and place his hopes for China's future in the Chinese Communist Party.

Building on the legacy of Edgar Snow, White traveled to Yan'an in 1944 and spent several weeks there.

The Yan'an White visited had undergone significant changes since Snow's visit in 1936. During the Sino-Japanese War, the CCP had quietly expanded its control beyond northern Shaanxi to encompass several northern provinces bolstering a population of 100 million.

In Yan'an, White met with top Communist leaders. Welcomed as an ally, he interviewed most of the Politburo and was deeply impressed by Mao, whom he portrayed as a visionary leader, and by the disciplined Communist troops. White's romanticized view of Yan'an and the CCP marked a turning point in his reporting—he became a vocal advocate for the Communists.

His 1946 book, *Thunder out of China*, delivered a scathing indictment of the corrupt and ineffectual Nationalist government while depicting the Communists as disciplined and principled. The book powerfully shaped American public opinion and influenced key policymakers, ultimately strengthening the CCP's position during the Chinese Civil War. It became a bestseller and earned White a Pulitzer Prize.

Despite later revelations about the brutality of the regime he had praised, White remained committed to his early impressions. After 1949, he repeatedly wrote to Mao and Zhou Enlai seeking to return to China, but his letters went unanswered. It wasn't until 1972—during Nixon's historic visit—that White returned as part of the U.S. delegation. At a banquet, Zhou Enlai greeted him warmly, calling out "Old friend, old friend!"[35]—a symbolic gesture that reflected the CCP's renewed interest in American support.

Gunther Stein, another notable figure, was an American journalist who visited Yan'an in 1944. During his visit, he had thirty hours of extensive personal interviews with Mao.[36] Stein reported positively on the CCP and its grassroots democracy, including the "bean voting" system—a method designed to allow illiterate peasants to participate in elections. Voters cast beans into bowls representing different candidates, providing a simple form of secret ballot. Stein highlighted this system as evidence of the CCP's efforts to promote what he saw as genuine democracy, referring to Yan'an as "China's Laboratory of Self-Government."[37]

Stein believed that the CCP's "agrarian revolution" was not truly Communist. During his interview with Mao, he naïvely asked whether it was possible to remove the "awful word Communist" from the party's name. Mao rejected the idea, explaining that what unites Communists worldwide is not a uniform social system, but a shared method of political thinking rooted in Marxism—adapted to each nation's conditions in pursuit of Communist ideals.[38]

His 1945 book, *The Challenge of Red China*, portrayed the Chinese Communists as pragmatic, disciplined, and deeply connected to the rural masses. His sympathetic account helped reinforce the emerging view among Western intellectuals and policymakers that the CCP offered a viable, even progressive, alternative to the Nationalists.

William Hinton occupies a distinct place among Western writers on Communist China. Unlike Edgar Snow and others who visited Yan'an and focused on party leadership, Hinton bypassed the political center and immersed himself in the countryside to witness the agrarian revolution firsthand.

Inspired by *Red Star over China*, he went to China in 1947 and joined a CCP-led land reform team in Long Bow Village near Yan'an, spending eight months closely observing and participating in the campaign. That experience became the foundation for his 1966 book, *Fanshen: A Documentary of Revolution in a Chinese Village.*

Fanshen documented how peasants, through land reform, dismantled the entire landlord class. Hinton portrayed the campaign as both chaotic and transformative—an epic of social justice in which oppressed villagers "stood up," or *fanshen*, to seize land and reclaim their dignity for the first time.

Although Hinton acknowledged the violence in land reform—including torture and executions of landlords and brutal public "struggle sessions"—he downplayed their significance, framing them as necessary steps in an inevitable class struggle, and justifying the brutality by comparing poor peasants to drowning men who lash out in desperation. What Hinton failed to understand is that violence was not incidental—it was the defining feature of the CCP's land reform, as shown by a harrowing atrocity that Hinton overlooked in a village near Long Bow around the same time he was there.

Niu Youlan, a progressive landlord who had supported the Communists financially and sheltered them during the Sino-Japanese War, became a target during the land reform campaign—like all landlords—simply because of his class. His past loyalty to the party meant nothing; he was branded an enemy and subjected to a brutal public struggle session.

Ironically, his son, Niu Yinguan—whom he had sent to the elite Tsinghua University—was radicalized and joined the Communist Party—a story that should feel all too familiar to many American parents today. By the time of the campaign, he was a senior CCP cadre overseeing the region. At the struggle session, which he personally supervised, a mob pinned Niu Youlan down and threaded an iron wire through his nose, mocking his surname "Niu," which means ox. Niu Yinguan was then forced to hold the wire and parade his father through the village. Humiliated, gravely injured, and in despair, Niu Youlan died three days later. His son was later promoted to vice governor of Jiangxi Province for his loyalty to the party.[39]

Stories like this played out across the country. In the end, more than 2 million landlords were killed during the land reform campaign—guilty of having more than their neighbors.

Hinton's moral relativism encouraged readers to overlook the human cost of the revolution in favor of its perceived justice. The same kind of moral relativism has taken root in America today—evident in the alleged cold-blooded shooting of United Healthcare CEO Brian Thompson by

Luigi Mangione, an act committed in the name of "social justice" and applauded by mobs of self-proclaimed justice warriors across the country.

Hinton did not publish *Fanshen* until 1966, more than a decade after returning to the United States in 1953. Upon his arrival, at the height of the Cold War, customs officials confiscated all his notes on suspicion of Communist influence, and his passport was revoked. It took him five years to recover his materials. By the time the book was finally published, the timing proved ideal—it resonated deeply with the 1960s counterculture movement, when many young Americans were disillusioned with capitalism and actively searching for radical alternatives.

I once met someone who shared his story with me: After reading *Fanshen*, he and his wife were starry-eyed with idealism and traveled to Hong Kong, hoping to obtain visas to enter China and witness the revolution for themselves. Their applications were naturally denied—there were no diplomatic ties with the United States at the time, and China remained closed to the outside world. I told him they would have been bitterly disappointed if they had made it in. By that time, all the land the peasants had fought for had already been confiscated by the state.

Ironically, it seemed never to occur to Hinton that, as a landowner himself who inherited and farmed land in Vermont, he would have been labeled a landlord under the very system he championed—his farm confiscated, and he himself likely denounced, publicly humiliated, and possibly executed.

Alongside *Red Star over China* and *Thunder out of China*, *Fanshen* became part of a foundational trilogy in American universities' China studies programs, profoundly shaping the views of those who would later influence U.S. policy toward China. Yet despite their enduring impact, all three were, at their core, propaganda works serving the Chinese Communist Party.

In 1971, Hinton and his family visited China at the invitation of Premier Zhou Enlai,[40] who referred to him as "an old friend of the Chinese people in times of adversity."

Hinton remained a committed Maoist to the end. After witnessing the Tiananmen Square Massacre in 1989, he denounced Deng Xiaoping's government in his book *The Great Reversal*, accusing it of betraying Mao's revolutionary vision by steering China onto the path of capitalism.

—

A critical question arises: Were there any American journalists who didn't fall for the CCP's deception? The answer is yes. Anti-Communist voices like Henry Luce, Freda Utley, and George Moorad offered early and clear-eyed warnings about the true nature of the Chinese Communist Party.

Luce, born in China to missionary parents and who became the influential publisher of *Time*, *Life*, and *Fortune*, used his media empire to support Chiang Kai-shek and sound the alarm about the CCP's totalitarian ambitions. He refused to publish pro-Communist journalist Theodore White's glowing report on Yan'an—and later fired him for pushing CCP propaganda.

Utley, a former Communist turned outspoken critic, exposed the brutality of both Soviet and Chinese Communism and challenged the romanticized image of the CCP being promoted by figures like Edgar Snow and Theodore White. She warned U.S. policymakers that the Communists were intent on seizing full control of China and establishing a Stalinist regime.

Moorad, a correspondent for the *Shanghai Evening Post and Mercury*, was one of the few American journalists in China who remained consistently pro-Nationalist and deeply skeptical of Mao's intentions.

Yet despite their credibility, firsthand knowledge, and moral clarity, these voices were marginalized and ultimately sidelined. They were drowned out by pro-Communist journalists who gained fame and influence by romanticizing the revolution, offering sensationalized reports shaped by exclusive access to CCP leaders. In the battle for narrative control, truth was eclipsed by spectacle—and America paid the price.

Sadly, today we see the same pattern playing out in journalism—and the latest case is a clear example: The entire legacy media appears eager to dismiss the systematic violence against white farmers in South Africa, eerily reminiscent of the killings of landlords during the Chinese Communist revolution, while vehemently attacking President Trump for daring to question President Cyril Ramaphosa during his visit to the White House.[41]

Edgar Snow's visit to Yan'an marked the beginning of the CCP's campaign to cultivate allies among American influencers, particularly journalists and writers. From there, the party steadily expanded its network of "old friends" to encompass government officials, military leaders, politicians, policymakers—and eventually, the upper ranks of major corporations and business elites.

One might argue that these influencers were merely deceived by the Chinese Communists. But the truth is far less forgiving—they were deceived because they wanted to be. They saw not what was real but what they longed to see. They heard not the truth but what confirmed their ideals and fed their convictions.

Though they came from diverse backgrounds, they shared one defining trait: a left-leaning political orientation—ranging from liberal sympathizers like Edgar Snow to committed Communists like Agnes Smedley and Anna Louise Strong. History has shown, time and again, that the ideological leap from liberalism to Communism is often alarmingly short.

These bleeding-heart liberals helped legitimize and elevate a regime that would go on to unleash unimaginable human suffering. Safely removed from the consequences, they never lived under the tyranny they helped glorify. Many never paused to reflect on the reality that every word they wrote in praise of the Communist Party came at the cost of real human lives—millions of them.

Words can kill, and the pen can be as deadly as any bullet. This tragic chapter of history must not be forgotten.

CHAPTER 4

LOSING CHINA TO COMMUNISM

Beginning in the years leading up to World War II, the United States became deeply entangled in China's fate—first by supporting its resistance against Japanese aggression, then by becoming a key player in the civil war between the Nationalists and the Communists. American leaders, diplomats, military officials, and presidents believed they were helping to shape a better future for China and safeguard freedom in Asia. Yet despite their efforts, China fell to Communism in 1949—a seismic geopolitical shift that shocked the American public and ignited one of the most contentious foreign policy debates in U.S. history, captured in the haunting question: "Who lost China?"

This chapter examines the key personalities behind that outcome—how their decisions, misjudgments, and ideological alignments contributed to the loss of China.

—

Once again, it is essential to highlight the historical context before introducing the key characters.

On July 7, 1937, Japan launched a full-scale invasion of China, expanding its aggression beyond Manchuria—occupied since 1931—and marking the start of the Second Sino-Japanese War.

The United States backed Chiang Kai-shek's government, beginning with limited official support in the late 1930s. One of the earliest and most visible forms of American involvement was the American Volunteer Group—better known as the Flying Tigers—led by retired U.S. officer Claire Lee Chennault and formed with quiet approval from the Roosevelt administration. Their heroic efforts made the Flying Tigers a legendary name in China and a celebrated story in the United States, even inspiring the Hollywood film *Flying Tigers* starring John Wayne.

When the United States entered the war with Japan in 1941 following the attack on Pearl Harbor, it significantly increased economic and military aid to China through the lend-lease program, including deploying advisors to support Chiang Kai-shek's forces.

Although the Nationalists were America's official allies, favorable views of the Chinese Communists began to take root within the U.S. government and among the American public—largely shaped by left-leaning journalists and writers who portrayed the CCP in a sympathetic light.

As the war dragged on, growing frustration with KMT corruption and ineffectiveness led some American diplomats and military leaders to advocate collaboration with the Communists, viewing it as a more promising way to advance the U.S. war effort against Japan.

This period showcases the CCP's strategic brilliance. By leveraging the newfound legitimacy gained through the Second United Front with the KMT, the CCP skillfully shaped the narrative, cultivated U.S. trust, and systematically undermined the Nationalists—driving a wedge between the KMT and the United States—while remaining laser-focused on its ultimate goal: not defeating Japan, but toppling the KMT and seizing control of China.

General Joseph Stilwell (1883–1946)

One of the most prominent figures of this period was General Joseph Stilwell.

Stilwell had a long military career that included service in the Philippines and France during World War I, and multiple assignments in China, where he became fluent in Chinese. His blunt demeanor gained him the nickname "Vinegar Joe." In 1942, Stilwell was appointed U.S. commander in the China–Burma–India Theater, overseeing U.S. supply operations and serving as Chiang's chief of staff.

Despite playing a vital role in reopening the Burma Road, Stilwell is best remembered for his contentious relationship with Chiang—a clash that led to his recall in 1944, in what became known as the "Stilwell Affair." Their conflict stemmed from personality differences and military disagreements. However, the main source of contention was the issue of the Chinese Communists.

Stilwell insisted that cooperation with the Communists was a viable way to strengthen the war effort against Japan, viewing the CCP as a more disciplined and reform-minded force. This belief stemmed from his shallow understanding of Communism, shaped by progressive journalists like Edgar Snow and Agnes Smedley, and reinforced by his liberal-minded aides.

More important, Stilwell's shift was driven by his growing disillusionment with Chiang's government. His firsthand experience left him deeply frustrated with the alliance, prompting him to describe the United States as being "forced into partnership with a gang of fascists under a one-party government similar in many respects to our German enemy," even going so far as to liken Chiang to Hitler.[1] Driven by the need for more fighting men, Stilwell naïvely proposed at one point adding twenty Communist soldiers to every hundred-man company in the expeditionary force he was training for Chiang. Hsiao I-shu, the force's chief of staff, warned that introducing 20 percent Communists into a unit would result in the entire company becoming Communist within two weeks.[2] Having lived under the CCP and knowing what I know, I believe it wouldn't even take that many—just one committed Communist would suffice. Using Marxist class struggle tactics, they would incite resentment and hatred of officers, turning soldiers against their own command. It was a risk the Nationalists couldn't afford, and Stilwell was forced to abandon the idea.

Yet Stilwell remained undeterred. Convinced that working with Chiang to reform the army and improve its combat efficiency was hopeless, he became even more drawn to the idea of collaborating with the Communists.

As the key figure overseeing U.S. supplies to China, Stilwell often used this leverage in his dealings with Chiang Kai-shek to advance his agenda. He even proposed that the Communists receive a share of the American-supplied resources.[3]

What Stilwell failed to understand was that the CCP had no real intention of fighting Japan; their true objective was to defeat the KMT and take control of China.

The Communists masterfully exploited Stilwell's disdain for Chiang, offering to fight under his command while refusing to submit to Chiang's authority as required by the Second United Front.[4] This deepened the rift and ultimately led Chiang to demand Stilwell's recall. President Franklin D. Roosevelt, unwilling to jeopardize the alliance with Chiang, agreed—framing the decision as a personality issue to avoid further diplomatic strain.

Stilwell's recall severely damaged U.S.–Nationalist relations and eroded American public support for Chiang's government. The beneficiary was the CCP, as Stilwell's influence helped shift sentiment within the U.S. State Department, ultimately contributing to the decision to withhold aid to the Nationalists.

As a tactically minded soldier, Stilwell overlooked the ideological stakes of the conflict. His naïve belief led him to describe the CCP as "agrarian liberals." In the end, he unknowingly contributed to the downfall of the KMT and the rise of the CCP.

Stilwell died in 1946, two years after his recall, never living to see the full consequences of his decisions.

Loathed by Chiang and the KMT, Stilwell is revered by the CCP. Recognizing his pro-Communist stance, the CCP converted his former residence in Chongqing, the wartime capital of KMT government, into the Stilwell Museum. In 2023, Xi Jinping replied to the letter by General Stilwell's grandson, John Stilwell, regarding a special exhibition commemorating the general's 140th birthday. Xi stated, "General Stilwell was an *old friend of the Chinese people*, providing active support for China's liberation and progress. He made significant contributions to fostering friendship between the Chinese and Americans."[5]

This is yet another example of the CCP's United Front strategy, which seeks to leverage historical accounts to shape the narrative of current "cooperation" with the United States in pursuit of its political goals. Tragically, eighty years after his death, Stilwell's descendants remain just as blind to the true nature of Communism.

The Dixie Mission (1944–1947)

General Stilwell's dismissal did not resolve the underlying issue. In fact, it strengthened the determination of those who shared his views to carry on his agenda.

John Paton Davies Jr., political attaché to General Stilwell and a prominent "China hand," came up with a proposal to send a U.S. Army Observer Group to Yan'an to assess the potential for collaboration with the Chinese Communists.

His proposal was inspired by the report of U.S. Marine Corps officer Captain Evans Carlson—later famous for leading Carlson's Raiders in World War II—and his firsthand accounts of Yan'an. In 1937, Carlson was sent to China as a military observer by his close friend President

Roosevelt, with the task of reporting directly on anti-Japanese resistance efforts.

While in China, Carlson met Edgar Snow and read the manuscript of *Red Star over China* before its publication, which sparked his interest in the Communist base at Yan'an. In 1938, he undertook a treacherous journey from Shanghai to Yan'an to witness it firsthand.

What he found exceeded his expectations. Carlson was deeply impressed by Mao, the Red Army, and especially General Zhu De. The CCP persuaded him that their primary focus was fighting Japanese aggression. He later told Snow that he would be glad to serve under Zhu De anytime. A devout Christian, Carlson believed he had seen in Yan'an a living example of Christian ethics and brotherhood in action.[6] Carlson's glowing report left a lasting impression—not only on diplomats like Davies but also on President Roosevelt.

In order to send an observation group to Yan'an, Davies and the Americans had to first convince Chiang Kai-shek. FDR dispatched Vice President Henry Wallace—widely seen as the most pro-Communist figure in the U.S. government at the time—to China to negotiate. In meetings with Wallace, Chiang firmly rejected the popular portrayal of the CCP as "agrarian democrats," insisting they were "more communistic than the Russian Communists."[7] Nevertheless, under pressure and fearing the loss of U.S. support, Chiang reluctantly agreed to Wallace's request.

The mission—later known as the "Dixie Mission"—marked the first official U.S. engagement with the Chinese Communist Party. Though limited in scope, it would later serve as a blueprint for the CCP's future interactions with the United States.

The Three Johns

Three key figures defined this early U.S.–CCP collaboration, known in China as the "Three Johns": John Carter Vincent, John Paton Davies Jr., and John Stewart Service. Like the Three S's, these men played critical roles in advancing the Communist cause. But while the Three S's were independent writers, the Three Johns were U.S. State Department officials with direct influence on American China policy.

John Carter Vincent was the highest-ranking among them—a seasoned China hand who served as director of the Office of Far Eastern Affairs in the State Department. A strong advocate for U.S.–CCP cooperation, Vincent accompanied Vice President Henry Wallace to China and pressured Chiang Kai-shek to approve the Dixie Mission. Dismissing Chiang's warnings that the CCP was more radical than the Soviets, Vincent argued that engaging with the Communists would strengthen the war effort and yield strategic intelligence. He believed China's size and nationalist sentiment would prevent it from becoming a Soviet satellite.[8] His views significantly influenced General George Marshall and laid the groundwork for the Marshall Mission—often seen as the continuation of the Dixie Mission.

John Paton Davies Jr., the first to propose formal contact with the Communists, was born in China to missionary parents with a deep knowledge of Chinese society and culture. It was he who coined the term "Dixie Mission," likening Yan'an to the American South during the Civil War—a rebellious region.

Though Davies himself wasn't a formal mission member, he visited Yan'an several times, meeting Mao and other top CCP leaders. He came away impressed, describing Mao's leadership as cohesive, pragmatic, and firmly in control. In reports like "How Red Are the Chinese Communists?" Davies concluded that the CCP was not very red and was open to cooperation with the United States. He even suggested the United States cut off aid to the Nationalists unless they stopped opposing the Communists.[9]

John Stewart Service, the third John, had the greatest influence. Like Davies, he was also born in China—in my hometown of Chengdu, to be exact—to missionary parents. He was fluent in Mandarin and three dialects and deeply immersed in Chinese culture—traits that uniquely positioned him to assess the CCP. During more than three months in

Yan'an as a member of the first Dixie Mission group, he held multiple meetings with Mao Zedong and Zhou Enlai, including an eight-hour marathon talk with Mao—the longest meeting any U.S. official had with the CCP leader at the time.

Service sent back glowing reports. In "General Impression of the Chinese Communist Leaders," he described them as physically vigorous, pragmatic, democratic, honest, incorruptible, and lacking in vengeance—italicizing these traits for emphasis. He claimed that their manners, habits of thought, and direct handling of problems seemed more American than Oriental.[10] He recommended direct U.S. military support for the CCP, even proposing the establishment of a U.S. consulate in Yan'an.[11] Through Service, Mao sent messages to President Roosevelt, urging balanced support and even proposing a visit to the U.S.[12]

The Three Johns were not alone. Their pro-CCP advocacy reflected a broader trend in the State Department, where CCP figures were increasingly referred to as "so-called Communists" and their territories as the "so-called Communist area."[13]

Unlike the Three S's, the Three Johns' analyses and recommendations directly influenced policy decisions in Washington—making their impact even more consequential.

The CCP did not forget their *old friend* Service. In 1971, Service was among a select group of Americans invited to visit China shortly before President Nixon's historic trip.[14]

Observing Yan'an

On July 22, 1944, the first Dixie Mission group—initially composed of nine members and later joined by nine more—arrived in Yan'an. The group was led by Colonel David Barrett (1892–1977), General Stilwell's assistant military attaché and a prominent China hand. Among the original members was John Service. Their official mission was to assess Yan'an for potential military and political collaboration against Japan, gather weather data for the U.S. Navy and Air Force, and collect intelligence on CCP force structure, capabilities, and Japanese troop movements.

This was the greatest gift the Chinese Communists could have hoped for.

The mission was warmly welcomed in Yan'an with a grand reception held in a large hall, featuring speeches, singing, and theatrical performances. Mao meticulously orchestrated every detail of the Americans' stay in Yan'an, from their food and lodging to their propaganda-laden entertainment.

On August 15, *Liberation Daily*, the CCP's official newspaper, published an editorial titled "Welcome, Comrades of the United States Army Observation Group!" The piece challenged the Nationalists' dominance over the wartime narrative, claiming the CCP had led the resistance against Japan. It also expressed confidence that the Americans would come to recognize the party's democratic values, commitment to the war effort, and worthiness as a U.S. ally.

Unbeknownst to the American observers, shortly after their arrival, Mao issued a directive highlighting that the visits from foreign journalists and U.S. military personnel marked a critical starting point for the CCP's international United Front operation and foreign diplomacy initiatives.[15] It meant the mission should be regarded as an ideal opportunity to employ tactics from the same playbook they had successfully used on Edgar Snow to build trust and secure support.

Barrett may not have been a typical Communist sympathizer like Davies and Service, but despite his deep knowledge of China as a China hand, he, too, failed to see beyond the surface. The "reality" carefully staged by the CCP left a strong, favorable impression on most members of the observation group—including Barrett himself.

Barrett was impressed by what he saw and struck by the lack of a visible police presence in Yan'an and the sight of Mao mingling freely with ordinary people, seemingly unafraid of assassination—a stark contrast to KMT's capital Chongqing.[16] However, what he failed to understand was that Yan'an was, in reality, a tightly controlled police state where individuals were under constant surveillance and routinely reported on one another—conditions often invisible to foreign visitors.

In his memoir, *Dixie Mission: The United States Army Observer Group in Yan'an, 1944*, Barrett later revealed that his group had accidentally discovered a concentration camp not far from their residence—used to detain "persons of doubtful political stability," or those the Communists did not trust. He learned of it through a young man from "some western country" who had just been released. However, Barrett did not press for details about the camp or the reasons for the man's imprisonment.[17]

What Barrett and the other American observers did not know at the time was that the Dixie Mission coincided with the Yan'an Rectification Campaign, which aimed to eradicate all dissenting voices and align everyone with Mao's version of Marxism. Those labeled as "thought criminals" were subjected to intense "thought reform," which sought to root out and eliminate all "incorrect" thinking. Individuals deemed irredeemable were sent to concentration camps, and some were quite literally eliminated through execution.

Yet Barrett's lack of curiosity blinded him to the most revealing truth about Yan'an: He was standing at the center of a totalitarian system. A key objective of the Dixie Mission was to establish contact with the CCP's intelligence network. Yet none of the Americans were ever aware of Kang Sheng, the head of the party's intelligence service. Kang, a KGB-trained spymaster, was notorious for his extensive use of torture and forced confessions during the Yan'an Rectification—a campaign to "root out spies," which instilled widespread fear. In Yan'an, Kang was virtually the second most powerful figure.[18]

The observation group, despite all its observations, failed to grasp the most critical truth: The CCP never had any true intention of fighting the Japanese. Instead, it used the invasion as a strategic opportunity to strengthen itself, a fact history has clearly confirmed.

Zhang Guotao (1897–1979), one of the CCP's original founders, defected to the KMT in 1938 after losing a power struggle to Mao and later immigrated to Canada. In his memoir, Zhang recounted that at the 1937 Luochuan Conference, Mao cautioned against being misled by patriotic zeal and rushing to the front as anti-Japanese heroes. Instead, he instructed the party to avoid direct confrontation with Japanese forces, focus on guerrilla warfare behind enemy lines, and strike where the enemy was weakest. Mao laid out a strategy centered on expanding the Eighth Route Army (the Red Army's rebranded name under the Second United Front), allocating 70 percent of resources to building CCP strength, 20 percent to countering the Nationalists, and just 10 percent to resisting Japan.[19]

This approach was validated by a striking fact: By the time Japan surrendered in 1945, the CCP's forces had grown from 15,000 after the Long March to 1.27 million.[20] Equally damning is this: From 1938 to 1943, Japan waged a relentless bombing campaign against Chongqing—the KMT's wartime capital—inflicting massive destruction and killing countless civilians. Yet Yan'an, despite being much closer to Japanese-occupied territory, was never bombed. This is further validated by the stark contrast in war casualty statistics between the Nationalists and Communists. Nationalist forces suffered more than 3.41 million casualties, including the deaths of 206 generals and more than 4,300 pilots, losing 75 percent of their military strength. In contrast, according to the CCP's own statistics—which were likely inflated—their reported losses were approximately 610,000 casualties, with only one general counted among the dead,[21] the result of avoiding as much fighting as possible.

The Dixie Mission ran from 1944 to 1947, with more than two hundred U.S. personnel participating at various points. Most left believing they had gained valuable intelligence and developed a highly favorable view of the Communists they encountered in Yan'an.

Yet not everyone fell into the trap. Colonels Wilbur J. Peterkin and Ivan Yeaton, who led the Dixie Mission at different times, exemplify this stark contrast in perspectives. Although both began as staunch anti-Communists, by the time Peterkin left the mission, his perspective had shifted and he began to view the Communists' peasant base as a potential force for good in China. Yeaton, however, held firm in his conviction that, regardless of any short-term gains Mao's regime might bring, any Communist regime would ultimately prove as harmful as another.[22]

Reflecting on Yeaton, Peterkin remarked, "He had no background on China or the Chinese but styled himself as an expert on communism. He apparently saw a secret agent behind every tree and around every corner."[23]

Peterkin's condescending description of Yeaton ironically offered sound advice for any anti-Communist dealing with Communism: Always suspect the possibility of a hidden Communist lurking behind every tree and around every corner, and never place trust in one—Chinese or otherwise.

The Dixie Mission accomplished little for the war effort. However, it succeeded in promoting the perception that the CCP was trustworthy and a viable potential ally for the United States.

As the first official engagement between the U.S. and the Chinese Communists, the failure of the Dixie Mission set a pattern that would repeat itself for decades to come: In every engagement, negotiation, and collaboration where the United States placed its trust in the CCP, the outcome remained the same—the CCP wins.

One Last "Favor"

By 1945, Japan had been defeated.

But instead of peace, a civil war loomed on the horizon. Immediately following Japan's surrender, the Dixie Mission provided one final yet crucial assistance to the CCP by flying twenty of its top generals—including Deng Xiaoping, the CCP's future paramount leader—from Yan'an to Changning, a Communist base area 186 miles east of Yan'an. The CCP initially approached the Americans with caution, but to their surprise, the Dixie Mission leader agreed to the request without hesitation, neither seeking authorization from his superiors nor verifying the identities of the twenty individuals.[24]

The Changning airlift lasted only four to five hours, a journey that would have otherwise required a grueling two-month trek. This seemingly routine flight played an extraordinary role in the decisive battles of the upcoming Chinese Civil War, significantly shaping the course of modern Chinese history.

At the time, most of the CCP's senior commanders and main forces were concentrated in Yan'an, not on the frontlines against the Japanese. Thanks to the airlifts, these commanders reached key future war zones ahead of the Nationalists, swiftly consolidated their forces by merging the Eighth Route Army with guerrilla units, and were able to choose battlefields and dictate the terms of engagement. This strategic advantage left the Nationalists on the defensive and paved the way for Communist victories.

This incident stands as yet another example of the profound naïveté of American observers. The Communists weren't hiding behind trees or around corners, to use Colonel Peterkin's words—they were right out in the open. Yet the Americans still allowed themselves to be manipulated by the CCP.

Even more consequential was another event that decisively tilted the balance in favor of the Chinese Communists—one that would profoundly shape the course and ultimate outcome of the Civil War.

The Yalta Treaty (1945)

President Roosevelt, who had served as assistant secretary of the navy under President Wilson, was deeply influenced by the Wilsonian liberal internationalism. However, he appeared unaware of the historical context and the disastrous consequences of Wilson's misguided foreign policy at the Paris Peace Conference—ultimately positioning him to repeat Wilson's mistakes.

During World War II, FDR prioritized the European front and saw Stalin as a vital ally, believing the Soviet Union was less of a threat than Nazi Germany. At the 1943 Tehran Conference, Stalin promised to join the war against Japan once Hitler was defeated. In his eagerness to please Stalin, FDR was willing to sacrifice China by offering the Soviets rights to Dairen (Dalian) and the Manchurian railroads.[25] By the Yalta Conference in early 1945, he had made further concessions, effectively placing Manchuria under Soviet influence.

At the final cabinet meeting before departing for Yalta, FDR asserted his determination to realize his predecessor Wilson's dream by securing Soviet cooperation in the creation of the world peace organization—the United Nations.[26] His actions at Yalta indeed mirrored Wilson's at the Paris Peace Conference. He totally ignored China's sovereignty by deliberately keeping Chiang Kai-shek in the dark for months about his negotiations with Soviet Russia and their potential impact on China's future.

When Chiang Kai-shek's foreign minister, T. V. Soong, was informed that the U.S. had committed to supporting the Yalta Agreement "as it stands," Soong retorted, "The question is, what exactly have you agreed to support?"[27] Soong was stating the obvious: How could China possibly take comfort in the U.S.'s commitment to a secret agreement about its future while being deliberately excluded from the negotiations?

The Yalta Agreement effectively transferred the control of Manchuria from Japanese imperialists to Soviet imperialists without giving China a voice in the decision. Once again, a victorious China treated as though it were a defeated nation.

Much like the Shandong Treaty in 1922, the Yalta Agreement severely undermined America's hard-earned prestige in China. This prestige had been built by the bravery of the Flying Tigers and the generous support and aid provided by the U.S. government and the American people during the Sino-Japanese War. The resulting anger and disillusionment among many Chinese intellectuals and students drove more of them toward the Communist camp.

On August 6 and 9, 1945, the U.S. dropped atomic bombs on Hiroshima and Nagasaki. That same day, August 9, the Soviet Union declared war on Japan and invaded Manchuria. Six days later, Japan surrendered. In return for just six days of fighting, the United States had effectively handed Manchuria to Soviet control. General Albert C. Wedemeyer, who succeeded General Stilwell as Chiang's chief of staff and was a staunch anti-Communist, later called it "our most costly strategic mistake in the Far East."[28]

The Soviet occupation of Manchuria profoundly shaped the outcome of the Chinese Civil War. After years of Japanese rule, the resource-rich Manchuria had become a heavily industrialized region and the hub of Japan's military-industrial complex—producing weapons and ammunition for campaigns across China, Southeast Asia, and the Pacific. It also contained vast stockpiles of arms, which the Soviets would later transfer to the Chinese Communists.[29]

With Soviet assistance, hundreds of thousands of Communist military and political personnel arrived in Manchuria earlier than the Nationalists, turning the important region into a Communist stronghold. At that time, whoever controlled Manchuria controlled the fate of all of China.

In addition to weapon supplies, the Soviet Red Army also provided military advice helping restructure the CCP's forces and train its troops to rapidly enhance their combat effectiveness.[30]

The CCP had now transformed from a ragtag force of "millet plus rifles" red bandits into a formidable army of over a million soldiers—well trained and equipped with advanced weaponry. Ironically, much of this equipment had originally been supplied to the Soviet Union by the United States during World War II. Now armed to the teeth with modern weaponry and rebranded as the People's Liberation Army, they were fully prepared to "liberate" China—with overwhelming force.

It is a tragic repeat of history: Woodrow Wilson's betrayal at the Paris Peace Conference sealed the fate of the Beijing government; FDR's betrayal at Yalta signed the death warrant for Chiang Kai-shek's Nanjing government.

The Marshall Mission

On April 12, 1945, FDR passed away, leaving Vice President Harry S. Truman to assume the responsibilities of the presidency.

Like FDR, Truman also viewed himself as a Wilsonian liberal internationalist. However, he ranked high among those U.S. presidents up until that time who had the weakest ties with and understanding of China. It turned out that he would be far less sympathetic toward the KMT government.

Facing the imminent outbreak of the Chinese Civil War, President Truman dispatched General George Marshall to China in late 1945 to mediate between the Nationalists and Communists. His mission aimed to broker the formation of a coalition government in an effort to prevent further conflict and bring peace to the country.

Marshall was tasked with an impossible mission.

Truman completely failed to grasp that the divide between the Kuomintang and the Communists was irreconcilable. By pushing for a coalition government, the United States effectively ruled out a Nationalist victory.

Secondly, Marshall failed to remain neutral, compromising his role as a U.S. envoy. His view of China was shaped by pro-CCP journalists, diplomats, and military leaders like Edgar Snow, Theodore White, Joseph Stilwell, and the China hands in the State Department. Despite this bias, he arrogantly believed he could reconcile two bitterly opposed camps. His mission was doomed from the start.

In December 1944, Marshall arrived in China and met with Chiang Kai-shek, but dismissed Chiang's warnings outright about the CCP's insincerity and Soviet support. He then met Zhou Enlai, whose charm—as it had for many Westerners—immediately captivated him. Zhou agreed in principle to a ceasefire and to accept Marshall's demand to recognize Chiang Kai-shek's government as the sovereign authority over all of China.

Encouraged by these early exchanges, Marshall moved quickly to formalize the negotiations. He formed a three-member committee with representatives from the KMT and CCP, effectively granting the Communists political legitimacy and equal status with the KMT. He also proposed a military restructuring plan favorable to the CCP, assigning them control of twenty out of sixty divisions and at least 30 percent of the navy and air force.[31]

After facilitating an initial ceasefire agreement, Marshall personally inspected various regions of China and visited Yan'an, becoming the highest-ranking U.S. official to do so. The CCP had long prepared to win him over. Accompanied by Mao Zedong, Zhu De, and Zhou Enlai, Marshall reviewed an honor guard of more than five hundred members of the Communist Army. The guard played a song written specifically for the occasion, "Let us extol your great spirit! You have used your power to extinguish the fire of war sweeping the plain. Oh! General Marshall, let the red troops pay you their highest salute. We Communists honor you."[32]

Applying democratic political logic, Marshall believed the CCP had "liberal" and "radical" factions, convinced the so-called liberals would act in the people's interest.[33] It is astonishing that someone with such influence over U.S.–China policy could hold such a naïve view. By then, all the so-called liberals within the CCP had already been "rectified"—brainwashed, silenced, or eliminated. The party demanded total conformity and submission.

The negotiations between both sides lasted for more than a year with no significant agreements achieved, while each side used the time to prepare for the inevitable conflict.

The negotiation inevitably collapsed. Marshall was convinced that there was no military solution, as he viewed Chiang to be "the worst advised military commander in history" and became impressed by the Communist leadership. Marshall urged Chiang to take a farsighted approach, suggesting that while his own mission for peace and unity had failed, Chiang still had the chance to lead China down a better path by winning the people's support and building a liberal party, rather than relying solely on military force. Marshall believed this could make Chiang "the father of the country."[34]

Frustrated by Chiang's resistance, Marshall imposed an arms embargo on the Nationalists in 1946. Ultimately, Marshall acknowledged to Truman that the mission was over, and it was now up to the Chinese to follow through.[35]

By 1949, the Truman Administration had adopted a passive "do-nothing" policy, arguing that the decades-long KMT-CCP conflict held no new developments.[36] In practice, this stance handed China to the Communists.

While Marshall's embargo crippled the Nationalists, the Soviets were actively strengthening the CCP's military capabilities, ultimately tipping the balance in their favor.

This was a terrifying prospect implying that the Second World War might have been fought in vain, as the combined strength of the Communists in China and the U.S.S.R. and Soviet-controlled Eastern European bloc would be even harder to deal with than the Axis powers had been.

Hu Shi, a leading figure among Chinese intellectuals advocating for liberal democracy, and the Chinese ambassador to the United States from 1938 to 1942, succinctly summarized the Marshall Mission:

> In plain language, the weapon was to be not military pressure or intervention, but the withholding of American aid to China. But this weapon could only checkmate the Chinese Government and had no effect whatever on the Chinese Communists, whose armies had been racing by land and by sea to Manchuria where they could obtain unlimited aid from the Soviet Occupation Forces and from the Soviet Union, now the contiguous, strongest base of revolution for the Chinese Communists. So, during the entire period of the Marshall Mission, the Chinese Communist delegation was constantly and successfully pressing General Marshall to stop or suspend American aid to China! And

> General Marshall and the United States Government did many times stop and suspend all American aid to China because of the loud protests of the Chinese Communists.

Hu Shi argued the United States was not "innocent of the blood" of fallen China.[37]

Who lost China? While the Truman administration blamed Chiang Kai-shek, Chiang's recently revealed diary tells a different story. He attributed his defeat to Stalin, Marshall, and his vice president, Li Zongren, who secretly pursued peace with the Communists. Chiang did not blame Mao, seeing the CCP's victory as a product of Soviet support and the loss of U.S. backing. Regardless of blame, the clear winner of the Marshall mission was the CCP.

After Marshall's unsuccessful mediation efforts in China, he was not held accountable but instead promoted to secretary of state and later secretary of defense, continuing to influence U.S.–China policy. President Truman praised him as "the greatest of the great in our time."[38]

Not everyone shared this view. During Marshall's senate confirmation for secretary of defense, Senator William Jenner called him "a living lie" and "a front man for traitors."[39]

General Douglas MacArthur, U.S. Supreme Commander of the Southwest Pacific during World War II, described Marshall's China policy as "the greatest political mistake we made in a hundred years"—one, he warned, "we will pay for...for a century."[40]

Although Marshall is best remembered for the successful Marshall Plan that rebuilt postwar Europe, Congressman Walter Judd, a former missionary in China and one of the most outspoken anti-Communists in Congress, highlighted the inconsistency in U.S. policy: "In Europe we insisted that in order to get our help the governments must keep the Communists out; but in China we insisted that in order to get our help the government must take the Communists in."[41]

Marshall eventually abandoned his remarkably naïve belief that "in China we have no concrete evidence that the Communist Party is supported by Communists from the outside," referring to Soviet Russia.[42]

But by then it was too late!

John Leighton Stuart (1876–1962)

Another notable "John" was John Leighton Stuart—a scholar-turned-diplomat born in China to missionary parents, who saw himself as more Chinese than American. Over fifty-five years, he rose from second-generation missionary to president of Yenching University—a leading Christian institution in China—and ultimately became the last U.S. ambassador to serve in mainland China under the KMT. Few Americans of his era were so deeply connected to China or left such a lasting legacy.

Ironically, Stuart is most famously remembered in China due to Mao Zedong's White Paper, *Farewell, Leighton Stuart*, published on August 8, 1949, which eventually became a staple of Chinese middle school textbooks. Mao mocked Stuart and portrayed him as a symbol of the complete failure of American imperialist policy in China. Adding to the irony, Mao timed the publication of the article to coincide with Stuart's departure from China, ensuring his "farewell" reached Washington before Stuart himself did.

In this white paper, Mao openly revealed his true stance toward the United States, condemning it as an enemy of the Chinese people and accusing it of backing Chiang Kai-shek to serve American interests and slaughter the Chinese.

Yet, just four years earlier in Chongqing during negotiations with Chiang Kai-shek, Mao had had a cordial meeting with Stuart. Stuart recalled: "When Mr. Mao saw me in the crowd, he greeted me with the remark that there were present many of my former students at Yan'an. I laughingly replied that I was well aware of that and hoped that they were proving a credit to their training."[43]

Among his students were John Davies—one of the Three Johns—and Huang Hua, who served as Edgar Snow's translator during his visit to Yan'an and later became the CCP's minister of foreign affairs.

Stuart seemed to miss Mao's sarcasm, which implied that Yenching University was producing future Communists for the CCP. He responded sincerely, noting that many Yenching students had joined the CCP by embracing the school's motto: "Freedom through Truth for Service." As Stuart wrote, "With my own passionate insistence on freedom, I could not but apply this to their right to choose their own experience."[44]

Stuart took pride in the influence the motto had on his students. He recalled, "I had students who went over to the Communists come back and tell me with starry-eyed enthusiasm what they were doing for the common people in trying faithfully to live up to this motto. In no other college of my acquaintance has the college motto had so vital and dynamic an influence upon the student body."[45] For many, Yenching's ideal of "freedom" meant the freedom to chart their own path—even if that path led them into the Communist movement.

Clearly, he failed to recognize that Communist ideology was fundamentally at odds with Yenching's Christian values—and could not foresee that his colleagues and students were marching into the grip of a totalitarian regime. Tragically, Yenching's transformation has echoed in America. Harvard, for instance, began as a Christian institution and has since become a hub of radicalism and a leading exporter of modern-day Cultural Marxism. As the founding president of Yenching University, Stuart led the institution under the influence of his liberal theology, believing that Christianity and socialism could be reconciled. Among the pro-CCP progressive faculty he recruited were Edgar Snow and missionary Randolph C. Sailer. Sailer, who chaired Yenching's Christian Fellowship and actively mobilized students for Communist causes,[46] was later praised by Zhou Enlai as an "*old friend of the Chinese people.*"

Stuart unwittingly made Yenching University a soft target for CCP infiltration, enabling the party to forge strong ties with student groups. These student activists played a pivotal role in the Chinese Civil War, helping to bring down the KMT regime—a strategy the CCP proudly called the "Second Front," waged behind the military frontlines. It's not hard to see that Marxists have effectively replicated this tactic in the United States, from the 1960s to today.

As university president, Stuart never discouraged students from embracing Communism. Yet this same man, with little grasp of its dangers, was appointed U.S. ambassador to China by Truman in 1946 on George Marshall's recommendation. By then, the KMT was in rapid decline, and the U.S. China policy was riddled with a history of costly mistakes. A scholar like Stuart was unlikely to change its course.

Stuart admitted his failure to assist General Marshall in persuading either side to achieve peace. Later in life, in his book *Fifty Years in China*, he reflected on this shortcoming, asking, "Were we too naive and unsuspecting as to the true nature of Communism wherever found?"[47]

When the Communist forces captured Nanjing, the capital of the Nationalist government, most Western diplomats followed the Nationalist government to Guangzhou. However, Stuart chose to remain behind, hoping to establish communication with the CCP through his former student, Huang Hua, who was now overseeing CCP foreign affairs under Zhou Enlai. Stuart aimed to persuade the CCP to maintain some form of diplomatic relationship with the United States.[48] But his goodwill had been met with profound hostility.

The U.S. State Department barred him from traveling north to negotiate with the Communists and urgently recalled him. On August 2, 1949, Stuart, at the age of seventy-three, quietly boarded a plane back to the United States, filled with a sense of melancholy.

On October 1, 1949, Mao Zedong announced the founding of the People's Republic of China, marking the beginning of a new Communist regime. Meanwhile, the Kuomintang, led by Chiang Kai-shek, retreated to Taiwan.

In 1954, Yenching University merged into Beijing University. Its last president, Lu Zhiwei, a scholar who had studied in the United States and earned a PhD in psychology from the University of Chicago, chose to stay in China to serve the new regime. His reward was political persecution. During the Cultural Revolution, his daughter publicly denounced him, and he was subsequently sent to the countryside to be "re-educated" through pig farming. He eventually died, tormented by hunger and illness.[49]

The downfall of Yenching University and Stuart's personal failure symbolized the larger collapse of American missionary work and U.S. foreign policy in China—both rooted in a fundamental misunderstanding of Communism.

The fall of China to Communism was not only a profound tragedy for the hundreds of millions of Chinese people—one-quarter of humanity—but also marked a turning point in Asia's political landscape, establishing a foothold for Communist dominance in the region. This shift set postwar Asia on a path of sustained conflict, with Communist insurgencies and ideological battles erupting across the continent. Ultimately, the United States became embroiled in two major wars to counter Communist expansion in Asia: the Korean War and the Vietnam War.

A provocative question is: Who truly won World War II? Before the war, the only Communist state was Soviet Russia. Following the end of the war, a third of the global population had fallen under the grip of Communism.

A more pressing question, however, is why so many influential American intellectuals, politicians, and policy makers believed the Chinese Communist Party's propaganda and viewed the Communists as mere "agrarian reformers," believing that the Communist movement was a populist uprising rather than a Marxist-Leninist revolution. This widespread belief cannot simply be attributed to naïveté. It stems from something much deeper—a left-leaning liberal worldview that made many susceptible to Communist deception. As Joseph Sobran, an American conservative journalist, insightfully remarked, "If Communism was liberalism in a hurry, liberalism is Communism in slow motion."

In truth, the American left is well aware that terms like "leftism," "Communism," and "Marxism" have long carried a negative stigma in the West. To mask their true intentions, they appropriated the label "liberal," presenting themselves as champions of freedom. In reality, they embrace totalitarianism, dictatorship, and tyranny, thereby tarnishing the true meaning of the word *liberalism*.

The consequences are stark. America not only "lost China" to Communism in 1949, but decades later, it now faces the unsettling prospect of losing itself to ideologies rooted in the same Communist doctrine. History is never truly behind us; it keeps repeating itself. Yesterday's liberalism has steadily morphed into the very Communism it once opposed, now creeping into American life under new names and guises. The failure to learn from history has left many Americans blind to the resurgence of Marxism—now repackaged for the modern era as Cultural Marxism, or more popularly, "woke" ideology.

For me, the fall of China was not just historical, but also deeply personal. Ten years later, I was born into the bondage of Communism and spent my first twenty-six years under its suffocating grip—while those China "experts" were safely back in America, never having to answer for the suffering they helped unleash.

CHAPTER 5

THE OPENING THAT SAVED THE PARTY

The events that unfolded in China after its fall to Communism in 1949 decisively answered the fundamental questions that had once divided Americans engaged with China: Were the CCP merely agrarian reformers or radical revolutionaries? So-called Communists or true Bolsheviks? More Chinese than Communist, or even more Communistic than the Soviets? And more.

The CCP's actions left no room for doubt. The answers were clear, unmistakable, and deeply sobering. Yet by then, those questions had been forgotten by those who once asked them—cast aside by the more immediate threat of the Soviet Union and the escalating Cold War.

By the end of his life, Mao had turned China into a living nightmare, carrying out atrocities—many still unknown to Americans—while also bringing the nation to the brink of nuclear war with his former master.

I wasn't just a witness to the hell Mao created—I lived through it.

Desperate for a lifeline, the party was in urgent need of salvation. Fortunately for them, a savior emerged from the most unlikely place—ready to pull China back from the edge.

Who Lost China?

The fall of China to Communism in 1949, fueled by the Cold War, sparked the Second Red Scare, the first one having been triggered by the 1917 Russian Revolution.

Intense domestic debates over the "loss of China" ignited in the United States as Americans grappled with questions of how and why China had fallen under Communist control.

Blame quickly fell on leftist journalists and writers whose credulous, sympathetic reporting amplified support for the CCP, as well as on the so-called China experts—or China hands—in the State Department, along with politicians and military leaders who crafted disastrous U.S. policies toward China. Americans wanted the truth and to hold them accountable.

McCarthy Was Right!

In the early 1950s, Senator Joseph McCarthy emerged as a central figure in the broader effort to investigate Communist infiltration in the United States.

Many of the figures discussed in the previous chapter—Snow, Smedley, White, Stein, Hinton, the Three Johns, and even General George Marshall—were drawn into these controversies, and for good reason. Their actions, writings, and policies undeniably contributed to the rise of the Chinese Communist Party.

In response to McCarthy, liberals countered with the claim, "China was not ours to lose." The truth they refused to acknowledge was that the United States lost more than just China—it lost to Communism itself.

While the methods and outcomes of McCarthy's investigations remain a subject of debate, the investigations themselves were clearly warranted, since they aimed to expose and address Communist infiltration, sympathy toward Communism, and the spread of Communist ideology within the U.S. government and institutions—a threat that legitimately jeopardized American values and national security. Evidence from various sources—including declassified Soviet archives—since the end of the Cold War in the early 1990s indicates that numerous cases of McCarthy's accusations were not false or exaggerated, but in fact accurate.[1]

McCarthy and his anti-Communist crusade were ultimately crushed, leaving the senator discredited and disgraced. His investigations and suspicions were labeled as "McCarthyism," a term that has become synonymous with political witch hunts and hysteria of any kind, regardless of context. The *American Heritage Dictionary* now defines McCarthyism as "the practice of publicizing accusations of political disloyalty or subversion with insufficient regard to evidence; and the use of unfair investigatory or accusatory methods in order to suppress opposition"—a narrative that ignores the historical anti-subversion, anti-Communist context of the term.

This brought back a vivid memory. In the early 1990s, still new to America and unfamiliar with its history, I happened to watch the 1991 film *Guilty by Suspicion*, starring Robert De Niro. It told the story of a Hollywood director who fell victim to McCarthyism. I remember feeling a strange sympathy for the character—while puzzled as to why anti-Communism was portrayed as something wrong. Fast-forward to today: Hollywood hasn't just defeated McCarthyism—it has become a full-blown propaganda machine for Communist ideology. This is a profound American tragedy. Anti-Communism was rebranded as "McCarthyism" and weaponized by liberals to demonize and silence their political opponents. Those accused were recast as martyrs—and, later, as heroes. What could have been a decisive effort to expose and root out Communism and its ideology was squandered. Its lessons were ignored, and the label itself became a rhetorical weapon for Communists and their sympathizers.

Path to Ruins (1949–1976)

The fall of China was followed by more than two decades of mutual isolation between the CCP and the United States.

Despite the loss, some clung to the illusion that Communist China might prove less radical than the Soviet Union and resist becoming a mere satellite under Moscow's control. They were to be swiftly and thoroughly disappointed.

Immediately after taking power, Mao launched one political campaign after another—often running several at the same time. These so-called campaigns were, in reality, mass movements of persecution targeting specific groups. Each wave claimed countless victims, inflicting widespread suffering and death across the country. In the end, there were no winners. Everyone—without exception—became a victim of the CCP's totalitarian rule. Most tragic of all were the stories of those who had helped make the victory of the revolution possible: the peasants, the intellectuals, and even loyal Communists.

Path to Serfdom

The CCP framed its revolution as a peasant movement, garnering support from millions of them who made up nearly 90 percent of China's population at that time. For the peasants, the promise of "free" land was their primary motivation for supporting the Communists.

Wasting no time after seizing power, the CCP launched a nationwide land reform—one of Mao's first major political campaigns to redistribute land. While land redistribution could have been managed administratively, the Chinese Communist Party opted for a violent campaign, pitting peasants against landlords and against one another. The CCP believed that through this class struggle, peasants would develop class consciousness and become more committed Communist supporters. The land reform campaign effectively turned traditional peasants into bloodthirsty revolutionaries and thugs, organized and directed by CCP work teams dispatched to each village.

What many failed to realize was that Mao's true revolution only began after the CCP assumed control—a process he referred to as the "Continuing Revolution."

In his groundbreaking book *The Bloody Red Land* (2019)—in stark contrast to William Hinton's *Shenfan*—author Tan Song exposes chilling accounts of the land reform in eastern Sichuan Province. Through interviews conducted between 2003 and 2017 with hundreds of survivors and participants, he unveils the brutal realities of this tumultuous period.

Here is a quote from Liu Zhixiong, one of the interviewees in the book, and a descendant of a landlord who died after a brutal struggle session:

> The Land Reform killed and persecuted people without any justification! If the land was to be confiscated, then take it—but if the landlords resisted, only then might suppression or violence be considered. But no! They didn't just seize the land and property; they had to kill as well! Not only were landlords executed, but their descendants were persecuted for decades. There is no justice in this—nowhere in the world does such logic exist.[2]

The land reform was engineered as a violent onslaught—a campaign of terror designed to instill fear so that no one would dare to challenge the new regime. The atrocities revealed in Tan Song's book, akin to what happened to Niu Youlan near Long Bow Village, where Hinton stayed as a land reform observer, were repeated throughout rural China.

As a landlord, my paternal grandmother had all her land and property confiscated. She was fortunate to escape the violence, having already resettled in the city of Xi'an. But her descendants, including me, inherited the permanent stain of her "landlord" status—branded as enemies of the revolution. I carried deep resentment and shame for her "sin" until after the end of Mao's era.

Even decades later, the truth about the land reform remains dangerous and taboo. Tan Song was forced to halt his interviews when the CCP intervened, resulting in dismissal from his university teaching position in 2017. He eventually immigrated to the United States. In an interview with Radio Free Asia, Tan emphasized that a central objective of the land reform campaign was the eradication of the gentry class—the traditional custodians of Chinese culture in rural areas and largely respected local leaders. The campaign aimed to replace them by establishing party branches in every village, no matter how remote, and imposing Marxist-Leninist ideology in place of traditional culture.[3]

The land reform campaign successfully eliminated the entire landlord class in rural China, resulting in the deaths of up to 2 million landlords and wealthy farmers.[4] Among the victims were not only landlords but also individuals in rural areas who did not engage in manual labor for their livelihood, such as teachers and practitioners of traditional Chinese medicine. Such was the CCP's arbitrary definition of guilt.

Initially, poor peasants—the beneficiaries of land reform—rejoiced as they received free land. Their joy, however, was short-lived. By 1958, the CCP introduced agricultural collectivization by establishing the so-called People's Communes. The state seized all land and farming tools in the name of the "people," while imposing strict state-controlled procurement and distribution of agricultural products. Peasants were left owning nothing and had no control over what they could plant. This policy plunged farmers into abject poverty—a condition that, in many areas, persists to this day. It stands as a stark warning: What the state gives, it can just as easily take away—a lesson Americans would do well to remember before trading their freedom for government handouts wrapped in promises. The CCP solidified its control of peasantry by imposing a strict household registration, or *hukou* (户口) system. Unlike earlier systems that merely required residents to register their place of residence, the CCP's *hukou* system locked individuals into a permanent status: once a peasant, forever a peasant. It bound peasants to the land, stripping them of their centuries-old freedom to move or settle in other areas, especially urban centers. Landless, immobile, and governed by a new overlord—the state—the peasants were effectively transformed into modern-day serfs.

In my first book, *Mao's America*, I shared the story of how, at age sixteen, I was forced to give up my urban *hukou* status and was sent to the countryside for reeducation—becoming part of the serf class.

Losing land to the state was only the beginning of the misery for Chinese peasants. In 1958, Mao launched the infamous Great Leap Forward campaign, aiming to rapidly transform China from an agrarian society into an industrial powerhouse. Peasants, degraded to slave labor, were mobilized to forsake agriculture for steelmaking in makeshift, wood-fueled backyard furnaces. This led to extensive deforestation and the smelting of every scrap of metal from their homes, from kitchenware to doorknobs, in a desperate bid to meet quotas imposed by the party.

While the steel-making effort failed disastrously, producing nothing but worthless metal, agricultural production also collapsed, leading to the Great Famine (1959–1961). Historian Frank Dikötter, in his book *Mao's Great Famine*, estimated that the catastrophe claimed up to 46 million lives, nearly all of them peasants.[5] The death toll from Mao's famine far exceeded that of the Ukrainian famine under Stalin in the 1930s. Yet, despite the staggering scale of this tragedy, it remains relatively unknown in the United States and the broader Western world.

I was born at the beginning of the famine. Though I have no memory of it, I grew up hearing harrowing stories from my mother—of severe food rationing and constant hunger. Everyone was swollen from protein deficiency. Yet she and other urban residents were the lucky ones. Nearly all the deaths occurred in the countryside, where peasants had no access to government rations, however meager they were.

War Against Free Thinking

In their struggle to rise to power, the CCP relied also on the support of the intellectuals and educated elites who played a critical role by leading student protests and carrying out propaganda efforts for the CCP. Despite their smaller numbers, their contributions were immeasurable in shaping public opinion and advancing the party's cause.

These intellectuals were encouraged to be "free" thinkers—free from traditional Chinese and Christian values, and free to embrace Marxism and Leninism—an outcome ironically demonstrated by John Stuart's motto, "Freedom through Truth for Service."

But now, these intellectuals posed a threat to the totalitarian regime. The reason was simple: The same "free" thinking that once led them to embrace Communism could just as easily be turned against it—challenging the rigid, monolithic ideology the CCP needed to impose its socialist transformation of China.

Mao's thought reform, or *sixiang gaizao* (思想改造), campaign served as the solution to this problem, much like land reform was for the peasants. Its goal was to reshape the minds of intellectuals by eradicating independent thinking and instilling absolute loyalty to Marxist-Leninist ideology and the CCP. In other words, thought reform was a brainwashing operation.

Just as land reform served as a revolution to transform rural China, thought reform aimed to reshape the minds of millions of Chinese intellectuals. And just as land reform was first implemented in CCP-controlled areas before seizing power in 1949, thought reform was first carried out in Yan'an as part of the rectification campaign, which I discussed in earlier chapters. By this point, the CCP was well versed in such methods and knew exactly how to execute them.

More specifically, the campaign sought to eradicate the Anglo-American educational ideology embedded in China's education system, particularly in higher education through missionary efforts. The goal was to replace it with Marxist doctrine and the Soviet model.

Li Jingduan, who enrolled at Tsinghua University in 1951, recalled witnessing the thought reform campaign, which aimed to transform professors and educators. The campaign required everyone to "wash out impurities" from their minds, likened to "taking a bath," by engaging in self-criticism. Those who failed to pass the "thought-cleansing" process in smaller meetings were required to repeat it at full university assemblies.

Li described witnessing the self-criticism of Professor Fei Xiaotong, a renowned anthropologist and longtime supporter of the CCP. Fei meticulously listed his "thought crimes," voluntarily escalating the severity of his offenses, and berating himself to the point of tears. His dramatic display earned him approval, and he successfully passed the evaluation.

In contrast, another professor failed his self-criticism even after multiple attempts. One significant reason was his prior affiliation with the Kuomintang and his work for the KMT government.[6]

The campaign didn't end with the professors; students were subjected to the same process once the professors were done.

By the time the thought reform campaign concluded in the fall of 1952, approximately 91 percent of teachers and 80 percent of students had undergone the "cleansing" process to purge incorrect thoughts from their minds.[7]

If these intellectuals felt any relief after two years of intense scrutiny during the thought reform campaign, they would not feel it for long.

In 1957, intellectuals faced an even greater calamity with the onset of the Anti-Rightist Campaign. In Mao's China, "Rightists" were defined as those who criticized the party, questioned its authority, or resisted its radical policies. In practice, being labeled a Rightist meant being branded an enemy of the party—and, by extension, the state.

Like all political campaigns under Mao, this one was also designed to instill fear. Mao arbitrarily declared that up to 10 percent of individuals in the cultural and educational sectors were Rightists. To meet—or even exceed—this quota, many organizations eagerly identified Rightists within their ranks, often without any evidence. According to declassified central archives, more than 3.17 million people nationwide were labeled Rightists, and an additional 1.43 million were categorized as moderate Rightists. Others were labeled suspected Rightists, or Rightist sympathizers. The youngest known individual labeled a rightist was only twelve years old.[8]

My mother, a loyal member of the Communist Party, was labeled a Rightist sympathizer for simply questioning what she saw as an unreasonable accusation against her co-worker. As a result, her career was effectively destroyed.

Those labeled as Rightists faced punishments ranging from dismissal, demotion, or assignment to a labor camp, to imprisonment and execution. Many individuals committed suicide or were tortured to death. In forced labor camps like Jiabiangou (夹边沟) in Gansu Province and Shaping (沙坪) in Sichuan Province, tens of thousands of Rightists were detained, and during the Great Famine, nearly half of these prisoners starved to death.

The remaining intellectuals faced continuous scrutiny and persecution, from the Cultural Revolution (1966–1976) to the present day. One could argue that over the years the CCP has successfully broken their spirit. The backbone of Chinese intellectuals has been crushed—most have learned to comply simply to survive.

I often wish I could strike every progressive liberal over the head with these tragic stories—to waken them to the reality that blindly following Woke ideology could lead them down the same path of self-destruction.

A Revolution to Take Down the CCP

Many Americans have heard of Mao's Cultural Revolution, but not everyone fully understands its purpose.

The Cultural Revolution had its roots in the aftermath of the catastrophic failure of the Great Leap Forward and the ensuing Great Famine—sanitized in CCP terminology as the "Three-Year Natural Disaster"—which claimed tens of millions of lives. Mao faced intense criticism from within the Communist Party and was compelled to relinquish much of his direct control over the government. In 1962, leadership shifted to more pragmatic figures, notably Liu Shaoqi (then president of China) and Deng Xiaoping (general secretary), who introduced policies focused on stabilizing the economy and recovering from the famine. These policies represented a clear departure from Mao's radical visions, emphasizing practical solutions and moderate reforms over endless ideological campaigns.

Mao viewed these developments as a betrayal of his revolutionary ideals and a threat to his absolute authority and became determined to regain power and take back absolute control.

In 1966, Mao launched his final and most destructive undertaking—the Great Proletarian Cultural Revolution—a ten-year catastrophe that marked my youth, ultimately transforming me from an elementary schoolgirl to a peasant undergoing so-called reeducation through hard labor in the fields for three very long years. Unlike previous political campaigns, this was a full-scale revolution aimed at dismantling the existing government, social order, and traditional culture. Its central theme was *duo quan* (夺权)—seizing power—by stripping authority from officials at all levels: central, provincial, and local, leaving Mao and his loyal allies as the sole holders of power.

Mao found the perfect "army" to carry out his revolution in the tens of millions of youths indoctrinated with blind loyalty to him—they came to be known as the Red Guards. Empowered by Mao with full authority, the Red Guards set out to obliterate Chinese civilization once and for all, targeting the Four Olds—old ideas, old culture, old customs, and old habits—and replacing them with the ideology of Maoism. Their most significant achievement, however, was the dismantling of the CCP bureaucracy itself. This aligned precisely with Mao's true intention: to purge his perceived rivals, thereby reclaiming his supreme dominance within the party.

The persecution of CCP officials was a replay of the brutal land reform campaign. The difference was that the roles had been reversed with CCP officials now targeted as the "landlords" and "rich peasants."

Li Jingquan, who governed Sichuan Province from 1949 to 1966, played a central role in several of the CCP's major political campaigns, including land reform. In 1947, he personally directed the land reform campaign in the "liberated areas" and ordered the public struggle session of landlord Niu Youlan, as previously described. It was Li who pressured Niu's son, Niu Yinguan, to prove his loyalty to the party by publicly denouncing his father—resulting in a brutal spectacle in which the son was forced to parade his father through the village.[9] Li later led both the Anti-Rightist Campaign and the Great Leap Forward, during which Sichuan suffered the highest famine-related death toll in the entire country.

During the Cultural Revolution, he and his family fell victim to the very system he had helped create. Li and his wife endured relentless struggle sessions, his wife committed suicide, and his son was beaten to death by the Red Guards. Isn't this a perfect example of "what goes around comes around"?

The ultimate prize for the Red Guards was the downfall of Liu Shaoqi, the president of China, whom Mao regarded as his archenemy. Branded as the chief "Capitalist Roader" and accused of betraying Communist ideals, Liu was publicly denounced, subjected to brutal struggle sessions, and stripped of all party positions. The Red Guards also targeted his wife, who was similarly humiliated and abused. Liu died in confinement, deprived of medical care. His death was officially recorded under a pseudonym, with his occupation listed as "unemployed."

As an ally of Liu Shaoqi, Deng Xiaoping was branded the number two "Capitalist Roader" and subjected to severe persecution, along with his entire family—a common tactic of the CCP. Deng's eldest son was accused of being a counterrevolutionary and detained by Red Guards. In a desperate attempt to escape, he jumped from a third-floor window, resulting in lifelong paralysis. However, unlike Liu Shaoqi—who was seen as a direct threat to Mao and ultimately perished in custody—Deng was exiled to work in a remote tractor factory rather than imprisonment. Mao spared Deng's life, believing he might prove useful in the future.

No one was immune to the Red Guards' wrath, including Xi Jinping, the current CCP's paramount leader. His father was purged by Mao, and the whole family suffered. Xi himself endured abuse from Red Guards, while his half sister, unable to bear the torment, chose to commit suicide.

Again, this bloody lesson must be learned: In a totalitarian regime, no one is safe—not even those who manage to rise to the very top of the power structure. The examples above are only the tip of the iceberg. The widespread violence of the Cultural Revolution claimed tens of millions of lives—not just CCP leaders, but also ordinary citizens and even many Red Guards themselves, who, caught up in the chaos, eventually turned on each other. After the Red Guards had fulfilled their task of destroying the Four Olds and seizing power from the Capitalist Roaders for Mao, he repaid them by exiling them to the countryside for so-called reeducation through harsh physical labor.

Mao did have a few allies among his old comrades, including Marshal Lin Biao. Lin played a pivotal role during the Cultural Revolution as Mao Zedong's closest ally and handpicked successor. As minister of defense, Lin helped consolidate Mao's power by using the military to support the Red Guards and enforce Maoist ideology. Lin played a key role in promoting the *Little Red Book* and elevating Mao's cult of personality to new heights, positioning himself as a staunch enforcer of Mao's directives.

However, Lin's relationship with Mao eventually deteriorated due to Mao's growing political paranoia. Allegedly, Lin plotted a coup to overthrow Mao, but the plan was discovered. In September 1971, Lin and his family attempted to flee to the Soviet Union, but their plane mysteriously crashed in Mongolia, killing all on board. This incident marked a dramatic turning point in the Cultural Revolution and severely undermined the legitimacy of Mao's regime.

This was a crushing blow to Mao, shattering his image as the all-knowing leader, as it became clear he had chosen the wrong successor.

After dismantling the lives of his former comrades, his party, his government, and his supporters, Mao found himself a broken man—isolated, with no one left to trust. His physical decline was unmistakable for all to see. It mirrored the state of the nation he now ruled absolutely—broken, divided, and teetering on the brink of total collapse.

Anyone with knowledge of both the Russian and Chinese Communist Parties has little difficulty concluding that the CCP outdid its teachers, driving the Communist revolution to even greater extremes.

International Fallout

Following the takeover of China in 1949, the Chinese Communist Party became the largest satellite state of the Soviet Union—a seemingly natural progression, given the decisive role Soviet Russia had played in the CCP's creation, development, and ultimate victory in China. In 1950, Mao signed the Sino-Soviet Treaty of Friendship, Alliance, and Mutual Assistance with Moscow, formally solidifying the alliance between Communist China and the U.S.S.R. and strengthening the Communist bloc during the early Cold War. While the treaty provided significant economic and military aid to Communist China, it also underscored China's subordination to the Soviet Union.

After twenty-eight years of fighting against so-called foreign imperialism, the CCP found itself a client colony of Soviet imperialism, a reality Chiang Kai-shek had predicted during his earlier observations of Soviet influence following his tour of Russia.

The early 1950s marked a honeymoon period for China and the Soviet Union. During Stalin's lifetime, Mao followed his lead meticulously. The Soviet Union was the only foreign country Mao ever visited. He knew his place in the Communist hierarchy with Stalin as the patriarch and himself as a dutiful son.

In 1950, Mao faced pressure from Stalin to get involved in the Korean War. Post-revolution China was extremely fragile after decades of military conflicts, including the Sino-Japanese War and the Chinese Civil War, and desperately needed time to heal and recover. Despite resistance within the party, Mao sent Chinese troops, branded as "volunteers," to directly intervene in the Korean War.

The cost to China was staggering, marked by immense casualties and a devastating loss of life. Among the wounded was my father. He was a reporter and suffered serious injuries when the truck carrying him and other soldiers plunged into a U.S. bomb crater at night, its headlights turned off to avoid attracting attention.

Mao also paid a personal price. His son, Mao Anying—his only heir apparent—was killed in an airstrike during the Korean War. Many Chinese believe that this loss inadvertently spared China from possibly following North Korea's path of extreme hereditary dictatorship under the Kim family.

Apart from human loss, the war deepened the challenges of economic recovery and modernization. The conflict also heightened tensions with the United States, solidifying its support for Taiwan and isolating China internationally.

To Mao, all these sacrifices were worthwhile, as he was handsomely rewarded by Stalin with Soviet aid and assistance in developing China's heavy industries.

The Chinese Communist Party modeled China after the Soviet Union, adopting a planned economy to drive industrialization. By the end of its First Five-Year Plan in 1957, China had laid the foundation for both its heavy industry and defense sector.

However, the honeymoon began to unravel after Stalin's death in 1953. Mao soon found that he did not see eye to eye with Stalin's successor Nikita Khrushchev, even though Khrushchev was economically friendlier toward China and expanded aid projects.

A major point of contention arose when Khrushchev shifted Soviet foreign policy toward advocating peaceful coexistence with the capitalist world. Mao, firmly opposed to any compromise, famously declared, "Either the East wind prevails over the West wind, or vice versa." Khrushchev, in turn, viewed Mao as a radical and was critical of his plan to fast-track socialist modernization through the Great Leap Forward campaign, dismissing it as a misguided and disastrous shortcut to Communism.[10]

Mao's resentment also stemmed from Khrushchev's opposition to Stalin's cult of personality, which directly clashed with the cult Mao was cultivating for himself. At the 20th Congress of the Communist Party of the Soviet Union, Khrushchev delivered his famous secret speech exposing Stalin's horrifying cult of personality and tyranny. Emboldened by Khrushchev's actions, critics within the Chinese Communist Party began pushing to remove references to *Mao Zedong Thought* from the party constitution.

Mao also saw himself—not Khrushchev—as Stalin's true successor and the foremost leader of the global Communist movement, viewing Khrushchev as a traitor to Stalin's legacy. Mao harbored a deep fear of a Khrushchev-like figure emerging in China. This anxiety became one of the driving forces behind the launch of the Cultural Revolution, aimed at purging leaders like Liu Shaoqi, whom Mao considered China's Khrushchev.

Meanwhile, Khrushchev increasingly regarded Mao as erratic, if not outright unhinged. Their mutual distrust only continued to escalate.

Despite Khrushchev's reluctance to continue the USSR's support of Mao's nuclear programs, China successfully detonated both an atomic bomb in 1964 and a hydrogen bomb in 1967. This success was largely attributed to Qian Xuesen (1911–2009), a U.S.-trained physicist and a recipient of the Boxer Indemnity scholarship who had played a significant role in NASA's early missile and nuclear programs. Accused of Communist ties during the Red Scare, Qian was expelled from the United States—a decision Secretary of the Navy Dan Kimball later described as "the stupidest thing this country ever did."[11] While Qian may have been a Communist sympathizer, this reckless decision ultimately became a great gift to the CCP.

In 1964, Leonid Brezhnev replaced Khrushchev, but Sino-Soviet relations continued to deteriorate.

The success of China's nuclear program emboldened Mao to take an increasingly hard-line stance toward the Soviet Union. Mao called for a critique of Soviet "revisionism," asserting that the Soviet Union had degenerated into a new imperialist power. Mao insisted that only China remained the true bastion of Marxism-Leninism, and the leader of the Communist world.

Yet the only Communist country to openly side with China was the small European nation of Albania. Even traditional "blood allies" like

North Korea and North Vietnam aligned with the Soviet Union. As a result, China found itself isolated on the international stage, rejected by both the Western bloc and the Communist camp.

In 1969, the Soviet and Chinese armies engaged in a small-scale military conflict at the northern border, known as the Zhenbao Island Incident. Similar conflicts occurred along the Xinjiang border. Both countries deployed more than a million troops along their shared border, each wary of the other.

The Soviet Union feared that China, in the throes of the Cultural Revolution, might become even more dangerous and reportedly considered launching a full-scale war, including the use of nuclear weapons.[12] In response, Mao ordered the construction of air-raid shelters in major cities across China. I was still in elementary school at the time, and we were tasked with digging trenches in the school playground, bracing for what was thought to be an impending Russian attack. This was much like the fear American schoolchildren experienced during the Cuban Missile Crisis and throughout the Cold War, when they practiced duck-and-cover drills under their desks in anticipation of a nuclear strike from the very same enemy: the Soviet Union. By this point, Mao had shifted his focus, viewing the Soviet Union, not the United States, as China's primary adversary.

Feeling encircled internationally and facing total collapse domestically, Mao realized that if this state of affairs continued, the CCP regime would disintegrate.

At this time, Mao felt compelled to adopt a strategy of aligning with the American "imperialists" to restrain the Communist Soviet Union. In 1970, after two decades of diplomatic estrangement, he took the initiative to invite Edgar Snow to visit China, viewing him as a channel to communicate with the U.S. government. On October 1, the CCP's National Day, Mao invited Snow to join him on the Tiananmen tower for the celebrations to signal his willingness to reconcile with the United States. Mao told Snow that "All Nixon has to do is board a plane, and he can come here."

Mao expressed his eagerness to talk to Nixon, saying Nixon could visit China either publicly or secretly, "as a tourist or as a president."[13]

Mao was betting that the United States would once again save him from an enemy—this time the enemy was the Soviet Union instead of the Nationalists.

Mao was not to be disappointed.

Nixon Goes to China

Since 1947, U.S. foreign policy had been guided by the principle of "containment" or "détente," aimed at preventing the spread of Communism and limiting Soviet influence beyond the territories it controlled after World War II. The core principle of the Cold War was anti-Communism, as President Dwight D. Eisenhower clearly articulated when he emphasized the ideological struggle at the heart of global politics: "The central fact of today's life is that we are in a life-and-death struggle of ideologies. It is freedom against dictatorship; Communism against capitalism; concepts of human dignity against the materialistic dialectic."[14]

While the primary focus was on the U.S.S.R., Eisenhower also warned of the threat posed by Communist China. He noted that Mao had openly declared his commitment to global revolution and the violent overthrow of all other forms of government. Eisenhower further stressed that Mao held absolute contempt for the principles of honor, decency, and integrity—values essential to the functioning of international law and order.[15]

Eisenhower's secretary of state, John Foster Dulles, shared this clear-eyed view of Communist China. In distinguishing Soviet Russia from Communist China, Dulles stated, "There are no doubt basic power rivalries between Russia and China in Asia. On the other hand, the Russian and Chinese Communist Parties are bound together by close ideological ties."[16] This reasoning emphasized why the United States should not ally with Communist China even if it was at odds with the Soviet Union. In 1954, during the Geneva Conference in Switzerland, Dulles famously refused to shake hands with Chinese Premier Zhou Enlai.

Anti-Communism or Anti-Soviet?

But President Richard Nixon and his national security advisor, and later secretary of state, Henry Kissinger deliberately chose to abandon this principle.

When Nixon first entered the American public spotlight, he was a Cold War warrior and one of the harshest critics of President Truman for "losing" China. As a freshman Republican congressman, Nixon condemned the Democrats for not doing everything they could to help the Nationalists fight the Communists, and he supported Senator Joseph McCarthy's domestic purges. In the famous 1959 Kitchen Debate with Soviet leader Nikita Khrushchev, Nixon passionately defended the superiority of free market and personal liberty over Communism.

Nixon could not have predicted that just a little more than a decade later, when he became the U.S. president, he would find himself becoming the very thing he had once fiercely condemned: the savior of the Chinese Communist Party.

Nixon's U-turn in the U.S. China policy was motivated by his strategic belief that the growing Sino-Soviet split could be exploited to weaken Communist unity, especially in Asia. He sought to engage China diplomatically, hoping this would diminish Chinese support for North Vietnam and ease the U.S. withdrawal from the Vietnam War, where the CCP had played a significant role in backing the Viet Cong. Both Nixon and Kissinger believed that improving U.S.–China relations would not only isolate North Vietnam but also help contain Soviet expansion—and position the United States as a key player in shaping Asia's future.

The Nixon-Kissinger approach was heavily influenced by a new perspective that emerged among American foreign policymakers during the Cold War. They came to view the Soviet Union as a modern incarnation of Russian czarist expansionist imperialism. Communism, as an ideology, was seen as a threat only insofar as it served as a tool for that expansion.[17]

These policymakers believed that while it was certainly true that the Chinese Communists were staunch Marxists, it was entirely possible that they were not Soviet imperialists.[18]

Nixon and Kissinger embraced this viewpoint, identifying the Soviet Union solely as the primary threat to the United States. This conclusion led them to place focus on the dangers of Soviet expansionism and minimize the role of ideology while taking a relatively tolerant stance toward what they considered "independent Marxism," which includes not only China but any Communist country that distances itself from the Soviet Union.[19]

It seemed like a sound strategy—leveraging your enemy's enemy against your primary adversary. Sadly, this age-old wisdom would eventually prove to be a gross miscalculation. The miscalculation was rooted in the failure to account for the vital importance of ideology in the equation.

Their belief led them to prioritize strategic alignment for the sake of geopolitics and maintaining the balance of power. Kissinger expressed this viewpoint succinctly, famously stating, "We have no permanent enemies; we will judge other countries, including Communist countries…, on the basis of their actions and not on the basis of their domestic ideology."[20] In the case of China, this meant being willing to overlook the deaths of tens of millions under Mao's regime.

Nixon and Kissinger's decision to align with Communist China raised profound questions at home: What was the true purpose of America's Cold War? If it was a fight against Communism, why forge an alliance with Communist China now? If not, what had Americans in Korea and Vietnam fought and died for? If the Cold War wasn't genuinely about combating Communism, then what was it really about? The uncomfortable truth was that there were no good answers.

One strategy that the Nixon administration employed was to convince the American public that Chinese Communists were somehow different from their European counterparts. Journalist and writer James

Mann noted that this idea reassured many, observing that the perception of Communist China was often "colored by romance and sentimentalism, a legacy of the American experience in China dating back to the trader ships and the missionaries."[21] This approach seemed to have worked.

Even though U.S. policy primarily focused on the Soviet Union before and during the Cold War, many Americans still lacked a clear understanding of Soviet Communism. The alliance with the U.S.S.R. during World War II further muddled public perception. This began to change in 1956 when Khrushchev delivered a shocking revelation, denouncing Stalin as a mass murderer and opening the floodgates to accounts of atrocities in the U.S.S.R. The 1962 Cuban Missile Crisis brought the Soviet threat directly to American shores, heightening awareness. In 1973, the publication of *The Gulag Archipelago* by Aleksandr Solzhenitsyn exposed the brutal realities of Soviet labor camps, revealing the horrors of Soviet Communism to the Western public.

The focus on the Soviet Union allowed the CCP to largely escape scrutiny, leaving the American public with little awareness of the far greater crimes and atrocities committed by the CCP against its people. Even among Americans who know about the Ukrainian Famine of 1932–33, many are unaware of Mao's Great Famine of 1959–62. Similarly, while "gulag" has entered the English vocabulary, few realize that the CCP's version, known as the *laogai* (劳改) system, is still in existence today. This lack of awareness weakened American resistance to the argument and significantly contributed to the acceptance of the notion that Chinese Communism was less severe than its Soviet counterpart, thereby justifying the new alliance.

Tragically, little effort has been made since then to educate Americans about the *other* "evil empire"—Communist China. While this may be due to negligence or flawed analysis, it increasingly seems to be a deliberate omission.

Nixon and Kissinger effectively redefined the Cold War as a conflict primarily against the Soviet Union, conveniently excluding Communist

China from the equation. Furthermore, they reframed Communism as merely an ideological tool for Soviet expansion rather than a global threat in its own right.

In all their analysis and calculations, however, Nixon and Kissinger overlooked a critical factor: Communist ideology was central to the Sino-Soviet split. Mao viewed the Soviet leadership as betraying true Marxism-Leninism by "revising" it into something diluted, positioning himself as the rightful heir to authentic Marxist-Leninist principles. It is worth repeating Chiang Kai-shek's assertion that the Chinese Reds are "more communistic than the Russian Communists."

On February 21, 1972, Nixon arrived in China to begin his historic week-long visit, becoming the first U.S. president to visit Communist China since "the loss of China" in 1949 and after over two decades of standoff. When Nixon shook hands with Premier Zhou Enlai after stepping off Air Force One in Beijing, Zhou must have relished it as a sweet revenge against Secretary Dulles, who had famously refused to shake his hand more than a decade earlier.

If Americans were stunned by Nixon's abrupt U-turn on China, the shock inside China was even greater. I was a middle school student when I saw the photo of that famous handshake. My first instinct was to ask why our leaders didn't seize the moment to capture the greatest enemy of the Chinese people. My classmates wondered the same. After all, we had been raised to see America as a mortal enemy. But the question didn't linger long—our trust in the party was absolute. We believed its decisions were always right, always wise.

In 1972, Mao's Cultural Revolution was still raging. Nixon, while he was cozying up with the CCP leaders in Beijing, willfully overlooked the harsh reality that Mao's current political campaign was tormenting millions of Chinese citizens. At any moment, individuals could lose their freedom, be imprisoned, or even executed by the CCP for perceived offenses.

During Nixon's visit, the CCP employed the same strategy they had used with the U.S. Observation Group in Yan'an—showing the U.S.

delegation and the press only what they wanted them to see. That approach hasn't changed since, and it appears to have continued to work.

While the press hailed the visit as "the week that changed the world," a more fitting description might be "the week Nixon saved the CCP."

Two years after his historic visit to China, Nixon was forced to resign over the Watergate scandal. Yet the CCP openly embraced Nixon's legacy, undeterred by the controversy. On January 1, 1976, Mao extended a remarkable gesture of hospitality by receiving Nixon's daughter Julie Nixon Eisenhower and her husband, David Eisenhower. They became the first foreign guests Mao met in the final year of his life—an unprecedented honor for private citizens on a semi-official visit.

In her book *Special People*, Julie recalled a farewell banquet hosted by Huang Zhen, the head of the Chinese Liaison Office in Washington. At the event, Huang quoted Nixon: "When I left office, I discovered who my friends really are." Then, turning to Julie, he added warmly, "We will never forget our *old friends*." Julie noticed the Chinese interpreter had tears in his eyes while translating those words.

The Nixon legacy continues. Christopher Nixon Cox—the son of Tricia Nixon Cox, and Nixon's grandson—followed in his grandfather's footsteps by actively courting China. He has been warmly embraced by Beijing as what the CCP fondly calls "the New Old Friend of the Chinese People." A lawyer and private equity CEO, Cox has visited China more than sixty times. His trips include leading a 2013 Nixon Foundation delegation retracing his grandfather's visit, and attending the seventieth anniversary of the founding of the People's Republic in 2019, where he observed a grand military parade. One can only imagine how deeply he has benefited from his enduring connections with the CCP.

Featured in the CCP's *People's Daily* documentary series "A Story Spanning 40 Years," Christopher Nixon Cox declared, "I would like to pick up the torch and carry it for the next generation of Chinese-American thinkers...The Chinese are very logical. You can make arguments to the

Chinese and change opinions if you do it based on logic and common interests. And that's really what diplomacy is all about."[22]

Stilwell and Nixon's grandsons may be just the tip of the iceberg when it comes to the unfortunate legacies still shaping U.S.–China relations.

—

The Nixon-Kissinger China policy set a new tone: fostering friendly ties with Beijing to counterbalance the Soviet Union, cooperating on East Asian affairs, and pledging not to challenge Communist rule in China. Subsequent presidents built upon this framework, making occasional adjustments but rarely questioning the flawed core principles. Over time, it replaced the original Cold War focus on containing Communism, redefining China from ideological foe to pragmatic partner.

One consequence of Nixon and Kissinger's realignment was paving the way for Communist China's entry into the United Nations. Although the United States officially opposed the move, it lacked the will and effort to mount a serious challenge, ultimately allowing the shift to happen. On October 25, 1971, the U.N. General Assembly passed Resolution 2758, recognizing the People's Republic of China as the sole legitimate representative of China and replacing Taiwan on the Security Council.

With this shift, Communist China and Mao emerged from international isolation. No longer trapped between hostility from both the United States and the Soviet Union, China repositioned itself on the global stage. Beijing's newfound legitimacy enabled the regime to promote a carefully crafted image of the "so-called Communist country"—a distinct, independent model of Communism, separate from the Soviet mold. This narrative proved powerful. China began to present itself as the leader of a new revolutionary path for the developing world—and eventually, as the leader in the global struggle against U.S. hegemony.

CHAPTER 6

FROM MISJUDGMENT TO SURRENDER: PRESIDENTIAL FAILURES ON CHINA

Decades after Nixon's opening to China, it is still hailed as a Cold War masterstroke—leveraging the Sino-Soviet split to counterbalance Moscow and ending decades of U.S.–China isolation.

Less acknowledged is how the move not only revived the CCP from near collapse, but also resurrected a long-standing false narrative among Western elites that Chinese Communism was not "real" Communism, but a pragmatic, nationalist offshoot. This view, shaped by early sympathizers like Edgar Snow, portrayed Mao's revolution as agrarian reform and distinct from Soviet-style totalitarianism, the same misconception that had contributed to the loss of China.

In short, Nixon set the template—and every president after him followed it religiously. The same delusional assumptions hardened into bipartisan dogma. As President Trump bluntly stated during a press briefing aboard Air Force One on May 4, 2025: opening to China was "the worst thing he [Nixon] ever did."[1]

Deng Xiaoping the Reformer

To many Americans and Westerners, Deng Xiaoping (1904–1997) is remembered primarily as a reformer. Britannica, for instance, states that he "abandoned many orthodox Communist doctrines and attempted to incorporate elements of the free-enterprise system into the Chinese economy." This enduring myth that the CCP were pragmatic reformers rather than radical Bolsheviks served Deng well.

Americans accepted this narrative largely because most had little historical knowledge of what transpired in China under Mao—and many still don't.

After Mao Zedong's death, Deng emerged as China's new paramount leader in December 1978, following a series of political maneuvers and internal power struggles. To consolidate his authority, Deng shifted blame for the disastrous Cultural Revolution onto the so-called Gang of Four, led by Mao's widow, Jiang Qing. After a high-profile show trial in 1980, the four were sentenced to prison. The Chinese people were told that justice had been served—and that it was time to move on.

Deng steered China toward economic reforms and modernization, but he was, in reality, a more orthodox Marxist-Leninist than Mao. While Mao had only a superficial understanding of Marxism-Leninism, often mixing it with traditional Chinese court intrigues and power plays, Deng was a trained Marxist.

Unlike Mao, who never left China except for two brief trips to Russia, Deng Xiaoping spent six formative years abroad—five in France, where he joined the CCP in 1926, and one in Moscow at Sun Yat-sen University, a Soviet training school for future Chinese Communists.* There, he was indoctrinated in Marxist-Leninist theory, Soviet organizational strategy, propaganda, United Front tactics, and intelligence work. These experiences set him apart from Mao and were crucial in shaping his

* Sun Yat-sen University in Moscow was founded in 1925 by the Comintern to train Chinese revolutionaries from both the CCP and the left wing of the KMT in Marxist-Leninist theory and revolutionary tactics. After the KMT-CCP split, the school came under CCP dominance before closing in 1930.

ideological foundation. Simply put, Deng was far better equipped to engage with the United States and the West. Deng Xiaoping was a loyal Maoist throughout the CCP's internal power struggles, consistently aligning with Mao. He led the Anti-Rightist Campaign and played a key role in executing the Great Leap Forward, prompting Mao to declare, "I am the commander, and Deng Xiaoping is the deputy commander."[2] During the Sino-Soviet split, Mao tasked Deng with denouncing the U.S.S.R. as "revisionist," leading to the drafting of the influential *Nine Critiques* against Soviet leadership.

Despite his staunch support for Mao, Deng Xiaoping was purged during the Cultural Revolution due to his association with Liu Shaoqi, the president of China, who was persecuted to death. However, Deng was allowed to survive. In the late stages of the Cultural Revolution, Mao "rehabilitated" Deng and assigned him important responsibilities to replace the ailing Premier Zhou Enlai.

The China that Deng inherited after Mao's death in 1976 was in total disarray. Facing the threat of inevitable collapse, Deng reluctantly opened China to foreign investment and technology, providing the Communist regime with vital transfusions to maintain its grip on power. Deng had little genuine interest in free-market economics or democratic political reform; his primary goal was to stabilize and strengthen the Communist system.

In declaring his four cardinal principles, Deng made it very clear he was not giving up on Marxism. These principles were:

- upholding the socialist path
- upholding the people's democratic dictatorship
- upholding the leadership of the Communist Party
- and upholding Marxism-Leninism and Mao Zedong thought

These principles defined the core issues that Deng considered non-negotiable for China's political structure and direction.

In 1978, under Deng Xiaoping, the Chinese constitution was amended to implement the one-child policy, stripping citizens of reproductive rights. The policy led to more than 336 million abortions between 1980 and 2009, according to official CCP figures.[3] It's safe to say that the majority were involuntary—or outright forced. The long-term consequences include a demographic crisis marked by population decline, rapid aging, and a severe gender imbalance.

In 1980, Deng abolished the Mao-era "Four Big Freedoms"—speech, expression, debate, and big-character posters.* Though originally used by Mao to mobilize the masses for political ends, Deng eliminated them for the opposite reason: to suppress a growing wave of dissent against the Communist system and his own rule.

In 1982, a constitutional amendment formally outlawed private land ownership, codifying what had been enforced since the late 1950s. All land was declared state property. The government permitted only long-term usage rights, typically seventy years for residential property. Ironically, the same American liberals who decry "stolen land" in other contexts often overlook the largest state land seizure in modern history.

The same amendment also banned strikes, further tightening state control over labor and economic life. Trade unions, while still formally in existence, were reduced to party-controlled entities, tools for enforcing state policy rather than protecting workers' rights.

On the issue of the Cultural Revolution, Deng Xiaoping's position was inherently contradictory. He denounced the revolution but not its architect, Mao Zedong—because to condemn Mao would implicate himself. A loyal Maoist and enforcer of Mao's policies, Deng had no interest in a full reckoning. As a result, the Cultural Revolution has never been truly confronted and condemned in China.

Deng's defense of Mao is why the butcher's portrait still hangs above Tiananmen Gate, despite his responsibility for the deaths of tens of millions of Chinese. In an interview with Italian journalist Oriana Fallaci,

* Big-character posters (大字报) were handwritten public wall displays for public viewing used during the Mao era to spread propaganda, denounce political enemies, and mobilize mass participation in ideological campaigns.

when asked whether the portrait would remain, Deng Xiaoping responded firmly: *"It will, forever."*[4] For anyone trying to understand China, Deng made it easy: Just look at Tiananmen Gate. As long as Mao's portrait still hangs there, China remains a Communist state.

In 1989, Deng reaffirmed his commitment to Communist rule by ordering the Tiananmen Square crackdown, killing thousands of unarmed protesters. His decisive and violent action demonstrated Deng's unwavering resolve to maintain the Communist Party's grip on power at all costs, aligning with his pragmatic, power-driven approach to governance. It is for this that he will forever be remembered as the Butcher of the Tiananmen Square Massacre. Given these facts, it's hard to argue that Deng Xiaoping intended to open China to a true free-market economy. Yet American media—much like Edgar Snow seventy years earlier—chose to ignore this reality, portraying Deng as a pragmatic reformer distinct from Mao and a potential U.S. ally. When he died in 1997, the *New York Times* called him "A Political Wizard Who Put China on the Capitalist Road," praising his pragmatism as free of history or ideology.[5] *Time* named him "Person of the Year" twice—one of only four non-Americans to receive the honor. This narrative obscured the reality that China remained, and still remains, a true Communist state.

As for political reform, Deng promoted concepts like "collective leadership," "term limits," and "peaceful transfer of power," which may have appeared to signal progress. In reality, these were largely deceptive facades. Deng personally engineered the ousting of two general secretaries—Hu Yaobang and Zhao Ziyang—both advocates of political reform, through informal meetings of Party elders held at his own residence.

Even after announcing his retirement from official positions, Deng continued to make key decisions from behind the scenes, asserting that the highest decision-making body of the Chinese Communist Party, the Politburo Standing Committee, could have only one boss—and that was him. He handpicked not only his successor Jiang Zemin (1926–2022), but also Jiang's successor, Hu Jintao (1942–).

Deng is famous for his doctrine "It doesn't matter whether a cat is black or white, as long as it catches mice," just as Henry Kissinger is known for stating, "America has no permanent friends or enemies, only interests." Both emphasized pragmatism over ideology—Deng in prioritizing economic results over ideological purity, and Kissinger in grounding U.S. foreign policy in national interest rather than ideological loyalty.

Once again, the CCP outmaneuvered the United States. Deng's doctrine allowed the party to harness foreign capital and technology to fuel economic growth—while retaining totalitarian control. Meanwhile, Kissinger's doctrine promoted a foreign policy that sidelined ideology and American moral principles in favor of cold strategic interests. History has shown that this approach enriched the CCP, but weakened the United States, and eroded its national security—setting in motion a long, steady decline driven by China's rise.

In defiance of fact and reality, a myth took hold and endured: that Deng and his successors were pragmatic economic reformers—not hard-line Communists like Mao. Only when Xi Jinping, empowered by the wealth the CCP had amassed, began to bare its teeth and reveal its true intentions did more and more Americans finally begin to wake up.

Continuing Nixon's Path

U.S. policy toward Communist China after Nixon's historic visit quickly became the prevailing orthodoxy: that China was different from the Soviet Union, ideology was secondary, and economic engagement would lead to political reform and serve American interests.

The phenomenon functions like political cruise control—once set in motion, it locks into place. Over time, this unexamined consensus shaped decisions, suppressed dissent, and blinded institutions to inconvenient truths.

U.S. presidents since Nixon followed this orthodoxy with only minor variations, steadily bringing America closer to the possibility of losing itself to Communist China.

President Jimmy Carter (Presidency 1977–1981)

Building on Nixon and Kissinger's break from the anti-Communist "containment" doctrine, President Carter pushed the shift further. He criticized prior administrations for supporting non-Communist authoritarian regimes and pledged to restore America's moral authority by making human rights the cornerstone of U.S. foreign policy—rejecting what he saw as an outdated Cold War mindset and its "inordinate fear of Communism."[6]

Carter's seemingly noble goal of promoting human rights was undermined by his fundamental misunderstanding of the intrinsic link between Communism and the denial of basic freedoms. While human rights abuses can occur under any regime, Communism by its nature rejects individual dignity—making the CCP one of the worst human rights violators in history.

Carter's view on Communism echoed the perspectives of the China hands often blamed for the loss of China. These China hands criticized the KMT government for its corruption and authoritarianism but failed to foresee the far greater atrocities under the Communists. Despite having the benefit of hindsight, Carter's liberal worldview led him to willfully ignore this inconvenient truth.

On December 15, 1978, President Carter announced that the United States and China had reached a formal agreement to establish diplomatic relations. On January 1, 1979, the two nations officially established ties. Following America's lead, other major Western countries quickly followed suit—creating what could be described as a domino effect.

As Western governments rushed to embrace China diplomatically, ordinary Chinese citizens seized the moment to voice their dissent at home. It was an exhilarating time. I had just entered college and vividly remember the sudden openness—once-forbidden topics were being discussed openly for the first time. Between 1978 and 1979, thousands of people in Beijing used big character posters to express their discontent with China's political and social issues. These posters were displayed on a long brick wall in the Xidan shopping district in Beijing, famously referred to as Democracy Wall. This movement marked a significant moment of public protest and a call for political reform in China. An open letter titled "To President Carter," written under the pseudonym "Citizen," was posted at Tiananmen Square. The letter directly addressed the issue of human rights in China and called on the entire Western world and the global community to pay attention.[7]

When Deng Xiaoping cracked down on the movement by taking down the Democracy Wall and jailed many who dared to speak out, Chinese dissidents appealed to Carter for help. But the Carter administration turned a deaf ear to them.

Carter's foreign policy inadvertently weakened American influence and contributed to a series of crises during his presidency. In Nicaragua, the authoritarian but anti-Communist Somoza regime—comparable to Chiang Kai-shek's in its staunch opposition to Communism—was overthrown and replaced by the Marxist, pro-Soviet and more oppressive Sandinistas, who openly sought to undermine America's allies in Central America. A similar situation unfolded in Iran, where the authoritarian U.S.-aligned, pro-Western shah was replaced by a radical Islamic regime known for its brutal human rights abuses. Adding to these challenges, the Soviet Union invaded Afghanistan in late December 1979, further destabilizing global geopolitics during Carter's tenure.

This has been a recurring pattern: authoritarian regimes being replaced by far worse totalitarian Communist regimes, as seen in Russia, China, Cuba, Vietnam, Ethiopia, and Nicaragua, to list a few. Yet Carter appeared uninterested in learning from history.

Carter held to the very end his belief that China's rise would not only benefit China but also promote peace and prosperity in East Asia and beyond. The sentiment seemed almost personal; he once noted that his birthday fell on October 1—China's National Day—prompting some to remark that his friendship with China was fate. In a *China-US Focus* interview on January 21, 2019, Carter said, "Deng Xiaoping thought that was quite significant, that fate would let me have my birthday on the same day as the birthday of the People's Republic of China." Carter continued, "It was a warm relationship between me and Deng Xiaoping, and also between Mrs. Deng Xiaoping and my wife, Rosalynn. Even between Deng Xiaoping and my daughter Amy who was then only about 12 years old."[8]

The CCP regard Carter an "Old Friend of the Chinese People." To Carter, Deng was practically a family friend.

Nixon sought to pit one Communist regime against another, while Carter reshaped the perception of Communism, downplaying it as no longer a significant threat to the United States and the free world, and reframing it as merely another form of authoritarianism. While his predecessors worked to contain its spread, Carter's policies arguably legitimized Communism and allowed it greater freedom to expand.

President Ronald Reagan (Presidency 1981–1989)

President Reagan will be remembered as an anti-Communist warrior who singlehandedly brought down the "evil empire" of the Soviet Union and ended the Cold War.

In stark contrast to Carter's downplaying the threat of Communism, Reagan declared, "The West won't contain communism, it will transcend communism. It won't bother to…denounce it, it will dismiss it as some bizarre chapter in human history whose last pages are even now being written."[9]

Reagan's staunch anti-Communism and anti-Soviet stance became the foundation of his foreign policy, which broke away from the traditional doctrine of containment, established during the Truman administration. Reagan's foreign policy, known as the "Reagan Doctrine," focused on supporting anti-Communist insurgents worldwide to combat Soviet influence by embracing the 1950s "roll-back" approach, which sought to actively diminish Soviet power. Unlike previous administrations, Reagan openly backed groups fighting Soviet control, exemplified by U.S. support for proxy forces like the Contras in Nicaragua and the Mujahideen in Afghanistan, who opposed Soviet-aligned governments and forces.[10]

President Reagan, along with Prime Minister Margaret Thatcher of the United Kingdom and Pope John Paul II, formed a powerful anti-Communist alliance that provided decisive leadership, ultimately contributing to the downfall of the Soviet Union. Their united efforts eventually brought about the end of the Cold War.

Unfortunately, even Reagan was not immune to the long-standing misconceptions about the Chinese Communist Party—misunderstandings that had endured since FDR's era. Despite his staunch anti-Communist stance, Reagan, like many U.S. leaders before and after him, underestimated the CCP's deep ideological commitment to Marxism-Leninism and its global ambitions. While pursuing a global anti-Communist agenda, Reagan and his administration took a conciliatory approach toward China. During his presidency, Ronald Reagan neatly redefined China as not really Communist, but a "so-called Communist" country.[11]

The 1980s marked a period of rapid reform and opening in China, characterized by economic openness—though this represented only a loosening of government control rather than genuine free-market reform—and greater engagement with the global community. This newfound openness provided access to previously censored information, including democratic and liberal ideas. Many, both in China and the West, including the Reagan administration, were hopeful that Deng Xiaoping's reforms would eventually steer China away from Communism and toward democracy.

When Reagan visited China in the spring of 1984, he was encouraged by the country's early economic reforms. The shift toward greater individual freedom in production and trade gave him hope that these changes were revitalizing the economy, improving lives, and laying the foundation for a more just society. Reagan argued, "It's a good thing for the world when those who are not allies remain open to each other. And it's good to remember that competitors sometimes have mutual interests, and those interests can make them friends."[12]

The Reagan administration's failure to fully comprehend the true nature of Chinese Communism led to the mistaken perception of the

PRC as a strategic partner. On April 21, 1984, Reagan authorized a National Security Decision Directive that classified Communist China as a friendly, non-aligned nation. This directive ensured arms sales to the CCP and further relaxed restrictions on the export of advanced technology. The administration broadly agreed that Deng Xiaoping was guiding China in a favorable direction, justifying U.S. support and encouragement.[13]

Michael Pillsbury, a foreign policy strategist who played a key role in these arms sales during the Reagan presidency, would later admit this grave mistake in his book *The Hundred-Year Marathon: China's Secret Strategy to Replace America as the Global Superpower* (2015).

It is a tragic irony that while President Reagan successfully defeated one brand of Communism—the Soviet Union—he simultaneously facilitated the rise of another, the CCP, which now poses an arguably greater threat than the Soviet Union.

President George H. W. Bush (Presidency 1989–1993)

If President Nixon revived the CCP from its deathbed, President George H. W. Bush resurrected it once more—this time from complete repudiation by the international community.

Bush's ties to the Chinese Communist Party began before his vice presidency, when he served as head of the U.S. Liaison Office in Beijing from 1974 to 1975. Photos of him and his wife bicycling through the city symbolized a friendly, personal diplomatic style. During this time, he met Mao Zedong twice and came away with a favorable impression.

Bush also formed an unusually close relationship with Deng Xiaoping. When asked on television who was the greatest leader he had ever met, Bush named Deng as a "very special leader."[14]

Only a few months after Bush took office, on June 4, 1989, Deng Xiaoping ordered troops and tanks to brutally suppress the peaceful pro-democracy student movement in Tiananmen Square, resulting in the deaths of thousands. Unlike the atrocities committed by Mao and the

CCP behind the Iron Curtain, this massacre was broadcast in real-time by Western media, allowing the world to witness the brutality firsthand.

I was studying in Florida at the time and, like the rest of America, watched the bloody crackdown unfold on television. Until the final moment, I truly believed Deng would never order the troops to open fire—I was still clinging to a lifetime of indoctrination that the People's Army existed to protect the people. The massacre didn't just shock me—it shattered me. In the days that followed, I joined protests against the brutality of the Chinese government. Representing Chinese students, I wrote an article for the local newspaper and was interviewed by a local TV station. That moment marked a turning point—a break from illusion and the beginning of a deeper understanding of the true nature of the regime under which I had grown up.

Amid international condemnation, Deng Xiaoping maintained a hard-line stance, expressing no remorse for the killings and making no effort to conceal the blood on his hands, stating that the Tiananmen incident was "an earthshaking event, and it is very unfortunate that the United States is too deeply involved in it…The various aspects of US foreign policy have actually cornered China…The aim of the counterrevolutionary rebellion was to overthrow the People's Republic of China and our socialist system. If they should succeed in obtaining that aim, the world would be a different one. To be frank, this could even lead to war."[15]

Just hours after the CCP opened fire on student demonstrators, Nixon called Bush, urging him not to let the episode derail U.S.–China relations. While Nixon described the massacre as "deplorable," he emphasized the importance of considering the "long haul" in the bilateral relationship. Bush agreed, stating that although he would impose some economic sanctions and temporarily pause the relationship, he would not recall the U.S. ambassador.[16]

On June 5, the day after the massacre, President George H. W. Bush stated during a press conference, "This is not the time for an emotional response, but for a reasoned, careful action that takes into account both our long-term interests and recognition of a complex internal situation in China."

Bush imposed some sanctions in response, but they quickly dissipated. In fact, he seemed more eager than Deng to restore communication channels between the two countries, as if the United States had somehow wronged China. He became the first Western leader to reestablish ties with the CCP after the massacre, undermining not only his own moral authority but also that of the United States. After Bush, the Tiananmen Square massacre was effectively erased from public discourse.

He later revealed to his biographer, "Had I not met the man [Deng Xiaoping], I think I would have been less convinced that we should keep relations with them going after Tiananmen Square."[17]

In 1990, as the Soviet Union's economy teetered on collapse, Mikhail Gorbachev sought assistance from the West, but his plea was declined. Meanwhile, Communist China, despite a poor human rights record, continued to receive Western aid. When questioned about this double standard, President Bush explained, "China and the U.S.S.R. aren't one and the same thing."[18]

Bush was right that China and the Soviet Union were different. In the late 1980s, Gorbachev showed restraint as pro-democracy protests spread across the Eastern bloc. He refused to use force, even when urged by East Germany and Romania, believing those days were over. Gorbachev was a genuine reformer; Deng Xiaoping was not.

It must have required immense courage, but in 1990, Gorbachev admitted that Soviet secret police were responsible for the massacre of thousands of Polish officers in Katyn Forest during World War II, calling it "one of the gravest crimes of Stalinism."[19] A sharp contrast to the CCP, which continues to deny or whitewash its atrocities against its own people.

Despite Gorbachev's tremendous efforts at decommunization, Bush stayed committed to the Nixon-era China policy, working diligently to restore relations with Beijing—including his annual push to extend China's most favored nation (MFN) status.

Ironically, when Gorbachev visited Beijing in May 1989 shortly before the massacre, the protesting students gathered in Tiananmen Square saw him as a hero. Some even held banners reading, "Where is China's Gorbachev?" The students believed that Gorbachev's bloodless reforms could serve as a model for China.[20]

After the fall of the U.S.S.R., Russia formally denounced Communism in its constitution. Meanwhile, China remains openly and proudly Communist. Yet it is Russia, now a regional power with an economy smaller than China's Guangdong Province, that continues to dominate the focus of Cold War–era experts and left-leaning politicians and the legacy media. Meanwhile, the far greater threat posed by Communist China is consistently downplayed—a continuation of Nixon's disastrous China policy.

The relentless "Russia, Russia, Russia" drumbeat stands in stark contrast to the near silence on "China, China, China."

Shortly after the Tiananmen Square Massacre, major American corporations resumed operations in China, lured by its cheap labor, lax regulations, vast untapped consumer market, and the rapid economic growth. Among the early wave of American businessmen returning to Beijing was Prescott Bush, brother of then-President George H. W. Bush, who arrived as early as September 1989, three months after the massacre. Defending his presence, he told the *Wall Street Journal* in Beijing, "We aren't a bunch of carrion birds coming to pick the carcass. But there are big opportunities in China, and Americans can't afford to be shut out."[21]

Competition with firms from Hong Kong, Taiwan, and Japan, already established in China, further spurred this influx. By 1993, investments from U.S. and multinational companies in China had reached record levels. Under pressure from Wall Street and the business community, the U.S. government faced mounting demands to decouple China's most favored nation trade status from human rights concerns.

Communist China's dismal human rights record has never been in doubt. In addition to the brutal 1989 crackdown on the Tiananmen Square protests, the regime had also violently suppressed prolonged uprisings in Tibet in the 1980s, even imposing martial law for a year from

1989 to 1990.[22] Despite such repression, the CCP successfully obtained renewal of its MFN trade status every year.

It was a historic reversal. With the Soviet Union gone, the United States formally stepped into the very role once held by its former rival—becoming the chief backer of the Chinese Communist Party and ultimately helping to create the most formidable adversary America has ever faced.

The CCP acknowledged Bush's contributions with appreciation. Upon his passing in 2018, *Global Times*, a publication under the CCP's official newspaper *People's Daily*, described Bush as a "long-time *friend of the Chinese people*" and positioned him as one of the most China-friendly U.S. presidents in history.[23]

Neil Bush, President George H. W. Bush's third son, and a businessman who has traveled to China more than 150 times since 1975, said in a 2024 interview with Chinese media: "Most Americans can't tolerate what I'll say about China: The Chinese system has worked for China," and went on to praise the country's progress over the past decades. Like Nixon's grandson, one can only imagine how much wealth Neil and his family have amassed from their ties to Communist China—a continuation of the Bush family legacy.[24]

President Bill Clinton (Presidency 1993–2001)

At the 1992 Democratic National Convention, Bill Clinton took a strong stance on China in his nomination acceptance speech, declaring, "An America that will not coddle tyrants, from Baghdad to Beijing."

After entering the White House in 1993, President Bill Clinton, who had criticized George H. W. Bush for coddling "the butchers of Beijing,"[25] issued Executive Order 12850, linking the renewal of China's most favored nation trade status to specific human rights improvements, including the protection of Tibetan culture and granting international human rights organizations access to Chinese prisons.

However, these efforts faced strong resistance from Beijing. Ahead of Secretary of State Warren Christopher's visit to China in March 1994, the

Chinese government arrested thirteen pro-democracy activists as a warning. Beijing made it clear that it would take whatever measures necessary to maintain political control.[26] Christopher returned empty-handed.

The resistance also grew from within. By then, a more "pragmatic" and "realist" view had taken over—overriding core American values and principles. Despite China's continued assault on human rights, the United States prioritized cooperation driven by economic interests and the illusion of regional stability.

In May of that same year, the Clinton administration reassessed its approach after failing to effectively engage with the CCP about its human rights violations. President Clinton announced the decision to decouple China's most favored nation trade status from human rights considerations. He acknowledged that, despite China's limited progress on the issues outlined in his 1993 executive order, maintaining a stringent human rights policy was hindering the United States from advancing other priorities—particularly economic interests. The message was unmistakable: Profit took precedence over principle. Once again, the United States gave in—and Beijing was rewarded for its defiance. In an attempt to remedy his capitulation, Clinton introduced a "new human rights strategy" based on voluntary business guidelines abroad, aimed largely at China. This strategy effectively offloaded responsibility onto private companies. But drawn by China's CCP-controlled cheap labor—with no worker rights or independent unions—American businesses had little incentive to follow these toothless policies, which amounted to little more than symbolic gestures.[27]

In 1999, the U.S. and China reached an agreement on China's entry into the World Trade Organization (WTO). The following year, the U.S. Congress passed legislation renaming "most favored nation" status to "normal trade relations" and endorsing China's WTO accession. In October 2000, Clinton signed it into law.

In his infamous address at Johns Hopkins University, Clinton not only made brazenly false promises but also attempted to reframe the history of U.S.–China relations to win over the American public:

> In the early 1900's, most Americans saw China either through the eyes of traders seeking new markets, or missionaries seeking new converts. During World War II, China was our ally; during the Korean War, our adversary. At the dawn of the Cold War, when I was a young boy beginning to study such things, it was a cudgel in a political battle: "Who lost China?" Later it was a counterweight to the Soviet Union, and now, in some people's eyes, it's a caricature. Will it be the next great capitalist tiger, with the biggest market in the world, or the world's last great communist dragon and a threat to stability in Asia?

In his reflection on U.S.–China relations, Clinton conveniently blurred the distinction between China's competing regimes. During World War II, the United States was allied with Chiang Kai-shek's Nationalists; in the Korean War, the United States was fighting against Mao's Communists. He also notably omitted the term "Communism"—a defining force in the geopolitical struggle between the two nations throughout the twentieth century.

As for the question he posed, the past two decades has made the answer clear: China did not become a capitalist tiger but remained the world's last great Communist dragon. Unsurprisingly, Clinton avoided addressing the one question that haunted a generation of American policymakers: *"Who lost China?"*

In his memoir *My Life* (2005), Clinton never once mentioned the Communist Party or Communism, as though the Communist Party wasn't governing China, and as though the preamble of China's constitution did not establish Marxism as its official ideology. Clinton even went out of his way to defend the Communist Party's rigidity, stating that given China's history, it's understandable that Chinese officials feared that greater openness could lead to social disintegration.[28]

Clinton was wrong. The CCP's rejection of political openness is not rooted in Chinese tradition but rather in the Communist Party's deep-seated fear of losing power.

Clinton's decision to let China into the WTO will be forever ranked among the most disastrous decisions: He let the fox into the henhouse, setting in motion a threat to the survival of America itself.

President George W. Bush (Presidency 2001–2009)

President George W. Bush continued the same China policy, emphasizing deeper trade and investment ties in the belief that economic engagement would encourage China's integration into the global system and promote liberalization—a doubling down on a mistaken assumption.

In the wake of the 9/11 attacks, Bush sought to align with China as part of his global war on terror strategy, failing to recognize that the CCP itself operates as a terrorist organization through coercion and suppression of its own people. Under the guise of anti-terrorism, the CCP launched its persecution of Uyghur Muslims in Xinjiang, using the global counterterrorism narrative to justify mass surveillance and reeducation prison camps. This critical miscalculation allowed the CCP to strengthen its global influence and accelerate its rise on the world stage. Today, the CCP stands behind nearly every major terrorist regime, using its economic power, military aid, and political influence to prop up totalitarian governments, destabilize entire regions, and undermine U.S. interests.

His most significant misstep regarding China was, however, his decision to attend the 2008 Beijing Olympics.

Despite a boycott movement protesting the CCP's human rights abuses—such as the repression of Tibetans, Uyghurs, Falun Gong practitioners, religious believers, political dissidents, and strict censorship—Bush remained determined to attend the event. Even presidential candidates John McCain and Barack Obama indicated they would not attend the games if they were president. At the time, European leaders were considering a boycott of the opening ceremony, but Bush's attendance was critical in quelling that momentum.[29] The CCP interpreted his decision as a significant gesture of support from the United States, strengthening their position on the global stage.

In his memoir *Decision Points*, Bush wrote, "The Olympics gave the world a chance to see the beauty and creativity of China. My hope is that the Games also gave the Chinese people a glimpse of the wider world, including the possibility of an independent press, open Internet, and free speech."[30]

This is deeply ironic. Bush believed that attending the games instead of boycotting them would encourage the CCP to grant greater freedom to the Chinese people. Contrary to his expectations, the Beijing Olympics—much like the Nazi-hosted Berlin Olympics—served as a propaganda victory. It enhanced a totalitarian regime's international prestige while enabling it to continue its domestic repression.

The Beijing Olympics marked the beginning of a historic turning point for China. From that moment on, China shifted away from Deng Xiaoping's guiding doctrine of maintaining a low international profile—summed up by his phrase *taoguang yanghui* (韬光养晦), often translated as "hide your strength and bide your time"—and began openly asserting itself as a rising great power on the global stage. At the games, President Bush positioned himself as the CCP's enthusiastic cheerleader.

The scene at the games of Bush standing in line waiting for an audience with China's president was a moment of symbolic humiliation, reflecting America's deepening dependence on Beijing.

President Barack Obama (Presidency 2009–2017)

President Obama traveled further down the same path. Upon taking office, Obama had to face the reality of China's growing international influence, which stood in sharp contrast to America's weakened position in the aftermath of the financial crisis of 2008. A Gallup poll conducted the same year showed that 40 percent of respondents believed China was the world's leading power, up from 10 percent in 2000, while only 33 percent thought it was the United States, down from 65 percent in 2000.[31] Unlike Reagan, who worked to restore American strength, Obama accepted America's declining power, and issued statements about America retiring as the world's policeman,[32] and apologized for its past actions. He sought joint governance with major powers, including Communist China.

During the Obama era, the concept of "Chimerica" gained traction as a framework for Sino-American interdependence. The term symbolized the symbiotic relationship between the two nations, where China focused on exports and savings, while the United States prioritized imports and spending.

This relationship was closely tied to the "G2 model," the idea of a U.S.–China dual leadership responsible for managing major global challenges. Obama embraced the idea, envisioning U.S.–China co-governance as a means to jointly build the twenty-first century, as reflected in his address at the U.S.–China Strategic and Economic Dialogue on July 27, 2009. In this address, he stated that the ability of the United States and China to partner with each other was a prerequisite for progress on many of the world's most urgent issues, including energy and climate change.

If Bush's attendance at the Beijing Olympics signaled America's enthusiastic acknowledgment of China's rise, Obama's address marked a deeper shift—one that signaled the U.S.'s quiet surrender to China's growing power. Obama clearly did not understand the CCP. Its ultimate goal is not to share power with the United States, but to replace it as the world's sole superpower.

Obama's constant kowtowing to the CCP only invited its disdain and disrespect. During the 2009 Copenhagen Climate Summit, Beijing sent a vice foreign minister to meet with a U.S. president, a significant snub,[33] marking the greatest diplomatic humiliation from China to the United States since they established formal relations. Obama simply accepted it without protest.

Obama's approach was, at best, deferential, if not outright submissive to China's growing assertiveness. Even the *New York Times*, a leading liberal newspaper that had long praised Obama, expressed dissatisfaction, stating: "This is no longer the United States-China relationship of old but an encounter between a weakened giant and a comer with a bit of its own swagger. Washington's comparative advantage in past meetings is now diminished, a fact clearly not lost on the Chinese."[34]

In Obama's second term, he encountered Xi Jinping, the most forceful Chinese leader since Mao Zedong, while Obama himself was seen as the weakest American president since Jimmy Carter. Xi, confident in both Communism and China's ascendancy, stood opposite a U.S. president who had not only lost faith in America's greatness but seemed to hold it in contempt. In such a confrontation, it is often the bolder, more resolute leader who prevails—and Xi capitalized on that dynamic.

On November 11, 2014, during Barack Obama's visit to Beijing, Xi Jinping hosted a late-night banquet that extended far beyond its scheduled time, symbolizing the height of their "personal exchanges." Chinese state media *China Daily* portrayed the meeting as a "vivid lecture on China's history," with Xi positioned as the teacher to Obama. Obama reportedly described the conversation as "the most comprehensive, in-depth understanding of the history of the Chinese Communist Party and its governance."[35] This framing was meant to be read by the Chinese reader as a lessening of Obama's and, by extension, America's status. And I can assure you: The history Obama learned that night was the same party-manufactured fiction I was taught under Mao.

One of the most humiliating incidents occurred on September 3, 2016, during Obama's visit to Hangzhou for the G20 Summit. Air Force One was not provided a rolling staircase, forcing the president to exit through a lower door. Chinese security blocked U.S. press access and clashed with American officials, even shouting, "This is OUR country, this is OUR airport." A Chinese social media account with 24 million followers posted a video of Obama descending a small staircase. Given China's strict censorship, this deliberate jab reflected the CCP's intent to humiliate Obama, exploiting what it perceived as his weakness.[36]

At the time, then–presidential candidate Donald Trump harshly criticized China's disrespectful behavior, claiming that, in Obama's shoes, he would have immediately turned around and left.[37]

In December 2016, just before Obama left office, China seized a U.S. underwater drone in international waters of the South China Sea and returned it five days later. The Obama administration's weak response—simply requesting its return—undermined U.S. credibility. As the *New York Times* noted, allies were confused, and China was emboldened by the lack of consequences, further accelerating its militarization of the South China Sea.[38] This was the real-world outcome of Obama's "Chimerica" vision—or the so-called G2 model in practice.

During what many—certainly including the CCP—viewed as Obama's third term under President Joe Biden, the Chinese Communist Party sensed a return of the weakness in American leadership and swiftly resumed its confrontational posture. At the March 2021 U.S.–China talks in Alaska—the first high-level diplomatic engagement of the Biden administration—Chinese officials openly humiliated their American counterparts. In a widely publicized exchange, they lectured the United States on human rights, democracy, and international relations, citing the Black Lives Matter movement as evidence of America's systemic racism and lack of moral authority. They declared the United States had no right to speak from a "position of strength" and dismissed Western values as unrepresentative of the global community—portraying China instead as the true defender of multilateralism and sovereign equality.[39]

It's a pattern we've seen time and again: The CCP advances when America is weak and retreats when America is strong.

Over the past decades following Nixon's trip to China, we have witnessed a dangerous unraveling: the decoupling of human rights from Communist China, the decoupling of the term "Communist" from China itself, and most significantly, the decoupling of Communism—once recognized as a deadly ideology—from its true meaning.

With Communism fading from the American mindset, China came to be seen as just another country with boundless potential for economic opportunities and global prosperity and everyone seemed to want a piece of the action.

Meanwhile, Communism has morphed into something far less recognizable. Globally, it is often seen as a relic of the past with the fall of the U.S.S.R., while Chinese Communism is frequently mistaken for capitalism. Domestically, it has reemerged in the guise of Woke ideology and stakeholder capitalism. Together, these forces—foreign and domestic—have brought Communism dangerously close to fulfilling its goal of destroying the United States from within.

It wasn't until 2020, when a full-blown Marxist-inspired movement erupted on American streets, that many began to recognize the ideological parallels between Neo-Marxism—commonly known as Woke ideology—and Communism.

By the time more Americans began to grasp this unsettling reality, it was almost too late.

CHAPTER 7

THE RISE OF THE CCP'S WEALTH

In December 2018, on the fortieth anniversary of China's reform and opening up, or *gaige kaifang* (改革开放), Xi Jinping declared that China had achieved in a few decades what took developed nations centuries to accomplish. He pointed to the country's remarkable economic growth and highlighted key milestones: lifting 740 million people out of poverty, offering a model for other developing nations, and becoming a powerful force for global peace and development. Xi described the reform as a revolutionary transformation that reshaped China's destiny and influenced the world.

As for how China achieved this so-called miracle, Xi gave a clear answer:

"The achievements of the past 40 years didn't fall from the sky, nor were they gifts from others. They were earned through the hard work, wisdom, and courage of the Chinese Communist Party and the Chinese people of all ethnic groups!"[1]

In other words, China achieved all of this on its own—and the CCP's leadership made such a miracle possible. The message is unmistakable:

China owes nothing to the United States or the world, and the party owes its success to no one.

A single question can dismantle Xi Jinping's narrative: When did the so-called Chinese miracle truly begin? The answer is unequivocal—it began only after the United States opened its door and after China was granted entry into the WTO. But the full story is far more complex than that.

How Did China Get Rich?

The turning point in China's unprecedented economic rise can be traced to a single, decisive moment: its entry into the WTO. This milestone unleashed a wave of growth that propelled China from the economic wreckage of Mao's rule to the world's second-largest economy in record time.

So what enabled a Communist regime to thrive in a global market built on free enterprise? What real competitive advantages did it possess? What were their "magic weapons"?

Dirt-Cheap Labor

China's greatest advantage was its massive and seemingly endless supply of cheap labor—so inexpensive and rights-free that it effectively amounted to modern slavery—a competitive edge unmatched by the United States or the rest of the world.

Just how cheap was Chinese labor, say, in 2003? About ¥3.8 per hour—roughly $0.46 USD. These workers averaged twenty-eight days a month, ten hours a day, with no benefits of any kind—not even paid holidays.[2] Most importantly, they were barred from organizing to defend their rights, demand safer conditions, or negotiate for better wages.

The source of China's cheap labor came from hundreds of millions of peasant workers, mostly from the country's inland and impoverished regions, who left their homes in search of work in cities where opportunities were available. For them, simply having a job and keeping their wages was a dream—something unimaginable under Mao's era of total state control, where peasants earned only work points through labor, which could be exchanged for food at harvest. Earning cash was nearly impossible. I know—because I was one of them during my reeducation years in the countryside. It is these landless peasant workers who created the wealth for the CCP.

Their struggles, however, often went unnoticed. I personally knew a few from my home province of Sichuan. One woman left her family behind to work in a factory in Shenzhen—a special economic zone near Hong Kong—making Christmas decorations. She described grueling hours and dormitories packed with bunk beds, with no proper facilities for bathing. They had to carry water in buckets to the restroom just to wash themselves. To save money, she often skipped the most important Chinese New Year holiday—the only chance to reunite with her family after a year of separation—in order to earn a little extra through holiday pay.

In 2010, a story from China finally captured international attention. At Foxconn, the electronics manufacturing giant producing parts for Apple, tens of thousands of workers were crammed into militarized factory campuses. In some cases, a single campus housed hundreds of thousands of peasant workers, whose daily lives resembled those of prisoners. In 2010 alone, fourteen workers at Foxconn's Chinese factories attempted suicide by jumping from buildings, with only two survivors. One of them was a young woman named Tian Yu, from a rural village in central China.

In February 2010, Tian Yu arrived in Shenzhen with 500 yuan from her father and a secondhand phone. She joined the army of 400,000 workers at Foxconn's Longhua campus, where her task on the assembly line was to inspect products for scratches, a monotonous job repeated 2,880 times a day. Despite working for over a month, Tian Yu never received her wage card. When she sought help, she was sent on a fruitless day-long journey between departments at another factory campus, only to be told her wage card could not be located. Penniless and exhausted, she walked fourteen kilometers back to her dormitory in tears. Her phone had broken, cutting off communication with her family. Overwhelmed with despair, the young girl struggled through the night before jumping from her dormitory's fourth floor.

Tian Yu remained in a coma for twelve days. When she finally woke up, she discovered she could no longer walk.[3]

How did Foxconn respond to the suicide epidemic at its factories? By installing suicide nets around its buildings to catch workers attempting to jump.

Amid Trump's tariff war with China, Apple CEO Tim Cook rejected the cheap labor narrative, insisting Apple manufactures in China not for low wages, but for its deep pool of skilled workers—skills supposedly hard to find in the United States. Yet the real question remains: What's the hourly wage? In 2024, it's about 26 yuan—or just $3.63. While no longer as low as the days of $0.46, it remains undeniably cheap.

While the struggles of peasant workers gradually drew public attention, one major group remained largely overlooked: their children. Lacking urban household registration (as discussed in Chapter 5), they were barred from attending city public schools. As a result, millions became "left-behind children," raised by grandparents or relatives back home in rural areas, often with minimal supervision or support.

Scott Rozelle, a Stanford University economist, uncovered a harsh reality in his study of left-behind children in China's impoverished rural areas. His study shows that more than half of eighth graders have IQs below ninety, making it difficult for them to keep up with the country's rigorous official curriculum. He further notes that over a third of rural children do not complete junior high. Rozelle delivers a stark warning—an estimated 400 million future working-age Chinese, he predicts, "are in danger of becoming cognitively handicapped."[4]

Without urban household registration, these peasant workers are also excluded from benefits such as healthcare. Their lives are of no concern to the municipal governments in cities where they often outnumber the local population.

As more peasant workers flocked to cities in search of opportunities, they increasingly came to be viewed as a nuisance, particularly in Beijing, where the government sought to maintain a pristine image as a thriving capital for the outside world. Labeled the "low-end population," these workers were seen as obstacles to this goal. In the dead of winter in 2017, Beijing launched a "Safety Evacuation Campaign," targeting migrant slums. Following a deadly fire in a migrant settlement, officials aggressively demolished allegedly unsafe and illegal buildings, forcibly evicting tens of thousands of peasant workers with little notice. The victims described their experience as being treated like pests by a city reliant on their labor, leaving them displaced and homeless in freezing temperatures.[5]

Let's not forget that the Chinese Communist Revolution claimed to be about liberating and empowering the peasants. Instead, the CCP has enslaved them, reducing them to mere resources for exploitation, then discarding them as inconveniences when they no longer serve the party's agenda.

Peasant workers provide the CCP with cheap labor, but this has been surpassed by an even cheaper workforce: prison labor, including political prisoners. In 2014, Karen Wisinska from Northern Ireland found a handwritten "cry for help" in a pair of pants she purchased three years earlier: "SOS! SOS! SOS! We are prisoners in Xiang Nan Prison of Hubei Province, China. Our job inside the prison is to produce fashion clothes for export. We work 15 hours per day, and the food we eat wouldn't even be given to dogs or pigs. We work as hard as oxen in the field."[6] Similarly, in 2019, a U.K. girl discovered a note inside a box of Christmas cards that read, "We are prisoners in Shanghai Qingpu Prison, China, forced to work against our will."[7] In both cases, the notes pleaded for intervention from international human rights organizations.

Environment Degradation

Another so-called competitive advantage for China is its lack of environmental protection regulations.

After decades of reckless exploitation, China's water crisis has reached a critical point. Thousands of rivers have vanished, and industrialization and pollution have contaminated much of the remaining water. Some estimates suggest that 80 to 90 percent of groundwater and half of river water is undrinkable, while over half of groundwater and a quarter of river water are unusable even for farming or industry.[8]

One such notorious polluter is China's rare earth industry—a critical geostrategic resource for the CCP. China's dominance in the rare earth industry has come at a significant environmental cost. The reckless and unregulated mining and refining of rare earth metals have led to widespread environmental destruction, including deforestation, the release of toxic sludge, radioactive contamination of groundwater, and severe soil degradation in agricultural regions.

China's air is often unbreathable; smog chokes its cities. The only clear blue sky I ever saw in China was during a visit to Tibet, more than 14,000 feet above the sea level. In preparation for the 2008 Beijing Olympics, authorities in Tangshan, an industrial city north of Beijing, shut down 267 factories, including steelmakers, cement plants, and power generators, to temporarily improve air quality. Beijing also implemented a traffic control system, removing half of the city's 3 million cars from the roads to reduce pollution during the games.[9] Air pollution in China is so bad that it even floats across the Pacific to California and the rest of the western United States.[10]

Air pollution fuels a surge in lung cancer among nonsmokers. A 2025 report reveals that China leads the world in deaths caused by lung adenocarcinoma, a form of lung cancer most commonly found in nonsmokers.[11]

On Earth Day, April 22, 2025, President Trump posted a series of photos on his Truth Social account showing massive floating plastic waste in the Pacific Ocean, calling it "a gift from China." According to GreenMatch, a U.K.-based renewable energy company, China produces 71,000 metric tons of plastic waste that ends up in the ocean.[12]

What is unfolding in China ranks among the gravest environmental degradations in human history. It is a bitter irony that climate globalists look to China as a partner in addressing environmental and climate challenges, despite its dubious ecological track record.

At tremendous human and environmental cost, China amassed immense wealth—on a scale and at a speed unmatched in history. But this is only part of the story behind how China became rich.

Industrial-Scale Technology Theft

In 2009, General Keith Alexander, National Security Agency director, called Chinese intellectual property theft "the greatest transfer of wealth in history."[13] It was no exaggeration.

Many admire Communist China's rapid rise and advancements in cutting-edge technology. However, a closer examination reveals a lack of meaningful innovation originating from China itself. Why? Because Communism and innovation are fundamentally incompatible.

Author James Pethokoukis articulates this phenomenon perfectly: "The main ingredient in the secret sauce that leads to innovation is freedom. Freedom to exchange, experiment, imagine, invest and fail; freedom from expropriation or restriction by chiefs, priests and thieves; freedom on the part of consumers to reward the innovations they like and reject the ones they do not...Innovation is the child of freedom and the parent of prosperity."[14]

Another critical prerequisite for innovation is the protection of private property, including intellectual property. When innovators are not rewarded for their efforts, there is little incentive to innovate.

As part of their "patriotic education," the Chinese people have long been taught to take pride in the "Four Great Inventions" of ancient China: papermaking, printing, the compass, and gunpowder. Today, they are encouraged to take pride in a new set of "Chinese inventions": high-speed rail, online shopping, mobile payments, and shared bicycles as symbols of modern progress. In truth, each of these was a copy of technologies developed decades earlier in the West.[15]

The reality is that Communist China excels only at copying, fueled by stolen technology. The CCP's Baidu mirrors Google, Alibaba (or Taobao) mirrors Amazon, WeChat and Douyin/TikTok mimic Facebook and X, and Youku replicates YouTube...While these Chinese platforms may appear to rival or even surpass their Western counterparts, they lack true core technological innovation. Their so-called success largely stems from China's massive user base and algorithms developed in an environment with zero privacy protections and total state control.

Imitation is not always the sincerest form of flattery. The CCP copies not to admire but to undermine and destroy—eliminating competition, consolidating control, and amassing vast wealth in the process.

Segway, once a symbol of American innovation, launched its self-balancing scooter in 2001. In China, a startup called Ninebot—backed by the state and tech giant Xiaomi—copied the product, bypassed years of R&D, and flooded the market with cheaper knockoffs. Despite legal challenges, Ninebot thrived. In 2015, it used its profits to buy Segway outright. By 2020, Segway's U.S. factory was closed, and China—using technology it didn't invent—had become the global leader in electric scooters. The imitator became the owner, and the innovator was erased.[16]

The same pattern of "rob, replicate, and replace" played out with Tesla. China initially offered the company generous incentives—free land in Shanghai, interest-free loans, and access to a vast market. At the same time, Tesla became a target of industrial theft, accelerating China's ability to build a competitive domestic electric vehicle (EV) industry.[17] Chinese EV giant BYD has now surpassed Tesla in global sales, solidifying China's dominance in the sector. Backed by state subsidies and a tightly integrated EV supply chain, China has left Tesla struggling to maintain its edge. But for consumers, the rise of cheaper Chinese EV imitations has come at a cost: A wave of recent fires caused by spontaneous vehicle combustion—including several involving BYD—has resulted in tragic deaths and injuries.[18]

Stories like those of Segway and Tesla have been repeated time and again with American businesses venturing into China. The only consistent winner in this game is Wall Street, which profits no matter who wins or loses—and for that reason, it remains one of the CCP's most loyal supporters.

Another major source for the CCP's technology theft is American university campuses. Since the late 1970s, following the normalization of U.S.–China relations, more than 3 million Chinese students have studied at U.S. universities. While most—including myself—came to learn and genuinely valued the opportunities, some, however, exploited America's goodwill and open and collaborative academic environment to steal advanced technology for the CCP.

According to the FBI's 2018 report *China: The Risk to Academia*, the annual cost to the U.S. economy from the CCP's theft—through counterfeit goods, pirated software, and stolen trade secrets—is estimated at $225 billion to $600 billion.

Liu Ruopeng, often called "China's Elon Musk," stands as one of the most dramatic cases. From 2006 to 2009, he studied under Professor David Smith—a pioneer in metamaterials research—at Duke University. During that time, Liu allegedly misappropriated U.S. Defense Department–funded "invisibility cloak" technology, even bringing Chinese colleagues into Smith's lab to take unauthorized photos and measurements. After returning to China, a replica soon appeared in Liu's lab. Armed with this technology, Liu founded KuangChi Science, built a $6 billion conglomerate, and became a billionaire—all while maintaining that he developed the technology independently.[19]

As most readers may already understand—but it bears repeating—all stolen technology ultimately serves the Chinese state. In Communist China, there is no such thing as privately owned innovation or patents—just as there is no such thing as privately owned land.

Break the Rules, Reap the Rewards

Another so-called competitive advantage the CCP has mastered is reaping the full benefits of WTO membership while disregarding its binding rules.

WTO trade rules are built on principles of non-discrimination, transparency, fairness, and legally binding commitments. But because enforcement depends largely on the good faith of its members, the system is inherently vulnerable to abuse. In essence, the WTO operates like a gentlemen's club. When a gangster was let in, the outcome was entirely predictable.

Since joining the WTO, the CCP has repeatedly violated rules, exploited loopholes, and systematically manipulated the open trade framework to gain unfair advantages, including:

- *Massive State Subsidies*: The CCP has weaponized state control to dominate key sectors such as steel, solar panels, and telecommunications. By funneling billions in hidden subsidies to domestic firms, it allows them to undercut foreign competitors with artificially low prices—driving rivals out of business and securing global market dominance.
- *Intellectual Property Theft*: As discussed earlier, China has engaged in widespread IP theft, targeting advanced technologies and proprietary innovations across industries.
- *Trade Barriers*: While demanding open access to Western markets, the CCP imposes opaque regulations, excessive red tape, tariffs, and arbitrary enforcement to restrict foreign competitors—especially in sensitive sectors like finance, media, and cloud computing.
- *Currency Manipulation*: By artificially devaluing the yuan, China makes its exports cheaper and imports more expensive, fueling trade surpluses at the expense of global competitors.
- *Abuse of "Developing Nation" Status*: Despite being the world's second-largest economy, China continues to claim develop-

ing country privileges within the WTO, securing preferential treatment and shielding itself from stricter obligations.

After decades of appeasement, it was President Donald Trump who finally confronted the issue head-on, rightly labeling the CCP as the "biggest abuser" of free trade.

The examples of the CCP's bad faith are countless—this being one of the more recent. In January 2020, China signed the Phase One Trade Agreement with the Trump administration, pledging to purchase an additional $200 billion in U.S. goods and services over two years. But instead of honoring the deal, the CCP unleashed the COVID pandemic on the world and then conveniently invoked the agreement's force majeure clause—citing the outbreak as an unforeseeable event to evade its commitments.[20]

In 2025, amid the tariff war, China refused to accept delivery of finished Boeing planes it had ordered. Trump remarked that Boeing should default on China, pointing out that this was just a small example of what China had been doing to the United States for years.[21]

There appears to be not a single multilateral or bilateral agreement that the CCP has not violated. By now, anyone who still expects the CCP to honor the terms of any agreement is engaging in self-deception.

Why did Clinton and his administration fail to anticipate the CCP's behavior when they brought China into the WTO? Because they fundamentally misunderstood Communism. By welcoming a totalitarian regime into a rules-based system, they helped undermine the very foundations of international free trade. In March 2025, the Trump administration responded by pausing U.S. financial contributions to the WTO—a long-overdue reckoning with a broken system.[22]

Marco Rubio, the newly appointed secretary of state under the Trump administration, captured the reality succinctly in his opening statement during his confirmation hearing on January 15, 2025: "We welcomed the Chinese Communist Party into the global order, and they exploited all of its benefits while disregarding its obligations and responsibilities. Instead, they have lied, cheated, hacked, and stolen their way to global superpower status. They have done so at our expense and at the expense of their own people."

As a result, the CCP is now deeply embedded in both the U.S. and the global economies—making any attempt to decouple both difficult and costly.

Is China a Capitalist Country?

This has become one of the most commonly asked questions about today's China—especially among the younger generation. To many, China appears to be a developed nation operating under capitalist principles and a market-driven economy, even perceiving it as superior to the United States.

China's modern landscape showcases an appearance of prosperity that dazzles onlookers, with gleaming high-rises, expansive highways, and cutting-edge bullet trains symbolizing its rapid economic transformation. Towering skylines in cities like Shanghai and Shenzhen rival those of the world's most advanced metropolises. The high-speed rail network, now the largest in the world, serves as a testament to China's ambition. One X account posted a video of a glowing Shanghai skyline at night with the comment, "There's good reason to be terrified of China and it has nothing to do with Communism, Politics or Morality. The Chinese are now doing 'our stuff' better than we can do it ourselves."[23] "Our stuff" obviously means capitalism.

Let's examine what defines a capitalist country. The most fundamental requirement for capitalism is the *protection of private property*—individuals and businesses must have the legal right to own, use, and transfer property freely, without undue interference by the state. In Communist China, however, all land and natural resources are owned and controlled by the state. This is clearly stated in China's constitution and in the speeches of its leaders, yet many Americans and Westerners choose to ignore it.

For real estate properties, individuals own only what is built above ground, while the land itself is leased from the state for terms of up to seventy years. Many of these leases are approaching expiration, and the government has yet to clarify what will happen next, leaving property owners in uncertain legal territory.

Another essential requirement is the rule of law—an independent judiciary that safeguards property rights, enforces contracts, and resolves disputes. In China, however, the rule of law is ultimately the rule of the party. Judicial independence is condemned as a misguided Western concept. The official argument is that if the principle of exercising judicial power independently were adopted, it would amount to rejecting the party's leadership over political and legal affairs.[24]

In Beijing's Fengtai District, there was once a place known as Shang Fang (上访) Village, or Petitioners' Village—a refuge for people from across China seeking to expose local government corruption and the injustices they had suffered. The practice of *shang fang* dates back centuries, rooted in the tradition of directly appealing to highest authorities when all other paths to justice had been exhausted. Each petitioner carried a heartbreaking story of suffering and persecution, clinging to the hope that high-ranking officials in the capital would hear their grievances and deliver justice. Yet, year after year, their pleas went unanswered. In 2007, the government dismantled the village, erasing what had become a powerful symbol of their struggle.[25]

On July 9, 2015, the Chinese government launched a large-scale crackdown on human rights lawyers, arresting and detaining more than three hundred legal professionals. This was the third such crackdown, following similar campaigns in 2005 and 2009.[26] In Communist China, the so-called People's Court exists to serve the party, not the people, and its authority cannot be challenged.

In a capitalist system, economic decisions should be driven by supply and demand with minimal government interference. In China, however, the Communist Party maintains control over everything. All elements of the market economy operate under party scrutiny and can be curtailed or canceled at any time if a business is perceived as posing a challenge or threat to state power.

The political, economic, and cultural structures of Chinese society under CCP rule fundamentally diverge from the principles of capitalism. Core features of a capitalist system—such as private property rights, the rule of law, and limited government—are all absent in China. Most critically, the defining hallmark of a truly capitalist society is missing: freedom of speech and freedom of the press.

Pony Ma, chairman and CEO of Chinese Internet giant Tencent Holdings, once famously remarked, "My money is the party's money." This candid statement, reflecting the CCP's overarching control over private enterprises, has since been scrubbed from the Internet.

Even defenders of Communist China inadvertently reinforce the argument that China is not a capitalist country. Eric X. Li, a Chinese venture capitalist and political scientist, explained in an interview: "In China, billionaires cannot control the Politburo or influence policymaking. While China has a vibrant market economy, capital does not rise above political authority or have enshrined rights. In America, by contrast, capital has surpassed national interests, and political authority cannot check its power. That's why America is a capitalist country, and China is not."[27] Li acknowledged the reality that in China, the party exerts absolute control over the market.

Billionaire Jack Ma is a prime example. The co-founder of Alibaba Group, once worth $23.3 billion, vanished in 2020 after publicly criticizing China's financial regulators.[28] When he reappeared, he seemed subdued and rehabilitated, echoing the party's narrative. Ma is just one of many wealthy entrepreneurs in Communist China who have faced the party's wrath, forced disappearances, or political rehabilitation when their influence was perceived as a threat to party control.

In 2022, Xi Jinping launched the "common prosperity" campaign to address wealth inequality by targeting the private sector. This modern version of the land reform campaign focuses on redistributing wealth through measures such as increased scrutiny, hefty fines, and pressuring tech giants like Alibaba and Tencent to donate significant sums to public welfare initiatives.

After Xi Jinping became party chairman, many super-rich Chinese have become former billionaires, with a significant number ending up in prison. While most not have been entirely innocent, their imprisonment often highlights the harsh realities of a repressive political system that spares no one, not even those it enriches.

A market economy thrives on freedom. One-party rule demands control. When these forces inevitably clash, the party always prevails.

One of the key lessons from American capitalism's engagement with Communist China is this: When capitalism is stripped of its Christian ethical foundation, it can become the very monster Karl Marx once condemned. Without moral boundaries, capitalism ceases to liberate and instead becomes a tool of oppression. In China, American capitalists face no moral restraint and no obligation to address labor abuses, human rights, or environmental harm, because the Party system shields and institutionalizes exploitation. The result is not merely a contradiction but a calculated alliance: a perfect marriage of state control and profit-driven greed—one made in hell.

This is the so-called China model—state capitalism in its most ruthless form.

Who Benefits from the Wealth

China's rapid economic growth made it the world's second-largest economy. While this boom significantly improved living standards for many Chinese citizens, the benefits have been unevenly distributed—often bypassing the hundreds of millions of peasant workers whose cheap labor fueled the country's economic success.

The result is an economy marked by high levels of exports and persistently low domestic consumption. But this is not a flaw—it's a deliberate feature of the CCP's model. At the heart of this imbalance is China's vast pool of low-wage labor, kept intentionally cheap to preserve the so-called competitive advantage. These workers produce goods for the world at minimal cost, fueling China's export dominance, yet their wages are so low that they lack the purchasing power to benefit from the very prosperity they help create. When Secretary of the Treasury Scott Bessent urged China to export less and consume more during the tariff war, he overlooked the fundamental truth: Under the CCP's model, that shift is structurally impossible. These Chinese sayings capture the reality: *guo fu, min qiong* (国富民穷) and *guan fu, min qiong* (官富民穷), meaning "rich state, poor citizens" and "rich officials, poor citizens," respectively.

Guo fu, min qiong encapsulates the reality of Communist China, where the state amasses the majority of the nation's wealth, channeling it primarily toward two objectives: securing and expanding its power. So where does the CCP spend the largest proportion of this wealth? Not on education. Not on healthcare. Not even on the military. Instead, the largest share goes to *wei wen* (维稳), or "maintaining stability" or "public security"—a euphemism for preventing and suppressing opposition and dissent and preserving the regime's grip on power. It is clear that the CCP sees its greatest threat not as external, but internal. And the primary target of its repressive apparatus? The Chinese people themselves.

It was estimated that China's 2019 stability maintenance budget was around 1.33 trillion yuan, with final expenditures expected to exceed 1.4 trillion yuan—surpassing the total national military expenditure of 1.28 trillion yuan.[29]

The maintaining stability expenditure extends beyond maintaining a large traditional law enforcement apparatus, with significant amounts directed toward targeting individuals. Here is a personal account from my co-author, Yu Jie, a well-known dissident:

> I was not only under strict police surveillance but also had a dedicated team assigned to monitor me. In 2011, during my last Christ-

> mas in China, the authorities forced me and my wife to travel to the southern city Sanya in Hainan Province, because we were members of a house church. The authorities feared our church might organize evangelistic activities during Christmas. Accompanied by eight plainclothes police officers, the trip was fully funded by the authorities, including accommodation in a four-star hotel. Three days later, after Christmas had passed, we requested to return to Beijing. The leader of the accompanying team informed us that a department head and two officers would accompany us back, while the rest of the team would remain in Sanya for a week-long vacation.
>
> On January 11, 2012, just before my family and I were finally allowed to leave China, the local police chief revealed to me that after my departure, their team would lose 2 million to 3 million yuan (approximately $414,000) annually in stability maintenance funds—funds allocated solely to monitor me and my family.

The second-largest spending category is military expenditures. The party no longer hides its ambitions—instead, it proudly broadcasts them. Xi Jinping revived the Soviet-style military parade as a spectacle to showcase China's growing military power on the world stage. Estimates place the cost of Xi's 2015 parade as high as $21.5 billion.[30]

Guan fu, min qiong—"rich officials, poor citizens"—underscores the oligarchic nature of China's political system, which primarily benefits princeling families—the offspring of powerful party elites and founders of Communist China—along with new party officials who consolidate wealth and influence within the ruling class.

This has ushered in an era Karl Marx could never have envisioned: a symbiotic alliance between Communist oligarchs, princelings, and Western multinational capitalists, all quietly amassing vast fortunes, while party officials remain firmly entrenched at the top of society.

Jiang Zemin, China's paramount leader after Deng Xiaoping, and his family are believed to top the list of China's elite wealth holders, allegedly controlling at least $1 trillion in state assets, with $500 billion reportedly laundered and hidden overseas.[31] This vast and rapid accumulation occurred primarily during Jiang's presidency (1993–2003) and his subsequent behind-the-scenes influence over his successor, Hu Jintao.

By comparison, Xi Jinping's family lags far behind. According to a 2025 Congressional Research Service report, Xi is estimated to control around $700 million in wealth—all carefully hidden, of course.[32]

Like all other political elites, the Jiang and Xi families neither invented nor created anything. The immense wealth they amassed came from what the Chinese people had built through their toil and sacrifices.

Corruption permeates all levels of government and officials, including the maintaining stability police operations mentioned above. In 2024, a leaked post revealed that officials of Zhuhai city in Southern China spent ¥800,000 (around $110,000) to censor online content about a car-ramming incident but later inflated reimbursement claims to ¥4.5 million (around $618,000), pocketing ¥3.7 million (around $508,000). The scandal came to light only when disgruntled insiders, excluded from the spoils, exposed the scheme to disciplinary authorities and social media, revealing both financial corruption and the abuse of censorship for personal gain.[33]

When Xi Jinping took power in 2012, he launched an anti-corruption campaign, framing it as an effort to clean up corruption within the Chinese Communist Party and restore public trust. However, it quickly became evident that the campaign was less about anti-corruption and more about eliminating political rivals and consolidating his absolute control over the party. The only way to fundamentally address the endemic corruption in this one-party kleptocracy is through systemic change—dismantling the one-party dictatorship.

Xi Jinping has repeatedly boasted that the CCP has lifted the Chinese people out of poverty. However, his former premier, Li Keqiang, openly disclosed that 600 million Chinese—nearly half of the country's supposedly 1.4 billion population—live on a monthly income of just ¥1,000 (approximately $136, or less than $5 a day).[34] This revelation directly challenges Xi's claims of poverty alleviation. To put it into perspective, ¥1,000 is only enough to cover a respectable dinner for four in urban areas.

Xi Jinping also conveniently omitted the fact that it was the Chinese Communist Party itself that had plunged the Chinese people into abject poverty. By the time of Mao's death in 1976, China was poorer than it had been before the Communist takeover in 1949, and per capita calorie consumption was even lower than in 1933.[35]

If Edgar Snow, William Hinton, Theodore White, and other leftist Americans who once placed their hope in the CCP were alive today, would they be shocked by the CCP's industry-scale corruption? Or would they, like so many leftists today, still rationalize and defend them?

Digital Totalitarianism

President Clinton confidently predicted that Internet and information technology would bring freedom and democracy to China. But the opposite has happened. With technology from the West, the CCP has created an unprecedented form of digital totalitarianism.

To counter the open Internet, the CCP swiftly built its "Great Firewall"—a digital fortress far more impenetrable than the Great Wall of ancient China. This system blocks the flow of information from outside the country and suppresses citizens' access to free and uncensored content—using technology originally provided by the American tech giant Cisco.[36]

Clinton severely underestimated the dual-edged nature of technology. The Chinese government has achieved what he once called the "impossible task" of "nailing Jell-O to the wall" by asserting active control over online society. China's social credit system is a state-run program that monitors and scores citizens' behavior to reward compliance and punish misconduct, including actions such as failing to repay debts, spreading "false information" online, or engaging in behavior deemed "disruptive." Individuals with low scores may be barred from booking high-speed rail or flights, banking, finding jobs, renting housing, or enrolling their children in certain schools or universities. A simple warning from authorities—linked to a person's phone number—can result in de facto blacklisting, turning that individual into a social outcast, cut off from full participation in society. This system makes the formation of civil organizations and opposition movements virtually impossible.[37]

The system is further reinforced by physical restrictions—the so-called fifteen-minute communities—which, while marketed as a convenience, often serve as zones of total surveillance and movement control, resembling open-air prisons.

Communist China has become a laboratory for totalitarian social control—and its model is now quietly and insidiously seeping into the United States and the broader West. Echoing China's social credit system, emerging frameworks like ESG (environmental, social, and governance) scoring for corporations—and even individuals—as well as "fifteen-minute communities" are being promoted as solutions to social injustice, climate change, and urban efficiency.

Decades of engagement with Communist China proved every single one of Clinton's promises wrong. Worse still, as the CCP became less like us, America began to look more and more like Communist China. It's an alarming reality that far too many Americans have yet to recognize.

—

While it's essential to understand the gangster nature of the Chinese Communist Party and how it amassed immense wealth, it's even more important to recognize the central role the United States played in that rise. After all, it was America that acted as the farmer who chose to save the snake—knowing full well it was a snake.

The enablers are no longer limited to political leaders, media elites, and so-called China experts. America's corporations have joined their ranks. Driven by short-term profits, U.S. companies abandoned core moral principles—outsourcing jobs, transferring vital technology, and cozying up to the Chinese Communist Party by turning a blind eye to human rights abuses, forced labor, and systemic corruption. The cost? Millions of lost American jobs, the hollowing out of critical industries, a weakened national security, and, in many cases, the collapse of their own long-term competitiveness and market share.

All the while, the American public has been assured that China's rise was inevitable—and America's decline, somehow, was just the natural course of history.

But none of this was true. The CCP grew strong because America lost its way—having strayed from the founding values that once made this nation great.

CHAPTER 8

CLAWS OF THE DRAGON REACHING INSIDE AMERICA

Many Americans who recognize the Chinese Communist Party as a political or military threat still view it as a distant, external force—be it military buildup, provocations in the South China Sea, surveillance balloons, or trade wars. But the danger is no longer just foreign; it is now deeply domestic. The CCP has gone far beyond economic influence, embedding itself in nearly every sector of American life—education, media, technology, politics, and even government. It has also cultivated an army of allies—so-called *friends of the Chinese people*—who share its goals and fight alongside it. This is no longer merely a geopolitical rivalry; it is a coordinated, multi-front assault unfolding within America's own borders—where the line between us and the enemy has been deliberately blurred.

Sun Tzu, the ancient Chinese military strategist, once wrote, "To fight and win a hundred battles is not supreme excellence; supreme excellence consists in breaking the enemy's resistance without fighting." The CCP has fully embraced this philosophy. After hollowing out America's industrial base, it has quietly set about hollowing out our institutions and our government.

Since Nixon's visit to Beijing, the path was laid for the CCP's deep penetration into America. Beyond opening our markets, one door after another was eventually unlocked, allowing the CCP's influence to seep into the very fabric of our society. How did Americans become so completely unguarded against Communist China?

The answer should be clear by now: Our political leaders persuaded the American people that Communist China could be transformed into an ally—a capitalist nation and a liberal democracy like the United States. Our business leaders assured consumers that Communist China would make America more prosperous with an endless supply of cheap goods. And those ideologically aligned with the CCP painted Communism as a noble ideal for all.

These forces worked in unison, leaving the nation defenseless and making it effortless for the CCP to wage its most effective weapon of subversion—its United Front operations—right here on American soil.

It is essential to recognize that many caught in the CCP's United Front operations are not innocent. These are willing captives, enticed by the prospect of power, wealth, or fame, and fully aware of what they stand to gain from serving Beijing's interests. As Jonathan Manthorpe, author of *Claws of the Panda*, argues, these "friends of China" take on their roles "knowingly, willingly, and often eagerly."[1] While Manthorpe's book focuses on CCP infiltration in Canada, its insights about this tactic apply just as well to the United States.

The Magic Weapon

Although the United Front strategy has been a recurring theme throughout the book, this chapter focuses specifically on the CCP's United Front operations within the United States.

The concept of the United Front, *tong zhan* (统战), originated with the Comintern in 1920s Communist Russia. Developed by Lenin and expanded by Stalin, it aimed to co-opt non-Communist groups to advance Communist goals. The CCP adopted and refined this strategy to serve its own ambitions, as seen forming tactical alliances with the Nationalists and working to win over American journalists and, eventually, the U.S. government throughout the 1930s and 1940s.

As early as 1939, Mao claimed the United Front strategy as one of the Communist Party's three "Magic Weapons" for gaining power and defeating adversaries, alongside Armed Struggle and Party Building.

After seizing control of China in 1949, the CCP formalized this operation by establishing the United Front Work Department (UFWD) to enhance and expand the strategy's effectiveness. The UFWD is one of the key departments directly under the Chinese Communist Party Central Committee and holds authority far above government ministries, with the full power to mobilize all resources. In 2019 alone, China's United Front budget exceeded $2.6 billion, surpassing the annual budget of China's Ministry of Foreign Affairs, the equivalent of the U.S. State Department.[2]

Though the term "United Front" remains unchanged, its scope has evolved from a domestic tool to a global strategy—now targeting the United States as a primary focus. It refers not only to the broad array of influence operations directed by the UFWD, but more specifically to a strategic tactic designed to entice individuals with offers they find irresistible, whether personal, financial, political, or ideological. Many become willing captives; others are merely naïve, unaware they've taken the bait and blind to how they are being used. Yi-Zheng Lian captured the deceptive nature of the United Front strategy perfectly in his article "China Has a Vast Influence Machine, and You Don't Even Know It":

> Rather than coercing, China manipulates, preferring to act in moral and legal gray areas. It masks its political motives behind laudable

> human-interest or cultural projects, blurring the battle line with its adversaries. When the job is done, the other side may not realize it was gamed, or that a strategic game was even going on.[3]

Crucially, the success of the United Front cannot be understood in isolation. It is deeply intertwined with the "long march through the institutions" carried out by American cultural Marxists, who are the ideological allies of the CCP. Both forces share a common objective: the destabilization and eventual destruction of the United States from within. They deploy similar tactics of infiltration, subversion, and soft penetration, and increasingly, they reinforce each other's efforts.

Elite Capture

Elite capture is a tactic frequently used by the CCP to manipulate and control political, educational, business, and cultural leaders in the United States, ensuring that their influence and decisions align with the CCP's interests. In other words, to turn them into "friends of the Chinese people."

For the CCP, capturing American elites is of paramount importance. Influential individuals advocating on its behalf often prove more effective, as they can shape opinions and policies from within.

Henry Kissinger (1923–2023)

Henry Kissinger is undoubtedly one of the most famous of these captured U.S. elites. He was the engineer of the opening of U.S.–China relations and engaged with every Chinese leader from Mao Zedong to Xi Jinping. Kissinger's affection for China seems to have exceeded his duty for the United States. After leaving public office as the U.S. secretary of state, Kissinger made more than a hundred trips to China over the course of four decades. Sometimes he continued his role as a political broker between U.S. and Chinese leaders, but more often, he acted as a businessman.

In 1982, Henry Kissinger founded Kissinger Associates Inc., a political consulting firm focused on helping clients navigate investment opportunities in countries like China. In 1988, he launched China Ventures in partnership with China's state-owned CITIC, aiming to facilitate and profit from investments in Chinese enterprises.

Following the 1989 Tiananmen Square Massacre, Kissinger sent a private message to Beijing, reassuring the regime of his continued support as an "old friend of China."[4] True to his word, Kissinger opposed U.S. government sanctions on Beijing, drawing criticism for prioritizing business interests over democracy and human rights.[5]

In his book *On China* and in many of his talks, Kissinger repeatedly linked the Chinese Communist Party to China's ancient heritage, portraying Mao and Deng as products of a millennia-old civilizational tradition rather than merely Marxist ideologues. While the Chinese civilization dates back thousands of years, Marxism began in 1848 with *The Communist Manifesto*. Kissinger was among the first to blur the line between China and the CCP—a dangerous distortion that still clouds public understanding today.

Kissinger enjoyed unparalleled privileges in China, celebrated as a "dear old friend of the Chinese people." This designation, rich with connotations of honor and elevated status in CCP culture, granted him unique access. Leveraging this position, he amassed a fortune lobbying for U.S. businesses in China—frequently prioritizing these ventures over America's broader national interest.

For decades, Henry Kissinger wielded unmatched influence over U.S. foreign policy, particularly in shaping relations with China. Successive American presidents sought his counsel, and many of his protégés ascended to powerful roles within the State Department. The only notable exceptions were President Reagan and President Trump, both of whom kept their distance. In 2020, Trump removed Kissinger from the Defense Policy Board, marking the definitive end of his decades-long dominance over U.S. policy toward China.[6]

In July 2023, at over a hundred years old and just months before his death, Henry Kissinger made his final visit to China and met with Xi Jinping. The Biden White House lamented that Kissinger, a private citizen, received more respect than their own officials.[7] They failed to grasp that the CCP viewed Kissinger as one of their own.

For many in the CCP, his death marked the end of the "golden era" of U.S.–China relations. I consider that a good thing. Kissinger viewed Communist China and the United States through the lens of power dynamics, treating the United States as just another player in the global struggle for influence. To him, power—not moral ideals—drove history, a perspective captured in his famous statement: "America has no permanent friends or enemies, only interests."

Kissinger's approach epitomized how U.S. political elites, motivated by self-interest, facilitated the CCP's rise.

The Biden Family

On November 28, 2020, Di Dongsheng, a CCP policy advisor, delivered a televised presentation during an online conference on international finance in China. In his speech, he boasted about the CCP's connections to "old friends" among the U.S. power elite. Di specifically mentioned Joe Biden, stating that "we see that Biden has come to power...You've noticed, haven't you? Trump accused Biden's son of having global investment funds—who do you think helped him set up those funds? Understand? There are deals behind all of this."[8]

The video clip quickly went viral, with Tucker Carlson highlighting it in detail on his Fox News evening show. While some dismissed the remarks as mere boasting, for those familiar with the CCP's elite capture strategy, it was a stark confirmation of an open secret.

Based on the report of the Congressional Committee on Oversight and Accountability, Hunter Biden's business dealings with Communist China began as early as 2013. These included his involvement with Bohai Harvest Partners, a private equity firm, and CEFC China Energy—ventures that reportedly earned him millions.[9] But this was not just about Hunter; it was a family enterprise. According to the House Oversight Committee, President Joe Biden met with nearly every foreign associate involved in funneling millions to his family,[10] contradicting his repeated denials. Notably, among those he met was Ye Jianming, Hunter's business partner and chairman of the Chinese energy giant CEFC, who has since vanished from public view.[11]

These ties weren't limited to business deals alone. Thanks to the Biden connection, the University of Pennsylvania—home to President Biden's think tank—received nearly $130 million in donations from Chinese entities and individuals between mid-2018 and mid-2023.[12]

Governor Tim Walz

Elite capture doesn't always target the top-most leaders. In 2020, Secretary of State Mike Pompeo warned governors that the CCP was closely monitoring them. He cautioned state officials that China was categorizing them as friendly, hard-line, or ambiguous in its efforts to shape U.S. policies.[13]

Governor Tim Walz was almost certainly labeled by the CCP as "super friendly," given his notable connections with Communist China. These ties gained national attention after he was chosen as the running mate for the 2024 Democratic ticket.

Walz taught English in China for a year right after the Tiananmen Square Massacre. After returning home, Walz organized many tours for high school students to visit China and told his students that "Communism" in China meant that "everyone is the same and everyone shares. The doctor and the construction worker make the same."[14]

After transitioning to politics as a congressman, governor of Minnesota, and eventually as the 2024 Democratic vice presidential candidate, Walz has consistently promoted the view that Communist China is not an adversary.[15]

Unlike other elites motivated mainly by profit—with no clear evidence he enriched himself through CCP ties—Walz appears to be a true believer, ideologically aligned with Communist principles. In many ways, he wasn't captured by the CCP itself, but rather by the Marxist ideology they share.

Unfortunately, the American political landscape is rife with captured elites like Kissinger, Biden, and Walz.

Business Elites

Many American business elites have openly expressed admiration for the CCP and its system of governance, despite the CCP's documented human rights atrocities and suppression of freedoms in China. Driven by business interests, some are willing to set aside core American values for profit and market access, choosing to overlook the inconvenient truths of the Communist regime.

China plays a critical role in Apple Inc.'s operations, as nearly all Apple products are assembled in China, and the Chinese market accounts for about one-fifth of its sales. In exchange for access to this essential market and manufacturing base, the Chinese government has exerted pressure on Apple executives to comply with CCP values. That did not seem to be a problem for Apple's current CEO, Tim Cook.

Apple's cooperation with the CCP includes storing Chinese user data with the state-run Guizhou-Cloud Big Data, effectively giving the regime access.[16] It also enforces CCP censorship by limiting iPhone apps to those approved by the party.[17] During the 2023 White Paper Revolution against Xi Jinping's brutal COVID Lockdown, Apple disabled AirDrop in China—used to evade censorship—prompting a hunger strike by U.S.-based activists at Apple's headquarters.

During his 2023 visit to Beijing, Tim Cook reflected on the company's long-standing cooperation with China, stating that Apple and Communist China had "grown together" over the past thirty years.[18]

Despite Cook's extensive efforts to comply with the CCP, the iPhone, as an American product, continues to pose a perceived threat to the regime. In 2023, the CCP banned government employees from using iPhones. This decision sought to close potential loopholes in the Great Firewall while boosting domestic competition, particularly favoring Chinese brand Huawei smartphones.[19]

Worse still, in April 2025, as Apple began shifting its supply chain to India due to uncertainty from Trump's tariff war, China retaliated by creating roadblocks—delaying or blocking equipment shipments without explanation. In some cases, Foxconn's export applications were outright denied; in others, approvals were delayed for months.[20] This was simply the continuation of a broader trend: It is becoming increasingly difficult to move money and business out of China. Foreign investors should take note—dealing with China now resembles dealing with a mafia state: Enter at your own risk.

As Apple works on shifting its factories from China to India, President Trump remarked that he had "a little problem" with Tim Cook—saying he wants Apple to "build here" in the United States. When a corporation's love of profit outweighs its loyalty to the country and its people, it's no longer just a little problem—it's a crisis.

Apple is not alone. Other U.S. tech giants, such as Microsoft and Google, have collaborated with Chinese companies by supporting startup incubator programs that developed policing or censorship tools used by CCP's law enforcement agencies, including helping the Chinese Communist Party establish a surveillance system in Xinjiang.[21]

Despite U.S. tech platforms being banned in China, Facebook CEO Mark Zuckerberg openly courted the CCP. At a 2015 White House dinner, he asked Xi Jinping to give his unborn child a Chinese name—a gesture widely seen as an attempt to gain favor.[22] Zuckerberg also displayed Xi's books on his desk to impress visiting CCP propaganda officials.[23]

Whistleblower Sarah Wynn-Williams, a former senior Facebook executive and author of *Careless People* (2025), revealed that in its failed bid to enter the Chinese market, Facebook worked "hand in glove" with the Chinese government, exploring ways to enable Beijing to censor and control content within China.[24]

Investment banker Robert Lawrence Kuhn went further than most business elites in his admiration for the CCP. He authored *The Man Who Changed China: The Life and Legacy of Jiang Zemin*, former president of China. The book became an instant bestseller in China, selling more than a million copies. However, one U.S. review remarked that the book "quickly departs from the realm of analysis and ends up somewhere close to cheerleading."[25]

Kuhn claimed his work was self-initiated rather than commissioned, stating that "Jiang didn't choose me; I chose Jiang. The book was my idea; I planned it, financed it, and wrote it to trace China's story through eight tumultuous decades of trauma and transformation."[26] In his book, Kuhn argued that Jiang's leadership had given Chinese people prosperity and more freedom than ever before.

However, Kuhn conveniently omits some critical facts, including Jiang's harsh suppression of groups like Falun Gong practitioners, Christians, Tibetans, and democracy activists. Kuhn's positive assessment of freedoms under Jiang clashes with the experiences of so many in China who encounter the reality of state control and repression daily.

America lost China to Communism in 1949 largely because too many decision-makers had no understanding of Communism and too many proved to be fellow travelers. Today, the situation is definitely far worse, as ignorance and ideological alignment with totalitarianism are rampant at the highest levels of American elites.

What distinguishes those who helped to lose China—like Edgar Snow, General Stilwell, John S. Service, General Marshall, and Harry Truman—from today's pro-CCP elites is intent. However misguided, the former believed they were helping the Chinese people. Today's elites support the CCP with full awareness of its atrocities, making their actions deliberate and indefensible. Cynical and self-serving, they have either lost faith in America, are indifferent to her fate, or despise her altogether. By ignoring the CCP's brutal record and enriching themselves, they betray their country.

When so many American elites defend the CCP, one might wonder if there are Chinese elites in China actively and openly promoting and defending the democratic values of the United States and the West. The sobering reality is that such individuals are most likely to be found either in prisons or in graves.

The Chinese Diaspora

This may seem jarring to Americans, but the Chinese Communist Party has long regarded all ethnic Chinese—including those of mixed heritage—as its subjects, regardless of their citizenship in Hong Kong, Taiwan, Singapore, the United States, or anywhere else in the world. As a result, ethnic Chinese individuals in America—estimated at around 2.5 million—are prime targets of the CCP's United Front operations, with a particular focus on influencing elites in positions of power and authority.

Although most Americans know about Republican Senator Mitch McConnell, few are familiar with the story of his wife, Elaine Chao, and her family's ties to McConnell's rise.

The Chao family's wealth comes from the Foremost Group, a shipping company founded by Elaine Chao's father, James Chao, who immigrated to the United States from Taiwan. James built the company into a global giant, thanks to his personal ties to former Chinese president Jiang Zemin, having been college classmates from Shanghai in the 1940s. Even before McConnell and Elaine Chao got married, political donations from the Chao family began flowing as early as 1989.[27] Over time, McConnell's rise in the Senate coincided with Foremost's growing profits from Chinese government contracts.

In 2004, McConnell and Chao's net worth was $3.1 million; a decade later, it had grown to between $9.2 million and $36.5 million, largely from gifts from James Chao.[28] The wife of the Senate majority leader, Elaine Chao rose to high office, serving as secretary of labor under Bush and secretary of transportation under Trump. While in office, Chao often defended Communist China, accusing U.S. media of demonizing it. She also earned up to $50,000 per speech at universities and forums in China.[29]

The connections run deeper: Elaine's late sister, Angela Chao, later took over management of Foremost, served on the board of CSSC Holdings—a major player in China's military-industrial complex—and was appointed to the board of the state-controlled Bank of China, becoming only the second foreign national to hold such a position.[30]

Since coming to power in 2012, Xi Jinping has intensified efforts to engage the Chinese diaspora through what is termed "overseas Chinese work"—CCP term for Chinese diaspora. At the 19th National Congress in 2017, Xi emphasized that the party will "maintain extensive contacts with overseas Chinese nationals, returned Chinese and their relatives and unite them so that they can join our endeavors to revitalize the Chinese nation."[31]

A 2024 *Wall Street Journal* article entitled "How Beijing Recruited New York Chinatowns for Influence Campaign" exposed Congresswoman Grace Meng of New York's 6th district and Linda Sun, a former aide to Governors Hochul and Cuomo. Sun was arrested by the FBI and charged with acting as an unregistered agent of the Chinese Communist government. She has pleaded not guilty. According to the indictment, Sun manipulated messaging from high-ranking officials on issues critical to China. This allegedly included ensuring that Governor Andrew Cuomo publicly praised China for its assistance with COVID-19, restricting access for Taiwanese government representatives, and facilitating unauthorized New York State proclamations for Chinese government officials.

In 2025, news broke that Boston mayor Michelle Wu—the daughter of Taiwanese immigrants—had received $300,000 in campaign contributions from a Chinese Communist Party operative during her 2022 race.[32] By then, the revelation was no longer shocking; it merely confirmed what many had already begun to suspect about the extent of CCP influence on American politics within the Chinese American community.

Soon after, an investigation by the Daily Caller News Foundation, conducted amid anti-ICE riots in Los Angeles, revealed a similar pattern involving Mayor Karen Bass. Adam Ma, a senior official in her administration, was identified as the son of Ma Shurong—a prominent figure in multiple CCP United Front organizations. Not only did Ma Shurong raise substantial funds for Bass's campaign, but he also maintained close ties to Chinese intelligence–linked groups, raising serious concerns about CCP infiltration at the local level.[33]

What had shocked the American public earlier was the revelation that the CCP had established numerous "overseas police stations" in major U.S. cities, including a prominent one in Manhattan's Chinatown. How did this happen? These stations were set up under the guise of service centers for Chinese nationals abroad, often embedded within Chinese hometown associations and diaspora organizations, particularly those linked to provinces like Fujian and Zhejiang. Far from benign, these so-called service centers have been used for harassment, intimidation, surveillance, and the coercion of dissidents.

One such dissident targeted was Yan Xiong, who ran for Congress in New York's 10th district in 2020. His involvement in the 1989 pro-democracy student movement in China made him a target of Chinese hometown associations in New York, which repeatedly denied him speaking opportunities. After he launched his campaign, the FBI warned him of potential physical threats. In early 2022, the Justice Department indicted a Chinese state-security officer for orchestrating a scheme to sabotage his candidacy.[34]

The CCP's United Front work has never been confined to Chinatown—it actively extends its influence far beyond. In a 2020 article, *Newsweek* reported that it had identified approximately six hundred Chinese or Chinese-affiliated organizations in the United States as being influenced by the CCP's United Front Work Department. These include alumni networks, hometown associations, Chinese chambers of commerce, and a wide range of community groups.[35]

I would venture even further: The CCP's reach likely extends into virtually every Chinese organization—including those most vehemently opposed to its rule, such as Falun Gong, and opposition groups of Uyghurs and Tibetans. The only question that remains is how successful these infiltration efforts have been.

While many members of those groups may be unaware of any foreign connection, these organizations are often in regular contact with Chinese diplomatic missions and aligned with CCP objectives—sometimes even competing for favor with party-linked entities.

One high-profile example featured in the *Newsweek* report is the Committee of 100—a nonprofit founded in 1990 by prominent Chinese Americans, including world-renowned architect I. M. Pei and celebrated cellist Yo-Yo Ma, with support from Henry Kissinger. The organization states its mission is to promote Chinese-American participation in U.S. public life and to "advance constructive relations" with China. Over the years, it has maintained close ties with Chinese government entities, including hosting meetings with senior CCP leaders and inviting Chinese ambassadors to its annual gatherings. Though it denies any foreign influence, its positions have often mirrored Beijing's narrative. In 2024, for instance, the committee joined other CCP-linked Asian American organizations in opposing the House's China Initiative—an effort to counter CCP espionage in the United States—arguing it fostered racial animosity. Such actions have raised growing concerns about its role in China's broader influence campaign.[36]

In December 2024, Asian Americans Advancing Justice submitted a letter to House leadership opposing the reauthorization of the House Select Committee on the CCP, accusing it of unfairly targeting Asian Americans and Asian immigrants—communities they claimed were already vulnerable to racial profiling, discrimination, and violence.[37]

Also in 2024, CCP-linked organizations—including United Chinese Americans—mobilized protests against Florida's SB 264, which banned citizens of Communist China and other totalitarian regimes from purchasing property within ten miles of military bases or critical infrastructure. Protesters condemned the measure as "anti-Asian racism" and likened it to the 1882 Chinese Exclusion Act.[38] What saddens me most is knowing some of the protesters personally—people with backgrounds and experiences much like mine, who also survived the brutal repression of the CCP, yet chose to stand with the very regime we once fled.

Through the examples above, a clear pattern emerges: United Front strategists have begun to wield another "magic weapon" borrowed from American Marxists—labeling any U.S. laws, policies, or actions they oppose as "racist" and "xenophobic," directly mirroring tactics popularized by the Black Lives Matter movement.

Another key target of the United Front is ethnic Chinese scientists in U.S. universities and research institutions, who are used to access America's advanced technology and intellectual property.

One person who stands out is Fei-Fei Li, a renowned AI scientist and former Google executive. Her appointment to Twitter's board as an independent director in 2020 drew scrutiny due to her ties to China's AI ecosystem and potential influence from the Chinese Communist Party.

Li played a key role in establishing Google's AI lab in China and served as an AI advisor to Tsinghua University, an institution deeply involved in China's military-civilian fusion programs. These affiliations have raised serious concerns about CCP influence within Western tech companies, particularly in AI development and governance.[39]

Among the many stories of the Chinese diaspora, this is one of the most revealing examples of the reach of the United Front operation. In August 2024, Tang Yuanyun was arrested in New York and accused of spying for China's Ministry of State Security since 2018, allegedly surveilling and reporting on Chinese dissidents living in the United States.

Who is Tang? Tang is a former pro-democracy activist who participated in the 1989 Tiananmen pro-democracy movement. For his involvement, he was arrested by the CCP and sentenced to twenty years in prison, though he was released after serving eight years. After his release,

Tang continued his activism in China, working in the pro-democracy movement and helping to establish the China Democracy Party. As a result, he frequently faced government surveillance and harassment.

In 2002, Tang fled to Taiwan by swimming from a Chinese fishing boat and later secured political asylum in the United States. For years, he was an active participant in overseas Chinese pro-democracy movements—until his recent arrest.[40]

If convicted, his story will stand as yet another tragic example of a dissident co-opted by the Chinese Communist Party, betraying the very ideals he once championed. Tang's case is not isolated; similar incidents have occurred and continue to surface.

The unsettling reality is that the CCP's United Front operations are pervasive across America. These efforts represent a modern extension of Mao's "people's war,"* infiltrating nearly every Chinese organization in the United States and seeking to influence or co-opt any Chinese individual deemed strategically valuable.

Within the Chinese diaspora, there is a special group: the offspring of CCP elites. According to the *Washington Post*, 74.5 percent of Chinese officials at the ministerial level or above—including retirees—have children with U.S. green cards or citizenship, and over 91 percent of their grandchildren are U.S. citizens.[41] Many enjoy vast wealth laundered abroad through corruption. It is safe to say their loyalties are in question, and they may have played a unique role in advancing the aims of the United Front.

Infiltration of American Institutions

While American Cultural Marxists have pursued their "Long March through the institutions" to infiltrate and seize control of American institutions, the CCP has been doing the same. Their goals align, and their efforts are often mutually reinforcing.

* A military strategy developed by Mao Zedong that mobilizes the masses for a protracted, asymmetric war, using guerrilla warfare, political indoctrination, and mass mobilization to weaken and ultimately defeat a stronger enemy.

Educational System

Having influence over a political leader is undoubtedly valuable, but influencing educators who can systematically shape generations of future political leaders, policymakers, and voters is even more powerful.

Harvard's ties with China date back over a century but deepened significantly in the twentieth century, particularly through figures like John King Fairbank (1907–1991), a leading American historian of U.S.–China relations. He authored *The United States and China* (1948), a foundational text on the subject, and established the Fairbank Center for Chinese Studies, which has trained generations of China experts in academia and government.

After studying at Harvard and Oxford, Fairbank conducted fieldwork in China from 1931 to 1935 and later worked for the U.S. government in Chongqing. Influenced by liberal journalists like Edgar Snow—a captive of the CCP's United Front—and pro-Communist academics, Fairbank came to view the CCP as China's future, based largely on reports from Yan'an.

After the war, Fairbank founded the East Asian Research Center in Harvard, which became a hub for China studies in the United States. He is recognized as a pioneer in the field, shaping both academic and governmental understanding of China.

In his book *The United States and China*, Fairbank argued that while Communism was unsuitable for the United States, it was appropriate for China, portraying the Communist Party's rise as historically inevitable. He reinforced the misconception, popularized by Edgar Snow, that Chinese Communism was distinct from Soviet Communism, framing it as agrarian reform adapted to China's rural realities. Fairbank advocated accepting Chinese Communism as a necessary development and engaging with it pragmatically.

As a renowned scholar and teacher, Fairbank trained a generation of East Asian specialists. By 1981, his students were teaching at seventy-five U.S. universities, many focusing on modern Chinese history under his guidance. Over time, Fairbank's influence—or rather, his pro-CCP stance—extended into key academic and political roles through his protégés, including Susan L. Shirk, who served as assistant secretary of state for East Asian affairs under Clinton. Shirk helped facilitate China's entry into the World Trade Organization and portrayed China as a "fragile superpower" posing no real threat to the United States.

Ezra F. Vogel (1930–2020), who succeeded John Fairbank as the head of Harvard's East Asian Research Center, continued Fairbank's work. He defended Deng Xiaoping's cold-blooded killing during the Tiananmen Square Massacre in his book *Deng Xiaoping and the Transformation of China*, by framing it as a tragic but necessary response to maintain stability and ensure China's long-term development.

Vogel also arranged for President Jiang Zemin to deliver a speech at Harvard University during his 1997 visit to the United States, offering the CCP a platform to promote its agenda. The event was tightly controlled, with no open floor for audience questions. Preselected individuals posed vetted questions, ensuring that no challenging or controversial topics were raised[42]—mirroring the CCP's approach to managing discourse in China.

While Xi Jinping's daughter attended Harvard, Ezra F. Vogel served as her mentor, offering guidance and support during her studies. Clearly, Xi Jinping trusted that her education would align more with CCP-friendly perspectives rather than the values of Western liberal democracies.

These roles earned Vogel the esteemed and politically significant title of "Old Friend of the Chinese People."

In recent years, Harvard University's Fairbank Center for Chinese Studies has partnered with several leading Chinese universities, regularly hosting government-affiliated Chinese scholars as visiting researchers.

But it gets even worse. The university has proudly earned the nickname of the "CCP's Overseas Leadership Training Camp." Since the early 2000s, Harvard—particularly the Kennedy School—has served as a training ground for rising CCP officials, receiving 4,000 carefully vetted party cadres, including future ministers, governors, and Politburo members. These officials study leadership, governance, media strategy, and crisis management in custom-designed executive courses. Among the most prominent alumni is Li Yuanchao, a former Politburo member and head of the very department responsible for selecting who gets sent.[43]

Even after the U.S. government imposed sanctions on Xinjiang for the ongoing Uyghur genocide, Harvard University discreetly provided training to members of the Xinjiang Production and Construction Corps—a designated "paramilitary organization."[44]

Harvard is so deeply entangled with the CCP that it punished students protesting China's human rights abuses during a speech by the Chinese ambassador on April 20, 2024, while letting the student who assaulted them off the hook—and even issuing him an apology. The incident prompted the Congressional Select Committee on the CCP to release a statement condemning Harvard.[45]

Doubtless to say, Harvard has been richly rewarded by the CCP. Between 2019 and 2022, Harvard received nearly $70 million from Chinese sources. Its financial ties to China stretch back further, including a $350 million donation in 2014 from the Hong Kong–based Morningside Foundation, with close ties to Beijing.[46]

Rivaling Columbia University, long home to the Frankfurt School of Cultural Marxism, today's Harvard University, deeply infiltrated by the Chinese Communist Party, has emerged as another epicenter of American radicalism.

The CCP's United Front extends beyond Ivy League campuses, notably through hundreds of Confucius Institutes across U.S. universities. Disguised as cultural centers, they spread propaganda, censor sensitive topics, monitor critics, and reward pro-China academics. After exposure made the name toxic, many universities rebranded these programs to retain CCP funding—which remains abundant. From 2004 to 2022, the CCP spent nearly $1 billion on Confucius Institutes alone.[47]

The CCP's infiltration extends into secondary schools, including both public and private schools, by offering millions of dollars in funding and various exchange programs. In one case, the elite Thomas Jefferson High School for Science and Technology in Virginia received more than $1 million in financial aid from CCP government-affiliated entities over the course of a decade.[48]

Based on a report by Parents Defending Education, the CCP spent nearly $18 million between 2009 and 2023 across 143 school districts, including twenty located near U.S. military bases.[49]

Muscatine High School in Iowa provides a notable example, thanks to its student exchange program and unique personal connection with Xi Jinping. After receiving a letter from the students, Xi responded by inviting them to visit China in March 2024, with all expenses covered by the CCP. As a gesture of goodwill, the students presented Xi with a Muscatine High School flag upon their arrival in Beijing, inscribed in Chinese with the words "Grandpa Xi, Here We Are."[50] This exchange was widely promoted in CCP media in China, emphasizing Xi's popularity among American youth.

Xi Jinping wants more American youths to share the same "enriching" experience as those from Muscatine High School. In 2023, he announced a plan to invite 50,000 young Americans to China for exchange and study programs over the next five years. So far, four additional student groups have toured China, fully funded by the CCP: graduate students from Columbia University; undergraduates from California State University, Long Beach; elementary school students from Utah; and ping-pong players from Virginia. The goal is clear: to shape future generations of young Americans into admirers of the CCP's totalitarian regime.[51]

While pouring money into U.S. schools to expand its influence, the CCP neglects China's own education system, especially in impoverished rural areas. The reason is simple: The CCP has never prioritized the welfare of its people—only the consolidation of its power, including over American institutions.

Media and Social Media

Although the CCP considers Armed Struggle, Party Building, and the United Front its three "magic weapons," it omits another critical tool: propaganda—particularly the strategic use of misinformation, disinformation, and malinformation. This fourth weapon is known as Da Waixuan (大外宣), or Big Global Propaganda—a sweeping campaign to shape international opinion, control narratives, and expand the party's influence by manipulating media and social media platforms around the world.

Amazingly, the CCP has managed to influence even the Voice of America (VOA)—a platform created to oppose it. Founded in 1942, VOA is a U.S. government–funded broadcaster promoting freedom and democracy worldwide. During the Cold War, it played a key role in countering Communist propaganda. Under Mao, VOA was labeled an "enemy station," and those caught listening faced harsh punishments, including execution. Still, many Chinese tuned in secretly to hear uncensored news. After Mao's death, the ban eased, and I became a regular listener. In 1989, during the Tiananmen crackdown, people in China depended on VOA for updates as the CCP tried to jam its signals. Deng Xiaoping despised it, famously calling it a "large rumor corporation."[52]

Not anymore. In the years since, the CCP has succeeded in turning VOA's Chinese service, once a beacon of light for millions of Chinese trapped behind the Communist information blockade, into a tool of influence through its United Front operations, effectively weaponizing the outlet against the very country that funds it.

On April 19, 2017, Voice of America abruptly cut off a live broadcast mid-interview with Miles Guo—a Chinese billionaire-turned-whistleblower and highly controversial figure. Sasha Gong, then chief of VOA's Chinese Service, who was allegedly ordered to halt the interview, later remarked, "I suspect somebody caved in to the Chinese government's demand because the timing itself was very suspicious." She later asserted that the directive undoubtedly came from the CCP.[53]

According to Gong, from 2023 to 2024, amid a migration crisis, VOA's leadership instructed its Chinese branch to send reporters to Central America and U.S. border zones to report on migration routes, asylum processes, and government assistance programs. As a result, VOA videos became notorious for serving as how-to guides for Chinese illegals on navigating and exploiting the U.S. immigration system.[54]

On March 15, 2025, news broke that President Trump had signed an executive order to shut down VOA and other U.S.–funded media organizations. What a fitting end for an agency that betrayed its original mission and transformed into a force of corruption.

But VOA wasn't alone. Across the broader media landscape, the CCP used financial influence to achieve similar results. By providing substantial sums for advertisements, it secured permission to insert special sections like "China Watch"—produced by China's Ministry of Foreign Affairs and Propaganda Department—into prominent U.S. newspapers such as the *New York Times* and the *Washington Post*. These sections often look indistinguishable from regular content, with only a small disclaimer in tiny print at the bottom stating that "the content is provided by China's Ministry of Foreign Affairs and does not reflect the views of this newspaper." Most readers miss this note and assume they are reading article content from the publisher. On one occasion, I came across four full pages of "China Watch" in the *New York Times*, featuring a large photo on the front page of Tibetan monks happily using iPhones in front of the Potala Palace, the former residence of the Dalai Lama and an iconic symbol of Tibet. The headline proclaimed something to the effect of Tibetan people enjoy full religious freedom. In reality, hundreds of Tibetans, including monks, have self-immolated across Tibet in protest against the CCP's suppression of their religious and cultural traditions.

Beijing attempts to outsource its propaganda, believing that information from non-Chinese sources is more credible to foreign audiences. American media outlets, eager to profit, readily provide platforms for CCP messaging, presenting it to unsuspecting American readers.

After the CCP-controlled investment group purchased a majority stake in Forbes Media in 2014, several instances of editorial interference on China-related stories have cast doubt on the magazine's editorial independence.[55]

The CCP has also been secretly acquiring American radio stations to expand its influence. China Radio International (CRI), a state-run, CCP-controlled entity, operates thirty-three radio stations across fourteen countries, including WCRW in Washington, D.C., using them to broadcast CCP-aligned narratives and shape public opinion in favor of Beijing. A 2020 Center for Strategic and International Studies report found most Chinese-language news outlets in the United States are CCP-linked, with growing influence on English-language media.[56]

Social media in the United States has also become a major target of the CCP's United Front operation. No other Chinese media outlet has had as much influence on American society as TikTok, which frequently injects the CCP's views on key political, economic, social, and cultural events in the United States. With more than 80 million active users in the United States, TikTok has become a major cultural force. According to the Pew Research Center, 67 percent of American teens aged thirteen to seventeen use the platform.

Beyond its cultural influence, TikTok also raises significant concerns about data security for tens of millions of users, posing a serious threat to U.S. national security. Efforts to ban the platform have so far failed, largely due to strong opposition bolstered by the CCP's United Front operations, which exploit America's democratic value of free speech while ruthlessly suppressing it at home.

After the congressional hearing on TikTok, Senator Tom Cotton faced criticism for persistently questioning TikTok CEO Shou Zi Chew about his citizenship and ties to the CCP. Shou insisted he is Singaporean. However, the reality is that Shou serves as a Singaporean face for the CCP's TikTok, presenting it as a supposedly neutral international corporation while it remains a tool of the CCP, designed to mislead

Americans. This incident revealed a troubling lack of awareness about the nature of the Chinese Communist Party among the American media, lawmakers, and public.

Domestically, the CCP tightly controls Douyin (抖音), TikTok's Chinese counterpart, enforcing strict regulations on children's access and usage—while in America, the same age group is specifically targeted, with little to no restrictions, shaping youth behavior in ways that benefit Beijing's strategic interests.

The CCP also actively uses the popular Chinese social media platform WeChat to spread its propaganda. Widely used by overseas Chinese to connect with family and friends in China, many also rely on it as their primary source of information.

Many Americans are unaware that in Communist China, all foreign media and social media platforms are banned. Anyone who has visited China knows the experience: disembarking from the plane only to discover that all search engines, media, and social media apps have gone dark—an immediate encounter with the CCP's Great Firewall.

While American social media platforms like Facebook and X are banned in China, representatives of the Chinese Communist Party actively use these platforms to disseminate misinformation, disinformation, and malinformation to the free world. The CCP has also launched the "Spamouflage" campaign, deploying fake accounts impersonating American voters and U.S. soldiers to post on divisive issues, with the goal of deepening societal rifts in the United States.[57] In addition, the CCP invests heavily in advertising on social media platforms to expand its influence worldwide.

Entertainment and Sports

Hollywood, led by studios like Disney, has long been a global powerhouse in cultural exports, yet it remains conspicuously silent on sensitive issues related to China. Why? Because the Chinese market has grown into the world's second largest.

During the Cold War, the James Bond series often portrayed the Soviet

Union as the villain. After the Cold War, adversaries shifted to countries like North Korea—but China has been carefully and consistently avoided.

To cater to China, the second-largest movie market after the United States, American film companies often invite officials from the CCP's Propaganda Department to Hollywood to review films before they are distributed in China. Any content that displeases Chinese authorities is either edited out or altered. The 2012 movie *Red Dawn* is an example: The villains were changed from Communist Chinese, as originally scripted, to North Koreans.[58]

Hollywood has learned to proactively appease Beijing by depicting Communist China as a hero. In the movie *Gravity*, Sandra Bullock's astronaut character is saved by the Chinese space station, where she ultimately finds refuge and safety.

Hollywood has effectively internalized China's censorship mechanisms, practicing self-censorship and even incorporating elements that glorify China in its films. The relationship between the CCP and Hollywood resembles a toxic dynamic between individuals; Hollywood constantly seeks approval from the CCP, while Beijing skillfully keeps Hollywood in suspense.

The CCP's censorship apparatus also has a direct impact on individual actors. Richard Gere, once a major Hollywood star, saw his career take a sharp downturn after starring in the anti-CCP film *Red Corner* and speaking out in support of a free Tibet. In 2008, he further drew Beijing's ire by calling for a boycott of the Beijing Olympics in protest of China's human rights abuses against Tibetans. As a result, Gere was effectively blacklisted from major film projects—particularly those with ties to the lucrative Chinese market.[59]

Another popular actor, Brad Pitt, has also been banned in China for the crime of starring in the 1997 movie *Seven Years in Tibet* about the story of an Austrian mountaineer's experience in Tibet during the Second World War.[60]

Isn't this a lot like the McCarthyism portrayed in Robert De Niro's film *Guilty by Suspicion*—only in reverse? After years of appeasing the CCP, Hollywood must be stunned to find itself among the first on Beijing's chopping block—banned from import alongside Boeing during Trump's tariff war. The irony couldn't be more glaring. Many conservatives cheered, as Beijing had unintentionally aided their cause by striking a blow against the Woke Entertainment Industrial Complex.

The sports entertainment industries, led by the NBA, have also become subservient to Chinese interests. Billionaire venture capitalist and part-owner of the NBA's Golden State Warriors Chamath Palihapitiya openly stated on the *All-In* podcast that "nobody cares about what's happening to the Uyghurs."[61]

When the then–Houston Rockets general manager Daryl Morey tweeted "Free Hong Kong," China retaliated by canceling broadcast contracts, resulting in losses worth millions of dollars.[62] Players, including James Harden and Russell Westbrook, quickly apologized, saying, "We apologize. You know, we love China. We love playing there."[63] Westbrook was celebrated as a hero by the CCP in China after wearing a traditional Chinese outfit to a press conference to issue his apology.[64] The question remains whether he and others realized they were apologizing to the CCP, not to the Chinese people.

There is no question, however, that their motivations were driven by profit, even if it meant turning a blind eye to the CCP's totalitarian suppression of freedom.

A Tool for Espionage

The CCP's United Front system has long served as a powerful tool of espionage. While the Ministry of State Security is the regime's official intelligence agency, the two often operate in tandem—blurring the lines between influence and intelligence work. As key components of the CCP's broader strategy of political warfare, their roles frequently overlap, intertwine, and are difficult to distinguish.

Through the United Front Work Department, the CCP cultivates networks of influence among foreign politicians, academics, business leaders, scientists, and diaspora communities. These relationships often serve to gather intelligence, access sensitive information, shape foreign perceptions, and recruit individuals who can assist Chinese state interests—knowingly or unknowingly.

Instead of traditional spy operations, United Front activities often involve soft penetration: building personal, financial, and political ties that make targets more willing to share information, lobby for pro-China policies, or suppress criticism of the CCP. In this way, the United Front blurs the lines between diplomacy, propaganda, and espionage, allowing the CCP to operate covertly within free societies under the guise of "cultural exchange" or "friendship."

In the minds of many Americans, CCP espionage is often associated with ethnic Chinese agents—most famously exemplified by Fang Fang, a suspected Chinese spy who cultivated a relationship with Congressman Eric Swalwell to gain access and intelligence. While this perception is not unfounded, it is equally important to recognize that many non-Chinese Americans have also betrayed their country on behalf of the CCP.

Notable cases include Dr. John Reece Roth of the University of Tennessee, convicted in 2009 for illegally transferring defense-related data to a Chinese national; Ron Rockwell Hansen, a former U.S. Army officer working for the Defense Intelligence Agency, arrested while carrying classified military information to China; Kevin Mallory, a former CIA officer sentenced to twenty years for passing national defense secrets; and Candace Claiborne, a former State Department employee convicted for hiding her ties to Chinese agents in exchange for gifts and internal documents.

These cases underscore the reach, success, and serious threat posed by the CCP's espionage operations within the United States.

After years of unchecked operations within the United States, this is the reality we face today: Through its United Front strategy, the Chinese

Communist Party has embedded its influence into every fiber of American society—corrupting institutions, infiltrating culture, undermining values, and threatening the very foundations of our nation. In effect, the CCP has built a vast fifth column inside the United States.

A crucial question must be asked: Is the United Front truly that "magical" and powerful? My answer is unequivocal: Its strength is not a testament to its genius but to America's moral decline. Our institutions—schools, media, and entertainment—have been captured by cultural Marxists and the so-called friends of the Chinese people, who are actively tearing down the founding values that built this nation. Through the warped lens of Woke ideology, the CCP is either dismissed as a threat—or worse, embraced as an ideological ally and welcomed as a source of wealth. Although almost too late, the CCP's political warfare is finally receiving the attention it deserves. On November 27, 2023, the House Select Committee on the Chinese Communist Party published a detailed report on the United Front on its official website, warning the American people of the growing threat.

On January 30, 2025, the U.S. Senate Foreign Relations Committee held a hearing titled "The Malign Influence of the People's Republic of China at Home and Abroad: Recommendations for Policymakers." During the hearing, Peter Mattis, president of the Jamestown Foundation and co-author of *Chinese Communist Espionage: An Intelligence Primer*, detailed the CCP's extensive use of United Front work as a central tool in its global influence operations.[65]

The tide is indeed turning. Americans are beginning to understand that we are at war with Communist China—an undeclared, shadowy, protracted, and unrestricted war, fought without clearly identifiable enemies. Our adversaries may wear uniforms, stand in the open, hide behind every tree and around every corner, or even be among those we trust as our own.

But far more people still need to awaken.

CHAPTER 9

TAIWAN: THE BETRAYAL AND GREAT TRIUMPH

To truly understand the complexity of U.S.–China relations, one must confront the trilateral reality of U.S.–China–Taiwan relations—with Taiwan as the indispensable linchpin. Since 1949, this fragile triangle has been shaped by shifting strategies, competing powers, and clashing interests.

Yet more than geopolitics, it is ideology that defines this dynamic. While China has remained a hard-line Communist state, Taiwan has undergone a profound transformation—from authoritarian rule to a vibrant democracy. It stands today as the living embodiment of a "Lost China" restored, where the century-long republican dream of self-governance has finally taken root.

Since the beginning, Taiwan's survival has depended on the United States. In return, it has endured a volatile mix of abandonment, disappointment, betrayal, and strategic support. Yet Taiwan persevered. And over time, shared democratic values—and the mounting threat from the CCP—have brought the two closer than ever.*

Taiwan Before 1949

Contrary to the Chinese Communist Party's claim that Taiwan has been part of China since ancient times, the island only came under Chinese rule in the late seventeenth century. Before then, it was inhabited by Austronesian peoples and briefly colonized by the Dutch and Spanish (1624–1662). In 1662, Zheng Chenggong (aka Koxinga), a Ming general, expelled the Dutch and established the Kingdom of Tungning, a regime that upheld the legitimacy of the Ming Empire.

In 1683, Taiwan was incorporated into the Qing Empire, though governance remained limited due to geographic isolation. After China's defeat in the First Sino-Japanese War, Taiwan was ceded to Japan in 1895. A short-lived attempt to resist this transfer resulted in the brief Republic of Formosa, which was quickly crushed by Japanese forces.

Under Japanese rule (1895–1945), Taiwan saw major modernization in infrastructure, education, and public health. Despite repression, living standards surpassed those of mainland China, and limited local self-governance emerged.

After Japan's surrender in 1945, Taiwan was handed over to the Nationalist government of Chiang Kai-shek. This transfer was agreed upon at the Cairo Conference (1943) by Roosevelt, Churchill, and Chiang—without Taiwanese input—effectively blocking any path to independence.

*Key terms for this chapter: The Republic of China (ROC) (1928–present), governed for decades by the Nationalist Party (Kuomintang, KMT), was once recognized internationally as "China" but is now more commonly referred to as Taiwan. However, since Taiwan's democratization in the late 1980s, the Democratic Progressive Party (DPP) has won five presidential elections (2000, 2004, 2016, 2020, and 2024) and governed Taiwan as a result. The People's Republic of China (PRC) (1949–present), ruled by the Chinese Communist Party, is now simply called China. The CCP views itself as "the real China," and that includes Taiwan. This shift in terminology reflects the evolving power dynamics and political realities of the past century.

Chiang saw Taiwan's return as a diplomatic victory, not foreseeing that he would soon lose the civil war and retreat to Taiwan, making it the last stronghold of the Republic of China. After taking over Taiwan from the Japanese in 1944, the KMT treated Taiwan as just another province, ignoring its unique colonial history and the aspirations of its people. Misrule, corruption, and exploitation quickly bred resentment.

The dissatisfaction and resentment culminated in the February 28 Incident of 1947, commonly referred to as the 228 Incident. Much like the Arab Spring, this incident was a small conflict—this time between police and an unlicensed cigarette vendor—which ignited widespread anger and escalated into island-wide demonstrations and revolt.

The Nationalist government swiftly deployed a large military force to crush the Taiwanese uprising. Nationalist troops carried out indiscriminate massacres across the island, killing no fewer than 30,000 people.[1]

Simultaneously, a systematic effort was made to target and eliminate Taiwanese leaders. Within a month, the island was forcibly subdued.

The uprising marked the beginning of the struggle against the KMT's authoritarian rule in Taiwan.

Tensions deepened following the KMT's Great Retreat to Taiwan after losing the mainland. Between 1949 and 1950, nearly 2 million people, including 600,000 KMT troops, fled to the island—amounting to 15 percent of Taiwan's total population. Concentrated mainly in urban areas, this sudden influx drastically altered Taiwan's demographics and fueled social and political frictions between the native Taiwanese (*ben sheng ren*, 本省人) and the mainland Chinese newcomers (*wai sheng ren*, 外省人).

These divisions, rooted in power imbalances and identity conflicts, would profoundly shape Taiwan's political and social development in the decades to come.

The Unsinkable Aircraft Carrier

By 1947, the Truman administration had adopted a do-nothing China policy, believing the CCP's victory was inevitable. The policy remained unchanged after the KMT retreated to Taiwan, leaving it at the mercy of the Communist tide.

The key policymakers in Washington believed that the Nationalist government was beyond saving due to its pervasive corruption and that any U.S. military effort to defend Taiwan could only temporarily delay a Communist takeover. The State Department openly regarded Taiwan as strategically insignificant, arguing that it was unlikely to affect the balance of power in East Asia.

George H. Kerr, the U.S. assistant naval attaché to Taiwan who witnessed the slaughter during the Taiwan uprising from the upper window of his walled mission compound where he had retreated with other foreigners, expressed his frustration: "President Truman knew nothing of Formosa, nor did his Secretaries of State. Younger men in the Department…appear to have made no effort to raise the Formosa question to levels of serious policy discussion for they were determined that there should be no such thing as a Formosa Question."[2]

Not everyone agreed with Truman's China policy. The heated "Who Lost China?" debate in Congress and Senator McCarthy's aggressive investigations into alleged pro-Communist sympathizers in the State Department fueled strong opposition to Truman's decision to abandon Taiwan. Some even proposed invoking the principle of self-determination to grant independence to the islanders. Kerr argued that the Allies should have placed Taiwan under trusteeship and then assisted in its independence.[3] They argued that Chiang Kai-shek's oppressive policies had alienated Taiwan's population, potentially driving them toward the Communists.[4]

But these voices were overshadowed by the dominant belief that America's primary focus should remain on Europe and the Soviet Union, avoiding entanglement in Asia's conflicts, and leave Taiwan's fate to unfold on its own.

Unexpectedly, June 25, 1950, changed everything.

On that day, the Korean War broke out. Within days, President Truman reversed his Taiwan policy, declaring that "the occupation of Formosa by Communist forces would be a direct threat to the security of the Pacific area and to United States forces performing their lawful and necessary functions in that area."[5] This decision marked a drastic turning point, shifting from the prewar policy of non-intervention and reluctance to actively supporting the Nationalist government.

General Douglas MacArthur (1880–1964), commander of U.S. forces in the Far East and during the Korean War, as well as Supreme Commander of the Southwest Pacific Area in World War II and Supreme Commander for the Allied Powers overseeing the occupation of Japan, consistently emphasized Taiwan's critical strategic importance, stating, "The geographic location of Formosa is such that in the hands of a power unfriendly to the United States it constitutes an enemy salient in the very center" of America's strategic dispositions in the Pacific, and he famously referred to Taiwan as an "unsinkable aircraft carrier."[6] His advocacy played a significant role in changing perceptions of Taiwan's strategic value.

MacArthur's stance on Communism was straightforward—he supported anyone who opposed it, including the Nationalist government and Chiang Kai-shek. He famously stated, "If he [Chiang Kai-shek] has horns and a tail, so long as he is anti-Communist, we should help him… we can try to reform him later."[7]

History ultimately vindicated MacArthur's position, highlighting the crucial distinction between authoritarianism and totalitarianism, which I will discuss later in this chapter.

Three days after the war began, Chiang offered to send 33,000 Nationalist troops to the Korean Peninsula. But Truman declined out of concern that such a move might provoke China and escalate the conflict and also Chiang might need the troops to defend Taiwan.[8]

Shortly afterward, on the morning of July 31, 1950, MacArthur paid a visit to Chiang in Taiwan. He informed the Department of Defense of his visit but deliberately excluded the State Department, which favored an appeasement policy toward the Communists. This visit marked the beginning of MacArthur's rift with President Truman and Secretary of State Dean Acheson, a split that ultimately led to his dismissal.

During his visit, MacArthur stated that Chiang's "indomitable determination to resist Communist domination arouses my sincere admiration. His determination parallels the common interest and purpose of Americans, that all peoples in the Pacific shall be free—not slave[s]."[9]

Truman's administration treaded cautiously around the Taiwan issue, seeking to avoid provoking China. Yet, in late October 1950, Mao Zedong sent Chinese troops into the Korean War under the guise of "volunteers," directly confronting U.S. forces.

General Douglas MacArthur was an American hero—a natural choice to lead U.S. forces in Korea. However, on April 11, 1951, President Truman relieved MacArthur of his commands, citing his defiance of administration policies and direct orders. Even today, Truman's decision remains a subject of controversy, with debates over whether or not it was justified.

Despite all this, one thing remains undisputed: MacArthur and Truman fundamentally disagreed on their views about Communism, and by extension, Taiwan. MacArthur argued for expanding the war against Communism in Asia, while Truman wanted to end the Korean War through diplomacy.

MacArthur saw the danger of Chinese Communism clearly, arguing that "Asia is where the Communist conspirators have elected to make their play for global conquest...we must win. There is no substitute for victory."[10]

Furthermore, MacArthur regarded both Communists and those advocating appeasement of Communism, including pacifists, as threats to U.S. national security.

On April 19, 1951, after returning to the United States, MacArthur delivered a powerful farewell address to Congress, stating: "There are some who, for varying reasons, would appease Red China. They are blind to history's clear lesson, for history teaches with unmistakable emphasis that appeasement but begets new and bloodier war. It points to no single instance where this end has justified that means, where appeasement has led to more than a sham peace."

MacArthur was absolutely right. Not long after the Korean War, the United States became entangled in the bloody Vietnam War, yet another conflict fueled by the failure to confront Communist expansion.

MacArthur's dismissal was historically ironic: One of the main reasons for the recall of both General Stilwell and General MacArthur was their differing stances on Chinese Communism—Stilwell being sympathetic toward it, and MacArthur vehemently against it.

MacArthur, like Stilwell, elicited opposite reactions from the two Chinas: despised by the CCP and deeply revered by the KMT. When the general passed away, Chiang Kai-shek mourned his death with profound praise, stating: "Even on his deathbed, he expressed the heartfelt wish to 'see the Republic of China triumph once again'—a sentiment that deeply moved us. His lifelong mission to eradicate Communism and his achievements in safeguarding Pacific peace command our highest respect and admiration."[11]

The Truman administration ultimately adopted elements of MacArthur's strategy to defend Taiwan. By May 1951, the Truman administration formally stated its policy of non-recognition of the Communist regime in China. The U.S. containment strategy, initially centered on Europe, was now extended to Asia to counter Communist China.

The Korean War gave Taiwan a lifeline, transforming a dire situation into a moment of salvation. This pivotal turn allowed the Republic of China to endure. Meanwhile the island became a symbol of resistance against Communist aggression, and its survival was assured by the Eisenhower administration's signing of the 1954 Mutual Defense Treaty.

Chiang Kai-shek, Chiang Ching-kuo, and Lee Teng-hui

To understand modern Taiwan, it is essential to recognize the influence of three pivotal figures:

Chiang Kai-shek laid the foundation of modern Taiwan by establishing a strong anti-Communist regime and maintaining martial law to preserve stability and resist CCP influence.

Chiang Ching-kuo, his son, initiated key political and economic reforms that transformed Taiwan into an industrial powerhouse and set the stage for democratization by lifting martial law and promoting native Taiwanese into leadership.

Lee Teng-hui, Taiwan's first native-born president, led the country through its full transition to democracy.

Ironically, all three shared an unusual trajectory—they began as followers of Communism but became staunch anti-Communists.

Chiang Kai-shek (1887–1975)

Before rising to lead the Kuomintang, Chiang Kai-shek was a loyal follower and later a protégé of Sun Yat-sen, deeply committed to his vision of a united republican China. This close relationship was pivotal to Chiang's ascent within the party.

Though Chiang spent most of his career fighting Communism, he was initially drawn to Marxist thought, even praising *Das Kapital.* In 1923, Sun sent him to the Soviet Union to study its political and military systems.

Chiang's view of Soviet Russia shifted by the end of his three-month tour. He concluded that Soviet Russia lacked sincerity, describing its policy as a new form of czarist imperialism aimed at annexing northern territories of China and intending to Sovietize China. He believed their ultimate goal was to help the Chinese Communist Party supplant the Kuomintang. "From my observations, the Russian Communist Party cannot be fully trusted. I once said we could believe only 30 percent of what the Russians claimed, but even that was an overstatement."[12]

His warnings were dismissed by Sun, but were later confirmed by his experiences with the CCP's United Front operations. In 1927, Chiang launched a decisive purge of Communists from the KMT, marking the beginning of his lifelong anti-Communist campaign.

Despite this stance, Chiang was pragmatic. As Japan's threat grew in the 1930s and Western powers failed to assist, he restored Sino-Soviet relations, culminating in the 1937 Non-Aggression Pact, making the Soviet Union China's largest arms supplier at that time.

After retreating to Taiwan, Chiang attributed his defeat not to the corruption but to insufficient autocratic control. He rebuilt the government along authoritarian lines, with his son Chiang Ching-kuo overseeing political warfare and preparing for succession. Upon his death in 1975, his son became president.

One of Chiang's overlooked legacies is the Chinese Cultural Renaissance, launched in Taiwan as a direct response to Mao's Cultural Revolution. While Mao's regime destroyed China's heritage, Chiang positioned Taiwan as the protector of traditional Chinese culture, using the movement to both resist Communism and distinguish Taiwan from the ideological chaos on the mainland.

Chiang Ching-kuo (1910–1988)

Chiang Ching-kuo had even deeper ties to Communism and the Soviet Union than his father. In 1925, at age fifteen, he joined a wave of idealistic progressive youth and went to Moscow to study at Sun Yat-sen University, where he was deeply indoctrinated by Communist ideology and even joined the Soviet Communist Party. After Chiang Kai-shek's 1927 purge of the Communists, Chiang Ching-kuo publicly condemned his father and declared a break in their father–son relationship. Despite this, the Soviets still distrusted him and held him like a hostage in the U.S.S.R. for more than a decade.

During that time, he endured brutal hardship—working on collective farms and in factories, spending nine months in forced labor at the Altyn gold mine in Siberia, and witnessing the terror of Stalin's Great Purge. While working at a heavy machinery factory in 1935, he met and married a Belarusian orphan, Faina Vakhreva, who later took the name Chiang Fang-liang.

Chiang Ching-kuo returned to China in 1937 after the Xi'an Incident, when his father was forced into the alliance with the CCP. To "reprogram" him, Chiang Kai-shek had his son study Chinese classics and Sun Yat-sen's teachings, and urged him to write about his time in the Soviet Union. The result was *My Days in the Soviet Union* (1937), in which Chiang Ching-kuo reflected: "After enduring twelve years of torment, I came to fully understand the cunning and malicious tactics used by the Communists to corrupt and destroy young minds. They first deceive young people with sweet words and enticing promises, manipulating and numbing their thoughts. Then, through terror and coercion, they strip away their dignity and destroy their individuality. Their ultimate goal is to eradicate personal free will, turning individuals into submissive slaves shackled by obedience."

Under his father's guidance, Chiang Ching-kuo began a political career focused on anti-Communist efforts and internal reform. Although he adopted a firm anti-Communist stance, the authoritarian features of Stalinism—central planning, ideological control, and suppression of dissent—left a lasting mark on his governance style.

After the KMT's retreat to Taiwan in 1949, Chiang Ching-kuo played a key role in consolidating power. In 1950, he became director of the Political Warfare Department, where he centralized intelligence and embedded party cells in the military. He later served as vice premier and premier, overseeing economic modernization, infrastructure development, and land reforms. His tenure as premier (1972–1978) brought both industrial growth and tight political control, paving the way for his presidency in 1978.

Lee Teng-hui (1923–2020)

Lee Teng-hui was born in a rural village near Taipei during Japanese colonial rule. In 1943, he entered Kyoto Imperial University to study agricultural economics—a field that would later underpin his focus on rural development and economic reform in Taiwan.

During his time in Japan, Lee became deeply immersed in Marxist ideology, drawn to its critique of inequality and imperialism. He planned to write his graduation thesis on *The Problem of Agriculture in Taiwan under Japanese Imperialism*, but due to the topic's sensitivity, he revised it to *A Study on the Problem of Farm Labor in Taiwan*. His studies were interrupted when he was drafted into the Japanese Imperial Army during World War II.

After the war, Lee returned to Taiwan in 1946 and enrolled at National Taiwan University. There, he witnessed the 228 Incident in 1947 and the brutal suppression of native Taiwanese by the KMT regime—an experience that profoundly shaped his political outlook and deepened his awareness of the divide between the mainlander government and the local population.

In 1952, Lee received a scholarship to study agricultural economics at Iowa State University, earning his master's degree in 1953. A decade later, he earned a doctorate from Cornell University. While in the United States, Lee's disillusionment with Marxism grew, and he found resonance in Christianity, culminating in his baptism in 1961. His faith became central to his personal and political life, later guiding his advocacy for democracy, justice, and reconciliation. In *The Road to Democracy*, he wrote:

> The greatest thing I have learned from Christianity is the idea of love...If that spirit of love is deep and affirmative enough to manifest divine love, society will be filled with compassion and vitality. This conviction is at the core of my political philosophy and underlies my basic stance as a political leader.[13]

Recognizing his intellect and expertise, Chiang Ching-kuo recruited Lee into government in 1971, promoting him despite opposition from within the Kuomintang. Lee rose steadily: from cabinet minister to Taipei mayor, provincial governor, and vice president. After Chiang's death in 1988, Lee assumed the presidency at age sixty-five—just as Taiwan entered a pivotal era of political liberalization and global realignment.

Taiwan's Political Transformation

After retreating to Taiwan in 1949, Chiang Kai-shek's regime overcame the factionalism and warlordism that had plagued the Nationalist Party on the mainland, establishing a centralized one-party authoritarian government—a system that bore some resemblance to Franco's anti-Communist regime in Spain.

In the aftermath of the 228 Incident, martial law was declared in 1948 under the provisions of the constitution of the Republic of China—"The Temporary Provisions Effective During the Period of Communist Rebellion." This martial law was kept in place until 1987, for a total of thirty-eight years!

The period of martial law, known as the White Terror, was marked by widespread political persecution. Thousands were imprisoned or executed on charges of being Communists, harboring Communist sympathies, or advocating for Taiwanese independence—a stance deemed anti–Chiang's government. The regime tightly controlled civil society, suppressing free speech and assembly.

In 1950, Chiang Kai-shek created the Political Department under the Ministry of National Defense and appointed his son as director. The following year, Chiang Ching-kuo established the Political Warfare Cadre Academy, cementing Nationalist control over the military. By 1957, Taiwan's armed forces employed 17,139 political officers[14]—and embedded Kuomintang cells within military units to ensure party loyalty. This consolidation of intelligence agencies and the policies of the White Terror echoed Stalinist purges.

On the one hand, Chiang sought U.S. recognition and protection while competing with Communist China for legitimacy, positioning Taiwan as "Free China."

Despite political repression, the KMT introduced economic modernization programs that spurred Taiwan's development, including support for small- and medium-sized enterprises and export-driven trade. These policies fueled rapid industrialization and created a prosperous middle class that later pushed for democratization. As part of broader reforms, the KMT also carried out significant land reform to redistribute land. Although administrative and peaceful, these measures could also be seen as intrusions on private property rights.

Throughout the 1950s and 1960s, the KMT maintained tight control, with little public participation in governance. After Chiang Ching-kuo became president in 1978, modest reforms began, and growing pressure from an increasingly empowered middle class accelerated Taiwan's path toward democratization.

One unexpected incident left a deep impact on Chiang Ching-kuo. During a 1970 visit to the United States, he survived an assassination attempt by Peter Huang, a Taiwanese student and pro-democracy activist. Huang's actions became a symbol of resistance to authoritarian rule, drawing international attention to Taiwan's repressive political climate under martial law. The incident intensified debate over the KMT's legitimacy, especially as Taiwan's global position weakened—culminating in the loss of its U.N. seat the following year.

The assassination attempt prompted Chiang Ching-kuo to acknowledge the urgency of political reforms. In 1972, he introduced localization policies aimed at allowing more native Taiwanese to participate in both the central government and the KMT. However, the reforms were limited in scope and fell short of broader democratization efforts, leaving underlying tensions unresolved.[15]

In 1979, the Carter administration announced diplomatic normalization with Communist China, a move that coincided with President Chiang

Ching-kuo's tentative steps toward opening elections in Taiwan. In response to the shock and uncertainty caused by the U.S. abandonment, Chiang issued an emergency decree suspending election activities. This triggered widespread protests by pro-democracy advocates and culminated in a government crackdown known as the Kaohsiung—or Formosa—Incident.

The incident took place on December 10, 1979, in Kaohsiung city in southern Taiwan, where activists from the opposition *Formosa Magazine* organized a pro-democracy rally to mark International Human Rights Day and challenge KMT authoritarian rule. The protest escalated into violent clashes with police, becoming the largest civil unrest since the 228 Incident. In response, the government cracked down, arresting and prosecuting key activists. The event became a turning point in Taiwan's democratization, exposing human rights abuses under martial law and galvanizing public support for reform. Many of those arrested would later become leading figures in the democratic movement.

Major political reform began in the mid-1980s, coinciding with Communist China's era of "reform and opening up." It was during this period that I, like many others, first began to learn about Taiwan. My entire education taught me Taiwan was a dark and oppressive place under the iron grip of the Chiang family. Discovering that Taiwan was in fact more free, more open, and more vibrant was nothing short of a shock. Young people on the mainland were quickly enchanted by the songs by Teresa Teng, or Deng Lijun. A popular joke back then captured the moment: There was a war between two Dengs—Deng Xiaoping and Deng Lijun—for the hearts of the Chinese people and it was the singer who was winning.

In 1986, defying the ban on opposition parties, pro-democracy activists founded the Democratic Progressive Party (DPP), signaling the rise of a credible opposition. Surprisingly, Chiang Ching-kuo allowed the party to operate, paving the way for political pluralism. The following year, martial law was lifted after thirty-eight years—a watershed moment in Taiwan's democratization. Freedoms of speech, assembly, and the press were gradually restored, and political life became increasingly open.

Chiang Ching-kuo is remembered as the strongman who chose to become Taiwan's last dictator.

Among Chiang Ching-kuo's most pivotal decisions was promoting Lee Teng-hui as his successor, and he became president after Chiang's death in 1988. By choosing Lee—a native Taiwanese—Chiang broke the Kuomintang's long-standing tradition of mainlander-dominated leadership, signaling a major political shift. This move eased tensions with the local population, addressed growing dissatisfaction, and fostered a sense of inclusion. By empowering a reform-minded leader, Chiang helped pave the way for a peaceful transition to democracy and reduced the risk of political unrest.

Choosing Lee Teng-hui as his successor also stemmed from Chiang Ching-kuo's belief that Lee's deep understanding of Communism was crucial to ensuring Taiwan's future security. Although Lee's appointment as vice president was initially a token gesture toward native Taiwanese, his role took on greater significance after Chiang Ching-kuo's death in January 1988, when he became the designated president. Despite strong opposition from KMT old-guard factions seeking to derail his presidency, Lee secured support from moderate voices within the party and successfully consolidated his leadership.[16]

The 1990s marked Taiwan's transition to full democracy, with the Wild Lily Student Movement in 1990 serving as a critical catalyst for reform. Thousands of students staged a six-day sit-in at Liberty Square in Taipei, from March 16 to March 22, calling for direct presidential elections and the abolition of the outdated National Assembly system. This authoritarian legislative body, dominated by a single party, had government positions filled through appointments rather than democratic elections.

In response, Lee adopted a measured, nonviolent approach, restraining police action—a stark contrast to Chiang Ching-kuo's harsh crackdown in the Formosa Incident in 1979 and an even more pronounced divergence from Beijing's brutal suppression of the Tiananmen Square protests just a year earlier.

On the sixth day of the protests, the same day Lee was elected president by the senior National Assembly members, he met with student representatives, recognizing the historical significance of the movement. He pledged to enact political reforms and followed through on these promises.

Unlike most politicians, he kept his word.

In June 1990, President Lee Teng-hui convened Taiwan's first National Affairs Conference, gathering 150 participants from across society—including opposition leaders—to chart a path for political reform. Lee emphasized the need to decisively implement reforms that respected public opinion.

In 1991, the authoritarian-era Temporary Provisions—the policies that had underpinned the White Terror—were abolished. The National Assembly was restructured with elected representatives, and political prisoners were released. Exiles returned, and laws criminalizing speech were repealed, marking a major shift toward democracy.

Taiwan held its first legislative elections in 1992, and by 1994, direct elections for governors and mayors further empowered local governments and deepened democratic participation.

Taiwan's democratization reached its pinnacle in 1996 with its historic first direct presidential election. Lee Teng-hui emerged victorious, becoming the nation's first democratically elected president. The election proceeded despite aggressive military threats from China, including missile tests near Taiwan's waters.

In the same year, Lee graced the cover of *Newsweek*, which called him "Mr. Democracy."

After completing his first term in 2000 as Taiwan's first popularly elected president, Lee chose not to seek reelection, focusing instead on ensuring a smooth transfer of power. He has since been revered as the "Father of Taiwan's Democracy."

Nearly a century earlier, Chinese intellectuals had championed "Mr. De" (democracy) and "Mr. Sci" (science) as the path to national renewal and liberation from foreign domination. Tragically, those ideals were extinguished by the rise of Leninism and Communism, plunging the Chinese mainland into totalitarian rule since 1949. In this context, Taiwan's success in turning democracy into reality stands as a historic triumph—one that cannot be overstated.

As a Chinese, I feel immense pride in this monumental achievement. It gives me hope that one day, "Mr. De" will also make mainland China his home.

Taiwan's peaceful transition to full democracy—often called a "Quiet Revolution"—proves that democracy is not only compatible with Chinese culture but can thrive within it. It directly challenges the CCP's claim that democracy leads to chaos, showing instead that it can foster stability and prosperity.

Since then, Taiwan's democratic system has ranked among the world's freest and most transparent, often seen as a model for democratization in non-Western societies. It consistently performs well in the Economist Intelligence Unit (EIU) Democracy Index, published by *The Economist*. In 2023, Taiwan ranked first in Asia and tenth globally, while Communist China lagged far behind at 148th place.[17]

This is the stark contrast we see today—the diverging outcomes of the two reforms that began in the 1980s: one focused on political transformation, the other solely on economic development.

Authoritarianism vs. Totalitarianism

Taiwan's transition from dictatorship to democracy raises a pivotal question: Could mainland China follow the same path? Why can't Xi Jinping be the next Chiang Ching-kuo? To answer this question, it is crucial to distinguish between authoritarianism and totalitarianism.

The *Encyclopedia Britannica* offers a clear and persuasive distinction between authoritarianism and totalitarianism: "Both forms of government discourage individual freedom of thought and action.

Totalitarianism attempts to do this by asserting total control over the lives of its citizens, whereas authoritarianism prefers the blind submission of its citizens to authority. While totalitarian states tend to have a highly developed guiding ideology, authoritarian states usually do not." Marxist ideology as upheld by the Chinese Communist Party goes beyond mere guidance; it functions effectively as a religion. In this sense, totalitarianism can be seen as a form of theocracy. Its ultimate aim goes beyond controlling the populace—it seeks to fundamentally reengineer society, police personal beliefs, and reshape human nature itself. Communists have a name for this system: the "Dictatorship of the Proletariat."

The KMT and CCP provide a textbook example of the differences between authoritarianism and totalitarianism, as seen in their respective "terrors": the White Terror and the Red Terror.

The goal of the White Terror was to suppress Communist influence and consolidate KMT rule on the island. The campaign targeted suspected Communists, supporters of Taiwan independence, dissidents, and anyone perceived as opposing the KMT regime. Rooted in anti-Communism, the White Terror focused on maintaining political control without radically reshaping society, preserving a relatively functional legal and economic system. Its repression included martial law, arrests, imprisonment, and executions, resulting in an estimated 140,000 victims, including approximately 4,000 executions.[18] After martial law was lifted in 1987, reconciliation efforts included compensating victims and publicly acknowledging the injustices that had been committed. Today, the National Human Rights Museum preserves the history of the White Terror, including Green Island Prison, a major detention site during the period, located on a remote island in the sea.

Mao's Red Terror aimed to radically remake Chinese society by abolishing private property, eradicating traditional culture and religion, dismantling families, and suppressing independent thought and individuality. Communist political campaigns targeted all dissenters—including party members and officials—unleashing waves of brutal violence that claimed tens of millions of lives and inflicted immense, lasting suffering. To this day, the Chinese Communist Party has never officially condemned these atrocities, and discussions on events like the Great Famine and the Cultural Revolution remain heavily censored. Most of the post–Tiananmen Square Massacre generation has never even heard of these horrific events.

History has proven that some authoritarian regimes, such as those in South Korea, Spain, and Portugal, as well as the Republic of China in Taiwan, have the potential and capacity to transition peacefully to democracy.

In contrast, totalitarian regimes like Communist China are fundamentally resistant to genuine political reform, relying instead on repression, censorship, surveillance, and violence to preserve their grip on power.

Historically, such regimes have collapsed only when confronted by overwhelming internal and external pressures. The fall of the Soviet Union is a prime example: It crumbled under the weight of a deep economic crisis, an unsustainable arms race with the West, growing domestic unrest, and failed foreign interventions.

History might have taken a different course had influential figures like Edgar Snow, Theodore White, Generals Stilwell and Marshall, and Presidents Roosevelt and Truman recognized this crucial distinction. The same holds true for every U.S. president from Nixon to Obama and Biden. One can only hope today's policymakers—regardless of party—truly grasp its significance.

U.S.–Taiwan Relations

U.S. involvement in Taiwan began in the mid-1800s, when Commodore Perry recognized its strategic value and urged a U.S. presence on the island.[19] In 1854, American ships surveyed coal in Keelung, and by 1855, U.S. diplomats proposed buying Taiwan from the Qing as a stable trade hub. The plan was ultimately rejected, ending the prospect of Taiwan becoming a U.S. territory.[20]

Following World War II, the United States played a pivotal role in shaping Taiwan's modern status but deliberately left its sovereignty undefined in postwar treaties. At the 1951 signing of the San Francisco Peace Treaty, also known as the Treaty of Peace with Japan, the United States excluded both the Republic of China and People's Republic of China from participation. The treaty required Japan to renounce sovereignty over Taiwan and the Penghu Islands but left their final status unresolved.[21]

Rather than holding a referendum on Taiwan's independence, the United States adopted a policy of strategic ambiguity, a stance that persists today and is often referred to as the "undetermined sovereignty theory."[22] This uncertainty is not the result of historical inevitability but a direct consequence of U.S. foreign policy decisions. It challenges China's claim that reunification is predetermined, highlighting instead that Taiwan's future has always been shaped by shifting geopolitical realities rather than inevitability.[23]

Since the Korean War in 1951, Taiwan has benefited from consistent U.S. military and economic support. This alliance was put to the test early on during the two Taiwan Strait Crises—and it held firm.

The First Taiwan Strait Crisis (1954–1955) began when Communist forces shelled the Kinmen Islands to weaken the ROC and pressure the United States to abandon Taiwan. In response, the U.S. helped evacuate personnel and, with Eisenhower signaling possible nuclear retaliation, China backed down.[24] That same year, the Sino-American Mutual Defense Treaty was signed, securing Taiwan's survival while curbing Chiang Kai-shek's plans to retake the mainland.

The Second Taiwan Strait Crisis (1958) saw a forty-four-day bombardment of Kinmen, with 10,000 shells fired daily—mostly Soviet-made.[25] Backed by U.S. military support, Nationalist forces mounted a strong counterattack, prompting Mao to order a strategic retreat and temporarily restoring peace.

As the Cold War proceeded, Taiwan's strategic importance became increasingly evident. Taiwan became an integral element of the U.S.

Pacific defense strategy, forming a critical link alongside Japan, South Korea, and the Philippines. Taiwan was viewed as a potential domino, whose loss could lead to the collapse of other regional allies, jeopardizing U.S. security interests and pushing America's defensive line back to Hawaii, evoking memories of the Japanese attack on Pearl Harbor.

In addition to providing substantial military support to fortify Taiwan's position, the United States also aided Taiwan economically to help stabilize its economy, reduce poverty, and counteract Communist influence. One notable program was the Sino-U.S. Joint Commission on Rural Reconstruction, often compared to the Marshall Plan, particularly for its role in Taiwan's economic and agricultural development. This initiative aimed to rebuild and modernize Taiwan's economy in the aftermath of conflict, laying the foundation for its transformation into a key regional player.[26]

During the Cold War, the Taiwan Strait emerged as a critical flashpoint between Communist expansion and U.S. efforts to defend its allies in Asia. Yet in 1971, this seemingly unbreakable U.S.–Taiwan alliance took a sudden and dramatic turn—one that Taiwan saw as a profound betrayal. The shift was led by none other than President Richard Nixon, once a staunch anti-Communist.

Nixon visited Taiwan twice—once as vice president in 1953 and again in 1964 as a private citizen—reaffirming support for the Republic of China. Even after opening secret talks with Communist China in 1970, he assured Chiang Ching-kuo, "I will never sell you down the river."[27]

But sell out Taiwan he did. Taipei was informed of Nixon's decision to visit to Beijing—an act considered to be an existential threat to the Republic of China—just twenty minutes before Nixon announced it on television.[28]

Nixon's realignment with Communist China stunned Taiwan. The first major blow came on October 25, 1971, when Taiwan lost its U.N. seat to China, which assumed its place on the Security Council. The ROC had earned that role through its World War II contributions, while the CCP had played little part. Since then, Beijing has used its U.N. seat to counter U.S. interests and gradually turn the organization into a tool of its influence.

Another blow came with the 1972 Shanghai Communiqué, in which Nixon pledged to reduce and eventually withdraw U.S. forces from Taiwan, acknowledging the CCP's claim that Taiwan is part of China.

In 1978, President Jimmy Carter made the decision to establish formal diplomatic relations with Communist China, dealing a devastating blow to the Republic of China. His administration informed Taipei of the decision just two hours before the official announcement, waking President Chiang Ching-kuo at two-thirty a.m. to deliver the news. This was a repeat of Nixon's earlier slight, yet even more disgraceful than the prior indifference. Chiang immediately lodged a protest with the U.S. Embassy in Taiwan.

In a subsequent public statement, Chiang condemned the United States for betraying its commitments to the ROC and declared that this decision would have a profoundly adverse impact on the entire free world. He firmly reiterated that Taiwan would never negotiate with Communist China, stating, "To do so would amount to self-destruction."[29]

Chiang's warning was grounded in his firsthand experience with Communism and his understanding that negotiating with the CCP was like bargaining with the devil. History has since vindicated his judgment.

In January 1979, the Carter administration formally recognized Communist China through the Joint Communiqué, severing official ties with Taiwan. Carter then unilaterally nullified the 1954 Mutual Defense Treaty, withdrew all U.S. military personnel, and closed military facilities on the island. He also imposed a secret one-year freeze on arms sales, which resumed under congressional pressure but at a reduced scale—further deepening Taiwan's international isolation.

Subsequent U.S. presidents largely followed a pattern of appeasing China at Taiwan's expense, with only minor variations in their approach. Even staunch anti-Communist Ronald Reagan disappointed Taiwan by signing the 1982 U.S.–China Joint Communiqué, in which the United States expressed its intent to gradually reduce arms sales to Taiwan.

The U.S. capitulation to Communist China did meet strong resistance in Congress. Led by Republican senator Barry Goldwater, Congress passed the Taiwan Relations Act (TRA) on April 10, 1979. The TRA affirmed the U.S. expectation that Taiwan's future be resolved peacefully and declared any attempt to change its status by force, boycott, or embargo a threat to the peace and security of the Western Pacific and a grave concern to the United States.

In 1996, President Clinton invoked the TRA during the Third Taiwan Strait Crisis, responding to Beijing's military intimidation aimed at influencing Taiwan's first direct presidential election. By deploying two aircraft carrier groups to the region, he effectively deterred CCP aggression—a clear reminder that Communists respond only to strength.

In 1998, the U.S. Senate unanimously passed the U.S. Commitment to Taiwan Resolution, led by Republican majority leader Trent Lott. The resolution condemned President Clinton's "Three No's" policy—no independence for Taiwan, no "two Chinas," and no membership for Taiwan in international organizations requiring statehood—as a dangerous concession to Beijing at the expense of Taiwan's international standing.

The rise and fall of U.S.–Taiwan relations serves as a mirror opposite to the rise and fall of U.S.–China relations—with Communism and anti-Communism as the underlying theme throughout.

Turning Tides

To the CCP's dismay—and Taiwan's delight—the tide began to turn.

In 2016, Donald Trump was elected president of the United States, and in 2024, he achieved an even greater victory, becoming the 47th president as well as the 45th. During his first term, Trump's Taiwan policy had already taken shape; in his second term, the trajectory of U.S.–Taiwan relations is expected to deepen further.

A story from three decades ago circulated among Taiwanese doctors in New York who often played golf and dined at Trump's New Jersey golf club. On one occasion, Trump himself approached them to say hello. Upon learning they were from Taiwan, he warmly remarked, "I know Taiwan very well, and I understand its situation." At that time, Trump was merely a businessman, but his genuine goodwill toward Taiwan was evident.

On December 2, 2016, Taiwanese president Tsai Ing-wen called President-elect Trump to congratulate him on his election victory. The call lasted over ten minutes, and Trump later publicly disclosed it on Twitter. When criticized by legacy media for potentially angering China, Trump responded with a tweet: "Interesting how the U.S. sells Taiwan billions of dollars of military equipment but I should not accept a congratulatory call."[30]

During Trump's first term, he signed multiple Taiwan-related laws, strengthening the legal basis for U.S.–Taiwan relations. One of these was the 2018 Taiwan Travel Act, which encourages mutual visits by U.S. and Taiwanese officials, including high-level officials.

Following President Trump's signing of the act, Secretary of State Mike Pompeo declared the removal of restrictions on interactions between U.S. and Taiwanese officials, stating, "Taiwan is a vibrant democracy and reliable partner of the United States, and yet for several decades the State Department has created complex internal restrictions to regulate our diplomats, service members, and other officials' interactions with their Taiwanese counterparts. The United States government took these actions unilaterally, in an attempt to appease the Communist regime in Beijing. No more."[31]

This firm stance was underscored by Trump's four-year tenure, which marked the highest level of arms sales to Taiwan since 1979.[32]

Other significant legislative measures followed. The Taiwan Allies International Protection and Enhancement Initiative (TAIPEI) Act aimed to support Taiwan's diplomatic alliances. The Taiwan Assurance Act of 2020 required the administration to ensure Taiwan's participation in international organizations and reassess engagement guidelines, emphasizing the shared values underlying U.S.–Taiwan relations and advocating for the peaceful resolution of cross-strait issues.

Trump's 2024 victory in the U.S. presidential election was decisive, as was the concurrent congressional election with the Republican Party securing control of both chambers of Congress. Key positions in the new administration—vice president, secretary of state, national security advisor, secretary of defense, secretary of homeland security, director of national intelligence, and CIA director—were filled by staunchly anti-CCP and pro-Taiwan hard-liners. The "Dragon Slayers" ascended, fully displacing the "Panda Huggers."

Only a few months into Trump's administration, significant shifts in U.S.–Taiwan policy were already underway—without major announcements. The State Department quietly removed the phrase "we do not support Taiwan independence," and the CIA updated its website to list Taiwan as a country.

At the Shangri-La Dialogue in Singapore on May 31, Trump's Secretary of Defense, Pete Hegseth, bluntly warned that any attempt by China to seize Taiwan by force would result in "devastating consequences," reaffirming that Asia remains the top strategic priority for the administration.[33]

One can only imagine how much more is yet to come.

This marks a critical turning point for both China and Taiwan, as the Trump administration stands ready to strongly counter the CCP's expansionism while opening new opportunities for Taiwan.

Taiwan Preparation for Renewal

Taiwan has not been in a more favorable position since Nixon's betrayal than it is with the Trump administration. There is a growing consensus among the American public that the CCP is an adversary and, by extension, that Taiwan is a true ally. Despite this shift, Taiwan faces two significant challenges that threaten its national security and survival, one external and one internal.

Ironically, Taiwan's challenges are exactly the same challenges that the United States and the western world are facing.

External Threat—The CCP

The external challenge is the extensive reach of China's United Front operations and infiltration efforts—a strategy dating back to the 1920s, which played a crucial role in the KMT's eventual defeat. Today, these efforts have deeply embedded themselves within Taiwanese society, influencing nearly every aspect of its political, economic, cultural, and social landscape. Both historically and geographically, Taiwan has long been the frontline of the CCP's United Front campaigns.

During the White Terror Era, the Taiwanese public was frequently bombarded with anti-Communist rhetoric and narratives about retaking the mainland. While these narratives were often used as pretexts to suppress opposition and justify oppressive government actions, the threat from Communist China was real, as demonstrated by the two Taiwan Strait crises.

Since the 1980s, Taiwan—like the United States and much of the world—was swept up in the tide of globalization. Despite persistent political tensions, trade between Taiwan and China expanded rapidly. With Taiwan's economic liberalization and China's reform and opening up policies, trade relations flourished, leading to heavy Taiwanese investment in China's manufacturing sector. Since Communist China has become its largest trading partner, Taiwanese investments have significantly fueled China's economic growth. Even during the global sanctions following the Tiananmen Square Massacre, Taiwanese businesses continued to invest in China.

By the 2000s, and as economic ties deepened, many in Taiwan began to downplay the Communist threat.

The KMT—once the staunchest adversary of the CCP—abandoned its values and history after losing power in 2000. Since then, it has degenerated into a subordinate political party of the CCP. Similarly, the Taiwan People's Party (TPP) has adopted a more pro-CCP stance, leaving the Democratic Progressive Party (DPP) as Taiwan's only major anti-CCP party.

Today, the Chinese Communist Party actively supports the Kuomintang and the Taiwan People's Party—both currently out of power—as part of its efforts to manipulate Taiwanese politics and undermine the ruling Democratic Progressive Party.

The CCP aims to forge a KMT–TPP coalition to challenge the DPP and advance pro-China policies in Taiwan. As hard as it is to believe, these politicians—willing to act as CCP proxies—have repeatedly worked to undermine Taiwan's defense by obstructing U.S. arms sales in the legislature while fueling anti-American sentiment across the country.

One of the CCP's most effective tactics is nationalism—the same strategy it used after the May Fourth Movement to pave the way for Leninist Communism in China. It seeks to convince the Taiwanese people that their future lies in national reunification and that their well-being depends on the rejuvenation of the Chinese nation. At the same time, it works to drive a wedge between Taiwan and the United States by invoking a powerful, historically grounded narrative: that the United States betrayed the KMT and later abandoned Taiwan—proof, they claim, that America cannot be trusted. The potential impact of this narrative should not be underestimated.

Over the years, hundreds of thousands of Taiwanese businessmen have not only set up factories in China but also established long-term residences by obtaining mainland residence permits, ID cards, and settlement documents. This trend has blurred national identities and aligned seamlessly with Beijing's strategy of using economic entanglement as a political weapon.

In December 2024, Taiwanese YouTuber "Potter King" released a viral documentary exposing the CCP's United Front operations in real time.[34] The video featured former pro-CCP rapper Chen Po-yuan, who went undercover in China to reveal how the CCP recruits Taiwanese influencers, youth, and entrepreneurs with financial incentives and enticing opportunities to win their allegiance. The documentary quickly went viral, garnering millions of views and igniting widespread public concern. It revealed the CCP's "Taiwanese-leading-Taiwanese" strategy—leveraging familiar local voices to legitimize its propaganda, fracture Taiwan's social cohesion, and erode public trust in democracy.

These influence operations are not limited to the cultural or economic realm. In early 2025, Taiwan was shaken by the revelation that retired Army Lieutenant General Gao Anguo and several others had reportedly been recruited by the CCP to form an underground organization intended to act as a fifth column in the event of a Chinese invasion. This was followed by another shock in March 2025, when a Taiwanese court sentenced four soldiers—including three former members of the president's security team—for spying on behalf of China.[35]

The CCP's United Front strategy is a multi-layered campaign that integrates cultural, economic, and psychological tactics with its military ambitions. These seemingly non-military efforts are designed to work in tandem with the PLA's hard power, advancing Beijing's goal of "peaceful reunification" under the ever-present threat of force. Ultimately, the strategy seeks to erode Taiwan's sovereignty and democratic resilience, laying the groundwork for eventual annexation.

This raises a pressing question: Will Xi Jinping attempt to "unify" Taiwan by force? Many Western analysts believe that under Xi's leadership, the risk of military action is at its highest since 1949, when the Nationalists retreated to Taiwan. The PLA Air Force frequently crosses the Taiwan Strait median line to harass Taiwan, while the Chinese navy conducts regular military exercises, including maneuvers simulating a blockade around the island.

The so-called unification of Taiwan is a core element of Xi Jinping's "Chinese Dream." His fixation on Taiwan appears deeply personal. Since rising to power, he has become the most powerful leader after Mao Zedong, and in 2017, he became the only leader besides Mao to have his ideology, Xi Jinping Thought, enshrined in the party constitution. Yet, one goal remains—bringing Taiwan under Communist rule, a feat even Mao failed to achieve. Xi's drive to cement his historical legacy and match or even surpass Mao's status in history may well be the force behind his ambitions.

Xi's ambition for Taiwan also reflects his broader geopolitical worldview of "East Rising, West Declining," in which China represents the ascendant East, while the United States and the free world symbolize a declining West. His ultimate goal is global domination, with Taiwan as the first and most necessary step toward achieving that goal.

While the timing and certainty of a military invasion remain unclear, it is increasingly evident that Xi is employing a dual strategy, combining military intimidation with long-standing United Front operations to influence and infiltrate Taiwan. Some within the CCP even argue that "buying Taiwan" through economic and political means would be more cost-effective than taking it by force.

Internal Threat—Woke Ideology

Apart from external threats posed by the CCP, the Democratic Progressive Party also faces a significant challenge from within.

The Democratic Progressive Party, a key driver of Taiwan's democratic transition, has thrived post-democratization, holding central government power three times: 2000–2008, 2016–2024, and currently. Advocating for Taiwanese localization and independence, the Democratic Progressive Party stands as a bulwark against CCP aggression. However, extreme leftist policies from the Tsai Ing-wen DPP–led administration posed a rather different threat.

The term "progressive," embedded in the party's name, resonates with leftist ideals. The rise of leftist ideologies in the West during the 1960s also influenced many Taiwanese intellectuals opposing KMT authoritarianism. These individuals adopted leftist ideals and later became foundational figures in the DPP. Despite their leftist leanings, most were moderate on social issues.

After Tsai Ing-wen was elected president in 2016, her administration closely aligned with progressive policies and "political correctness" trends from the West, particularly those championed by the Democratic Party in the United States. These policies, often associated with contemporary

Woke ideologies, included initiatives on transgenderism and climate change. Tsai's approach sparked considerable debate and backlash within Taiwanese society, reflecting deep divisions over these issues.

The Tsai administration, rather than adopting a free-market approach, used government power to forcibly implement its so-called green energy policies, following the model of the Biden administration's Green New Deal. Instead of solving Taiwan's energy shortage, these policies led to a new wave of green energy corruption, severely damaging the credibility of the Democratic Progressive Party government.

In May 2024, President Tsai invited Taiwanese drag queen Nymphia Wind to perform at the presidential office in celebration of his victory on *RuPaul's Drag Race*, making it the first presidential office in the world to host a drag show.[36]

Tsai's alignment with the U.S. Democratic Party, which historically has been less supportive of Taiwan, naturally led to a certain distancing from and even opposition to the genuinely pro-Taiwan Republicans.

In the 2024 election, Lai Ching-te won the presidency as Tsai Ing-wen's successor, but the Democratic Progressive Party suffered a sweeping defeat in both parliamentary and local races—largely due to its progressive leftist agenda. This electoral setback severely weakened the party's governing capacity and undermined its ability to resist infiltration by the Chinese Communist Party, as the opposition-controlled legislature recklessly slashed government budgets—particularly by blocking critical national defense spending vital to Taiwan's survival—pushing the government to the brink of paralysis.

Similar to the United States and the West, Taiwan's mainstream media is also dominated by left-leaning intellectuals, many of whom criticized President Trump as harshly as CCP propaganda. These media outlets include state-controlled platforms such as Taiwan Public Television, the Central News Agency, and Radio Taiwan International, which frequently echo Ivy League perspectives and align with Western media like the *New York Times* and CNN.

It is crucial that the Democratic Progressive Party and the broader anti-Communist camp recognize that Western leftist ideologies share common roots with Communism, and that leftist movements tend to escalate toward increasingly radical positions. In many cases, they ultimately advance toward Communism with accelerating momentum. To truly oppose Communism, one must also confront the leftist currents that lead to it.

The critical task for those committed to defending democratic values is to understand the true nature of Communism—and, more importantly, to recognize Woke ideology for what it is: a mutated form of Communism, designed to subvert Western-style democracies from within, including Taiwan.

Taiwan, like most Western countries, faces the challenge of younger generations lacking a deep understanding of the true history and ideology of Communism—particularly Chinese Communism—and the atrocities it has committed against its own people. Without this knowledge, younger generations do not understand the threat it poses, not only to Taiwan but to the entire world.

In the face of a national crisis—marked by a pro-CCP legislature and China's open threat to seize Taiwan by force—Taiwan's civil society has risen to the occasion. Citizens have launched an unprecedented grassroots effort known as the "Great Recall Movement" to remove KMT legislators from office. Although the first round of recalls on July 26, 2025, failed to remove any of the twenty-four targeted KMT legislators, it showcased the vitality of Taiwan's democracy. This unprecedented civic participation marks a milestone in Taiwan's democratic maturity and should be regarded as a success.

This movement has not only mobilized voters—it has rekindled a long-dormant sense of national clarity. The term "anti-Communism," nearly forgotten during Taiwan's three decades of democratization, has returned with force, uniting people across generations and backgrounds. "Anti-Communism to Save Taiwan" is no longer just a slogan—it has become a national rallying cry, uniting citizens in defense of their freedom, sovereignty, and democratic way of life.

Over the past century, the United States, China, and later Taiwan have been deeply intertwined. With the benefit of hindsight, one dominant theme emerges: the ideological struggle between Communism, anti-Communism, and freedom.

After facing indifference from the United States, Taiwan defied the odds, transforming from an authoritarian regime into a democracy. In stark contrast, Communist China, once on a trajectory of reform and opening since the late 1970s, has regressed into a Mao-era-style totalitarian dictatorship under Xi Jinping. This divergence highlights the vastly different paths taken by these two systems—authoritarianism and Communist totalitarianism. One eventually embracing freedom and democracy, the other tightening its grip on power and suppressing dissent.

The economic contrast is even more striking. Despite decades of Western investment and engagement, Communist China's economy is faltering in the 2020s, plagued by one crisis after another. The endless construction of skyscrapers and massive residential complexes with few buyers cannot continue indefinitely, foreshadowing a real estate collapse of historic proportions. As Trump's tariff war rapidly shatters the illusion of the China miracle, it also highlights Taiwan's strategic position as a global economic powerhouse—particularly in semiconductors and high-tech industries—cementing its vital role on the world stage.

The story of Communist China and democratic Taiwan is ultimately the story of an ideological battle, highlighting the triumph of democracy and freedom over totalitarianism and tyranny. To overlook this reality is to miss the core lesson of their intertwined histories: Systems that find their way to liberty and openness are far more likely to endure than those built on repression and control.

CHAPTER 10

THE TRUMP REVERSAL: AMERICA FIGHTS BACK

From Wilson to Obama and Biden, over a century of U.S. engagement with the Chinese Communists has followed the same disastrous pattern. Time and again, America was misled, deceived, manipulated, cheated, and attacked by the very snake it helped to nurture. Now fully revived and emboldened, the snake was poised to deliver its final and deadly strike.

But to its dismay, the plan began to unravel. At last, one American president saw through the deception, recognized the full scope of the Communist threat, and dared to fight back. That president was Donald J. Trump, who chose to fight for America when no one else would.

America Strikes Back

Trump clearly identified China as an adversary—not a competitor and certainly not a partner. He did not fall for the "Chinese Communism isn't REAL Communism" narrative that deceived so many presidents before him.

Trump's counterattack against Communist China began with trade. In his book *Crippled America: How to Make America Great Again* (2015), he stated:

> There are people who wish I wouldn't refer to China as our enemy. But that's exactly what they are. They have destroyed entire industries by utilizing low-wage workers, cost us tens of thousands of jobs, spied on our businesses, stolen our technology, and have manipulated and devalued their currency, which makes importing our goods more expensive—and sometimes, impossible.[1]

While many elites had lost faith in America, Trump had not. He was determined to push back and defend America against the ungrateful, striking snake.

Interestingly, Trump also used the story "The Snake" to warn about the dangers of open borders and taking in unvetted migrants—illustrating how those who welcome threats in good faith may ultimately be betrayed and harmed.

One of the key highlights of Trump's first administration was his trade war with China, which aimed to counter China's unfair trade practices, reduce the trade imbalance, and safeguard U.S. intellectual property and industries. Through tariffs on hundreds of billions of dollars in Chinese goods, Trump sought to disrupt China's "Red Supply Chain" and reduce its economic exploitation of the United States. The strategy also included pressuring China to reform practices like forced technology transfers and state subsidies, while encouraging the reshoring of American manufacturing to revitalize the U.S. economy. Despite mixed outcomes, the trade war marked a dramatic shift in U.S.–China relations, sending a clear message to the CCP that the days of fleecing the United States and "eating our lunch" were over.

The Trump administration also launched investigations and countermeasures against China's theft of U.S. trade secrets. From late 2018 to

February 2020, the FBI conducted around 1,000 investigations into China's theft of trade secrets, exceeding the total investigations during the entire Obama administration. John Brown, the FBI's Counterintelligence Division assistant director, stated, "We believe no country poses a greater threat than the Chinese Communist Party. From our vantage point, the U.S. hasn't faced a threat of this scale since the Cold War with the Soviet Union. Today, investigations linked to the Chinese government make up a larger portion of our counterintelligence workload than at any other time in FBI history."[2]

President Nixon viewed Soviet Russia as czarist, expansionist, and imperialist. However, Nixon ignored a deeper reality: Communism itself—regardless of the country or ethnicity of its adherents—is inherently expansionist and imperialist, driven by the belief that Communists must "liberate" all of humanity.

In sharp contrast to his predecessors, President Trump stands as the first U.S. leader to take decisive action against expansionist Communist China. Trump clearly recognizes CCP's imperial ambitions, which mirror, and in many ways surpass, those of Soviet Russia.

During his first term, President Trump adopted the Indo-Pacific Strategy, replacing the outdated Asia-Pacific framework and marking a historic shift in U.S. foreign policy. This strategic reorientation acknowledged the growing threat posed by China and recognized India's rising importance in one of the world's most critical regions.

Early in his second term, Trump advanced this vision by hosting Indian prime minister Narendra Modi at the White House in February 2025. Their joint statement outlined a sweeping strategic partnership across defense, technology, trade, and security—solidifying a common front for global stability and prosperity. Vice President Vance later visited India to further deepen and operationalize this growing alliance.

Unlike Nixon's ill-fated gamble of allying with Communist China, Trump built alliances framed around shared democratic values and strategic interests. While not all partners live up to every ideal, this time

America chose more wisely—aligning with nations inclined toward freedom.

After winning the election in 2024, even before reentering the White House, Trump proposed bold initiatives such as reclaiming the Panama Canal and annexing Greenland. While these ideas may seem unconventional, they are clearly strategic moves aimed at countering the CCP's growing global influence. For years, the CCP has aggressively expanded its influence in Latin America, particularly at key strategic hubs like the Panama Canal, where Chinese state-linked companies have secured significant footholds. In 2018, China declared itself a "Near Arctic State" and launched the "Polar Silk Road"[3]—a strategic extension of the Belt and Road Initiative into the Arctic, named after the ancient Silk Road, a trade network linking China to Europe.

Immediately after returning to the White House, President Trump resumed the tariff war with Communist China as expected—but also threatened to raise tariffs on Mexico and Canada. Also viewed as unconventional, this move was a calculated strategy to counter the CCP's use of origin laundering—the practice of mislabeling a product's country of origin to evade tariffs and sanctions, particularly in connection with fentanyl trafficking into the United States via its neighboring countries.

On April 2, 2025, President Trump announced sweeping new tariffs on U.S. trading partners, declaring, "It's Liberation Day in America." China now faces crushing tariffs. The move marks a bold escalation in Trump's economic war against the CCP and a decisive step toward reclaiming American industrial sovereignty.

In this context, Trump's announcement that tech companies investing in U.S. manufacturing would be exempt from the 100 percent tariffs on imported chips further encouraged firms like Apple to bolster their domestic operations. We are witnessing a growing shift of turning "Made in America" into a reality as more companies commit to strengthening their U.S. operations.[4]

However, Intel—one of America's largest chipmakers—recently appointed Lip-Bu Tan, a Malaysian-born Chinese executive with deep ties to Chinese businesses, including firms linked to the Chinese military. On August 7, 2025, President Trump called for his immediate resignation, citing potential conflicts of interest stemming from those investments. Trump's message was clear: To protect America's interests, we must clean house![5] The CCP understands, perhaps better than most Americans, that Trump's tariffs are not merely a trade war. They strike at the core of the regime's economic lifeline and pose a direct threat to its existence. Xia Baolong, the top CCP official overseeing Hong Kong policy, put it bluntly: "The US isn't after our tariffs, it's after our very survival." In the same speech, he sought to demean the American people, mocking them as "peasants" and "country bumpkins."[6] The CCP is growing desperate, because it knows that losing its status as the "world's factory" would sever the lifeblood that sustains its economic power to challenge the United States, pursue global dominance, and—most critically—maintain its tyrannical grip on the Chinese people.

And Trump made clear that the tariffs were just the beginning. He did not forget one of the CCP's gravest crimes: unleashing the deadly virus on the United States and the world. On April 18, 2025, his administration replaced the federal covid.gov site with a new platform titled "Lab Leak: The True Origins of COVID-19," presenting the Wuhan lab leak not as a theory but as the most credible explanation. It emphasized that a lab-related incident involving gain-of-function research is now widely considered the most likely origin—signaling a renewed commitment to uncovering the truth and holding the CCP accountable. In May, President Trump issued an executive order restricting federal funding for gain-of-function pathogen research.

As a victim of the CCP virus who spent ten days in intensive care and still struggles with lingering complications, I want answers. I believe the virus's true origin is far darker than we've been told.

Most important, President Trump reignited American awareness that Communist China and Communist ideology itself had risen to become the number one threat to the United States. This marks a profound cultural and ideological shift in the nation.

In a remark commemorating National Victims of Communism Day, November 7, 2020, President Trump condemned Communism as an "oppressive ideology that, without fail, leaves in its wake misery, destruction, and death." He argued: "While Marxism promises equality, peace, and happiness, in practice it results only in inequality, violence, and despair."[7]

Those words were music to my ears—a rare moment of truth spoken without apology.

One of the decisive actions taken by the first Trump administration to counter Communism was the issuance of an immigration policy alert barring current and former members of Communist parties from applying for U.S. immigration benefits, including green cards. The policy has historical precedent dating back to 1918, when similar restrictions were enacted to guard against "external threats of anarchism and communism" from the Soviet Union. After decades of admitting Chinese Communists and the children of CCP elites, it is long overdue for the United States to take firm action to keep them out. As Trump declared at the 2023 Faith and Freedom Coalition conference in Washington: "We're going to keep foreign, Christian-hating communists, Marxists, and socialists out of America."

The revival of the 1918 policy is not just a nod to history—it's a stark warning that after more than a century the fight against Communism is far from over. If anything, it has entered its most dangerous chapter yet. The 2024 presidential election transcended being merely a contest between Trump and Harris or a battle between Republicans and Democrats. Trump boldly labeled Kamala Harris a "Communist," mockingly referring to her as "Comrade Kamala," and accused her of promoting policies rooted in Communist ideology. He asserted, "She's a Marxist. Everybody knows she's a Marxist. Her father is a Marxist economics professor, and he taught her well."[8]

Trump also questioned whether Democratic leaders had fully considered Harris's background and ideological leanings when selecting her for a leadership role. Clearly, they had not—or, more likely, they had and wanted her for that very reason. Her running mate, Tim Walz, was also pro-CCP, who likened socialism to "being neighborly."[9] For survivors of Communism like myself, it was jaw-dropping to witness the Democratic Party openly embracing socialism and Communism.

Trump framed the 2024 election as "a choice between Communism and freedom"—the very warning I have been shouting from the rooftops and sounding even louder with my book *Mao's America: A Survivor's Warning* to wake up the American people.

Trump's historic victory sent a powerful message to American Marxists, Communist China, and their friends—both old and new: The United States is back, determined to defend freedom and strike back against Communism.

Despite the victory, the 2024 election stands as a stark reminder: Nearly half of America, knowingly or unknowingly, voted for Communism.

—

With President Trump back in office, the United States finally has a fighting chance against Communism—both abroad and at home. But to secure lasting victory, the American people must first understand how we got here.

Now is the time for serious reflection. We must confront a fundamental question: Why has the United States, time and again, repeated the fable of the Snake—rescuing, aiding, and enriching the very regime that seeks our downfall, or as President Trump bluntly put it, "rebuilding China"?

History Lessons, Not Learned

The German philosopher Georg Hegel famously said, "The only thing we learn from history is that we learn nothing from history." By failing to learn history's lessons, we remain blind to recurring patterns and doomed to repeat the same tragedies.

The American encounter with the Snake did not begin with China.

Before Edgar Snow and his *Red Star over China*, the Russian Communists had an American advocate in journalist John Reed. His *Ten Days That Shook the World* is a firsthand account of the 1917 Bolshevik Revolution, written with an openly sympathetic tone that casts the revolution in a positive light, glorifying what would later become one of history's most repressive and murderous regimes. Later in the 1930s, Walter Duranty, the *New York Times*'s Moscow correspondent, notoriously downplayed Stalin's atrocities, including the state-engineered Ukrainian famine, earning a Pulitzer Prize while serving as a de facto apologist for the Soviet regime.

American capitalists, ignoring the clash of ideologies and the brutality of the regime, rushed into Soviet Russia, lured by the promise of a vast new market. Who helped implement Stalin's First Five-Year Plan (1928–1932)—the foundation of Soviet industrial modernization? The answer: the United States, its industrialists, engineers, planners, and corporations. Companies like Ford Motor Company, International Harvester, General Electric, and Koppers & Co. built factories, tractor plants, hydroelectric stations, and steel complexes that jump-started Soviet industrial power.[10]

But that market turned out to be a trap. Despite formal agreements, the Soviets routinely ignored patent rights, copied American designs without permission, and engaged in outright technological theft. A prime example was the Stalinets tractor—a direct copy of a Caterpillar model, built using stolen blueprints and technology. American engineers frequently reported the Soviet Union's blatant disregard for intellectual property.[11]

Beyond industrial mimicry, the Soviets escalated their efforts—using espionage to steal critical U.S. technologies. Soviet agents infiltrated major American aviation firms, including Douglas, Bell Aircraft, and

Wright Aeronautical, to copy, steal, and reverse-engineer designs that became the foundation of the Soviet air force.[12] Their espionage didn't stop there. Soviet spies ultimately penetrated the United States' most closely guarded secret: the atomic bomb. By stealing American nuclear technology, they shattered the U.S. monopoly on nuclear power and ushered in a perilous new era of global rivalry.

As Sean McMeekin, author of *To Overthrow the World: The Rise and Fall and Rise of Communism*, aptly put it, "The Soviet Communist superpower that contested the Cold War and brought the United States to the brink of nuclear war in 1962 could not have emerged without the contributions, both voluntary and involuntary, of American capitalists."[13]

In the end, Americans unwittingly proved Lenin's grim prediction: "The capitalists will sell us the rope with which we will hang them."

The Russian Communists, too, showed little gratitude for America's goodwill, charity, and generosity. America has a long history of extending help to Soviet Russia in times of crisis. In 1921, under the leadership of Herbert Hoover, the United States provided massive humanitarian aid to the Soviet Union, saving millions from starvation during a devastating famine.[14] Even before officially entering World War II in December 1941, the United States had already sent arms and equipment to the Soviet Union—totaling $11.3 billion, or roughly $231.4 billion in 2025 dollars.[15] Without U.S. aid, it would have been nearly impossible for the Soviet Union to withstand—and ultimately defeat—the Nazi invasion.

And what did America get in return? The Cold War—and the looming threat of nuclear annihilation.

President Roosevelt allied with Communist Russia against Nazi Germany. President Nixon allied with Communist China against the Soviet Union. Did the outcomes differ?

Not at all. The reason is simple: Both regimes viewed the United States as their mortal ideological enemy. No amount of goodwill, charity, or strategic partnership could change that. In the end, a snake is a snake—its nature cannot be changed.

Communist vs. Nazi

This leads to another uncomfortable truth: Why are the crimes of the Nazis universally condemned, while those of Communist regimes are so often ignored? The answer is not historical oversight—it is deliberate. The radical left has worked tirelessly to erase Communism's bloody past, sanitize its deadly ideology, and obscure the reality that both Nazism and Communism share the same totalitarian roots.

In the process, even the teaching of Nazi crimes was manipulated. The acronym "Nazi" was severed from its full name—the National *Socialist* German Workers' Party—to hide the reality that both Nazism and Communism are radical far-left ideologies. As a result, Nazism was rebranded as a purely right-wing phenomenon, and conservatives have been routinely smeared as Nazis or Hitler wannabes—a tactic especially wielded against figures like Donald Trump, Elon Musk, and the late Charlie Kirk.

While most Americans are familiar with the atrocities of the Nazis, especially the Holocaust, the opposite is true when it comes to the horrors committed by Stalin, Mao, and Pol Pot, whose regimes were responsible for more than 100 million deaths through purges, political repression, and forced famines. Hollywood has extensively depicted the crimes of the Nazis in acclaimed films like *Schindler's List* and *The Pianist*. Yet major films exposing the mass atrocities of the Soviet Union or Communist China are virtually nonexistent—aside from *The Killing Fields*, which portrayed the Khmer Rouge genocide in Cambodia.

The Nazi regime lasted only twelve years and was thoroughly defeated in 1945. Afterward, laws were enacted in Germany and much of Europe that made defending, denying, or even questioning Nazism a criminal offense.

In contrast, Communism, particularly Chinese Communism, has endured for over a century. With the help of the United States, it has not only survived but thrived, its crimes dismissed as misunderstandings or excused as mere "mistakes."

The Nazi swastika is universally reviled, yet the hammer and sickle rarely provoke the same outrage among Americans. Worse, in recent decades, some members of younger generations have come to admire it. Communist flags are now a common sight at radical protests across the United States and the West, including Black Lives Matter rallies and pro-Hamas demonstrations. More troubling still, the Communist Party USA (CPUSA)—founded in 1919, two years before the CCP—has seen a rapid surge in membership in recent years.[16]

It is time to establish a global tribunal for Communism, just as the Nuremberg Trials exposed the crimes of the Nazis. The public must also be made fully aware of Communist atrocities: Stalin's Great Terror, Mao's Great Leap Forward and Cultural Revolution, and Pol Pot's genocide in Cambodia.

Following Florida's lead, we must mandate that K–12 students learn the full truth about the atrocities of Communism—so that future generations understand the deadly cost of totalitarian ideology and never repeat its horrors. I've been advocating for the establishment of an Anti-Communism Month to help educate the American people. We have Black History Month, Women's History Month, Pride Month, and many others dedicated to identity groups—yet nothing that confronts one of the most destructive ideologies in modern history, an ideology that has oppressed all of those very groups. It's time we dedicate a month to exposing the evils of Communism. I hope this idea soon becomes a reality.

In exposing the evil of Communism, we must also confront its modern mutations, including identity politics, critical race theory (CRT), diversity, equity, and inclusion (DEI), and transgenderism.

Chinese or Communists?

For decades, Americans and Westerners have mistakenly believed that Chinese Communists are first and foremost Chinese of Confucian culture, and secondly Communists. As a result, the Chinese Communist Party has been seen as a Confucian-style Communist Party, a more moderate and benevolent Communist Party compared to the Soviet Communist Party. This misconception has fueled the persistent illusion that Chinese Communism is not *real* Communism, but rather a uniquely Chinese adaptation—a *so-called* Communism. In adopting this illusion, they overlook a crucial fact: While China's history spans thousands of years and is deeply rooted in Confucianism, the CCP's history dates back only to 1921 and is grounded in Marxism-Leninism.

During the tariff war with the United States, the CCP repeatedly employed its familiar tactic of conflating the party with the Chinese nation itself. This was evident in a 2025 BBC interview with Victor Gao, vice president of the Beijing-based Center for China and Globalization, where he declared: "China has been here for 5,000 years. Most of the time, there was no United States, and we survived...and we expect to survive for another 5,000 years."[17]

It must be made clear that the CCP is the offspring of Soviet Communism, not the heir of traditional China. Its remarkable adaptations for survival have not lessened its evil—if anything, they have made it even more dangerous.

From the very beginning, the Chinese Communist Party's objective has been to impose Marxist ideology on China. While systematically dismantling the positive values of traditional Chinese culture, it also pushed China's imperial totalitarian culture to its extremes. Mao Zedong claimed to be a combination of Karl Marx and Qin Shi Huang—China's first emperor and one of the most brutal and feared tyrants in Chinese history.[18] Mao's Cultural Revolution marked the peak of this destructive and tyrannical vision.

Chiang Kai-shek's warning to Vice President Henry Wallace in 1944—that the Chinese Reds were more Communistic than the Soviets—has been repeatedly proven true. Yet, time and again, this warning has been ignored. This fundamental misunderstanding has enabled the CCP to manipulate American political leaders and elites, advancing its agenda while obscuring its true nature.

Is It About Ideology?

The reality is even worse than merely failing to recognize Chinese Communists as orthodox Communists. Many of our political leaders and elites do not believe ideology plays any role in U.S.–China relations at all.

John Mearsheimer, a prominent American political scientist and international relations scholar, argued in a 2024 interview with the CCP's media outlet *China Daily* that tensions between the United States and China stem from shifting power dynamics rather than ideological differences. According to Mearsheimer, when American elites accuse China of authoritarianism and Communism, it is merely to paint China as the "bad guy." He further claimed that within China, ideology is secondary to traditions like Confucianism and a cultural emphasis on harmony—extending, as he put it, to China's approach to fostering international stability.[19]

The profound ignorance of people like Mearsheimer is truly stunning. They not only ignore the CCP's own constitution, which explicitly declares China to be ruled by Communist ideology, but also seem to forget that the United States was founded on its own ideology—one rooted in liberty, individual rights, and government by consent—ideals that are diametrically opposed to Communism.

In 1992, following the collapse of the Soviet Union, political scientist Francis Fukuyama published *The End of History and the Last Man*, positing that the fall of Communism signified the endpoint of humanity's ideological evolution and the universal triumph of liberal democracy as the final form of government. However, his conclusion has since been challenged by the rise of another Communist regime—the Chinese Communist Party, which asserted in its official platforms: "Westerners eagerly proclaimed that history had ended with the triumph of capitalism. Yet the remarkable success of socialism with Chinese characteristics ultimately marked the end of the 'end of history' thesis."[20]

The CCP reaffirms the fact that the conflict with the West represented by the United States is ideological, a clash between capitalism and socialism, and between freedom and totalitarianism.

Anti-CCP Equates to Anti-Communism?

Although more Americans are awakening to the reality that the United States is in a new Cold War with Communist China, the battle lines remain blurred, and the objectives unclear. Is America's true enemy solely Communist China, or is it Communism itself?

It is easy to recognize that pro-CCP politicians exist in both political parties, Republican and Democrat, but it is more difficult to grasp that being anti-CCP does not necessarily mean being anti-Communism. Former House Speaker Nancy Pelosi, for example, is a well-known supporter of the Tiananmen Square pro-democracy protesters. During her 1991 visit to Beijing, she went to the square without her Chinese hosts' permission and held up a hand-painted banner that read: "To those who died for democracy in China."[21] Pelosi also established herself as a staunch supporter of Taiwan, with her 2022 visit to the island drawing sharp condemnation from Beijing.

Yet she led a Democratic Party whose policies have moved so far toward Maoist and Communist models that they are becoming almost indistinguishable—embracing the oppressor-oppressed narrative, identity politics, the destruction of tradition, the suppression of free speech, lawlessness, and an ever-expanding government. In essence, the Democratic Party has become the driving force behind the American version of the Chinese Cultural Revolution.

This applies even to those who have suffered under Chinese Communism. Although they vehemently oppose the CCP regime, many Chinese immigrants fail to recognize the ideological kinship between Wokeism and Communism. Embracing a new identity as victims of so-called white supremacy, they seek protection from the Democratic Party—often aligning with the very Woke agenda they should instinctively resist. I've seen this firsthand in more than a few individuals. They would do well to remember the old saying: "Fool me once, shame on you. Fool me twice, shame on me."

To safeguard our freedom, we must resist both the Chinese Communist Party and the American form of Communism, which now hides behind the banner of social justice.

By studying the Chinese Communist Party, the American people can gain a deeper understanding of Communism. Defeating the CCP is not just a geopolitical necessity, it would also help better equip America to confront Communism within its own borders.

A Hundred-Year Marathon

The CCP has always pursued a long-term strategy focused on surpassing and countering the United States. Recall the anti-Christian campaign launched in 1922, shortly after the Party's founding? From the very beginning, the CCP identified Christianity, capitalism, and the United States as adversaries to be defeated.

More than a century later, nothing has changed. Xi Jinping has actively advanced this vision through the doctrine of the Two Centenaries:

- 1921–2021: The 100th anniversary of the CCP's founding, marked by the goal of transforming China into a strong economic power—a milestone the regime now claims to have achieved.
- 1949–2049: The 100th anniversary of the founding of the People's Republic of China, with the ultimate objective of achieving global dominance—a goal Xi is determined to realize.

This is the Chinese Communist Party's "Hundred-Year Marathon"—a grand strategy, despite shifting tactics, that has remained fundamentally unchanged. The CCP believes the turning point is now, as Xi Jinping frames it: amid the "great changes unseen in a century."

These "great changes" signal the CCP's belief that the world is entering a new era—one where China's rise and the West's decline are inevitable, and where China can finally assert itself as the new global master. In other words, the CCP is supremely confident the moment is near when Communism defeats capitalism—now that capitalism is dying by the very rope it sold to Communists for profit.

Time is a weapon for the Chinese Communist Party, especially in its strategy for confronting Trump's tariff war. The CCP believes time is on its side: It faces no term limits, no elections, and no need to answer to voters. As former CCP Vice President Wang Qishan reportedly said, "The Chinese people can survive by eating grass." In contrast, the Trump administration had not four, but effectively only two years to act before the midterm elections. The CCP's strategy was clear: stall, delay, and wait for American resolve to weaken. This exposes a fundamental vulnerability—how democratic systems struggle to confront totalitarian regimes that believe they can wait indefinitely.

The CCP has always played the long game—and that strategy has brought us to where we are today. If Xi Jinping's Project 2049 becomes reality, the United States—and the international order it built—could be dismantled by the Chinese Communist Party. America may face the unthinkable: becoming a colony of the CCP. And the world that follows could be even darker and more oppressive than the dystopia imagined in Orwell's *1984*.

Freedom vs. Totalitarianism

Instead of arriving at the end of history predicted by Fukuyama, we now stand at a historic moment—a decisive showdown between the United States and Communist China, a defining clash between two fundamentally opposing systems.

Only months into the tariff war, it was already clear that President Trump faced powerful internal obstacles and entrenched opposition intent on derailing his agenda.

It's no surprise that the usual suspects—the radical left, the entire Democratic Party, and the legacy media—oppose Trump no matter what, even if it means siding with Communist China.

One of the more surprising voices of opposition came from Republican senator Rand Paul, who joined Senate Democrats in a failed attempt to block President Trump's tariff and trade policy. In a CNBC interview, Paul insisted that all voluntary trade is mutually beneficial, dismissed the idea that "China rips us off" as a fallacy, and declared that trade is always a win-win.[22] While Senator Paul is correct in principle, he ignores the glaring reality that, over the decades, the CCP has successfully corrupted, dismantled, and weaponized the global free trade system to serve its own agenda. He seems unaware that in Beijing's view, "win-win" with the United States simply means China wins twice.

Although Paul was one of only three Republican senators to side with the Democrats, he revealed in the interview that several other Republican senators privately shared his view but chose to vote along party lines.

It is a tragedy that we still have conservative political leaders like Paul who fail to grasp the deeper stakes behind the free trade and tariff debate—a battle not just over economics, but between two irreconcilable systems: capitalism and Communism. In this, Paul unwittingly echoes the same naïve China hands whose blindness helped deliver China into Communist control in the first place.

Another obstacle came from the American public, many of whom see themselves primarily as consumers rather than citizens—focused solely on their personal bottom line. They complain about the potential price increases of consumer products that tariffs might bring. In response, I posted the following on X, on April 29, 2025:

> During World War II, Americans were called upon to fight the totalitarian Nazi regime. Over 400,000 brave young men gave their lives for the cause of freedom—and secured victory. Today, we face a new totalitarian threat: the Communist regime of China. This regime has been responsible for the deaths of hundreds of millions of its own people—including victims of political

persecution, man-made famine, and 360 million* unborn children—and over a million Americans, through the Korean War, fentanyl, and COVID-19.

Yet, we're told it's too much to ask to spend a little more to avoid buying Made-in-China products?

Americans, never forget—freedom is never free.[23]

Winning the war against Communist China will take more than President Trump and his administration—it will require all of us, united, willing to stand up, make sacrifices, and fight for freedom.

Looking Back to See Ahead

For too long foreign policy has remained the guarded domain of a small circle of so-called elites, while the American public remained largely in the dark, unaware of the context, the decisions made behind closed doors, and their far-reaching consequences that have shaped our nation's destiny.

But the American people deserve to know the truth: how U.S. presidents, the entrenched bureaucracy, intellectual elites, and the media conspired to commit one of the greatest strategic blunders in our nation's history: aiding the rise of the Chinese Communist Party.

Tracing the actions of these presidents and their policies highlights the path that brought us to where we are today.

Since President Woodrow Wilson helped set the stage for the creation and rise of the Chinese Communist Party, his successors—Warren G. Harding, Calvin Coolidge, and Herbert Hoover, spanning 1921 to 1933—largely leaned toward isolationism, particularly in their approach to China. They viewed China as a vast but impoverished country, unworthy of serious American attention, while they overlooked Soviet efforts to influence and ultimately control China's future.

It was not until after the mid-1930s that the Japanese invasion forced

*I meant to say 336 million.

China back into America's strategic focus, with the ensuing conflict making China a central front in the United States' war effort.

The era of President Franklin D. Roosevelt marked the beginning of America's engagement with the Chinese Communist Party. From the very start, the United States consistently misread Chinese Communism—a costly mistake that went uncorrected until the arrival of President Trump.

Although Roosevelt led the United States to victory in World War II, he ultimately empowered Stalin and facilitated the expansion of the Soviet empire. His failure to grasp the true intentions of the Chinese Communists laid the groundwork for the Communist takeover of China—the "loss of China."

President Harry Truman took it a step further by sanctioning Chiang Kai-shek, thereby cementing the Communist victory in China. The complete communization of China in turn precipitated the Korean War and the Vietnam War. In response to growing Soviet expansion, Truman later introduced the "Truman Doctrine," laying the foundation for a global policy of containment.

After the fall of China in 1949, the CCP became a Soviet satellite state, severing all ties with the United States and the West. It remained isolated until it broke with its former patron and, facing hostility from both superpowers and looming internal collapse, sought a way out through renewed engagement with the United States.

In the later years of the Cold War, President Richard Nixon, who had historically been viewed as a staunch anti-Communist, seemed to lose confidence in the superiority of the American system and institutions. After setbacks in the Vietnam War and falling behind the Soviet Union in areas including space and nuclear technology, Nixon and other U.S. policymakers began to believe that America could not defeat the Soviet Union alone—and that an alliance with China was necessary.

This led him to take steps toward thawing relations with China after more than two decades of mutual isolation, thereby saving a chaotic,

Cultural Revolution–ravaged China from collapse. Nixon's approach was akin to Roosevelt's alliance with the Soviet Union against Nazi Germany, a strategy that ultimately proved to be shortsighted and self-defeating.

President Jimmy Carter spoke of promoting human rights diplomacy but turned a blind eye to China's systematic and atrocious human rights abuses, which were worse than those in the Soviet Union. In a rush, Carter established formal diplomatic relations with China, which amounted to a form of appeasement. As he admitted in a 2019 interview, "I decided to do that [establish diplomatic ties with China] before I was president."[24]

President Ronald Reagan, the most staunchly anti-Communist U.S. president of the Cold War era and a key figure in the Soviet Union's collapse, also overestimated China's potential for liberalization—just as his predecessors had. He permitted the sale of a significant number of advanced weapon systems and technology to Communist China. Yet the CCP made it clear to the world that it never intended to liberalize, as evidenced by the 1989 Tiananmen Square massacre.

President George H. W. Bush, who once served as an envoy to Beijing and considered himself an expert on China, chose to overlook the true nature of the Chinese Communist regime. Even in the wake of the bloody Tiananmen Square massacre, he refused to adopt a tough stance against China and instead took a conciliatory approach, maintaining relations with the Chinese government.

President Bill Clinton was a proponent of modernization theory—the idea that economic development would naturally lead to democratic reform. This theory has proven valid in non-totalitarian contexts such as Taiwan and South Korea. However, in Communist China, calls for political liberalization were systematically and brutally suppressed. Clinton's misreading of Communist totalitarianism shaped trade negotiations with the CCP and led to China's entry into the World Trade Organization, integrating it into the global economy. This decision accelerated China's rise while setting the stage for America's decline over the next three decades.

President George W. Bush, in the wake of the 9/11 attacks, sought to align with China as part of his global war on terror strategy, failing to recognize that the CCP itself operates as a terrorist organization through coercion and suppression of its own people. Under the guise of anti-terrorism, the CCP launched its persecution of Uyghur Muslims in Xinjiang, using the global counterterrorism narrative to justify mass surveillance and reeducation prison camps. This critical miscalculation allowed the CCP to strengthen its global influence and accelerate its rise on the world stage.

President Barack Obama declared that the United States "welcomes China as a strong, prosperous, and successful member of the community of nations,"[25] signaling a willingness to share global leadership with Communist China. He completely overlooked the reality that a "strong, prosperous, and successful" totalitarian regime poses a threat not only to the United States but also to the Chinese people and the entire world.

During President Donald Trump's first term, his administration identified China as the greatest strategic threat to the United States, marking the first time since the Nixon presidency that such a stance was formally established. After President Biden took power, he was forced to partially continue Trump's policies, such as semiconductor export bans and other sanctions on China. However, the Biden administration significantly weakened many of Trump's hard-line measures, attempting to return to the Obama-era approach of maintaining a superficial peace with China.

And that was the state of affairs before President Trump returned to the White House.

As for the question who is to blame for the "loss of China" and the later "rise of the Chinese Communist Party"? History has made the answer clear: The blame lies squarely with the United States. The CCP, and the immense threat it now poses to America, was, indeed, made in America, because America brought in the snake, fed it, sheltered it, and watched as it grew strong enough to strike its clueless benefactor.

—

For the United States, defeating modern totalitarian China is an unprecedented challenge—more formidable than World War I, World War II, the Cold War, or the War on Terror. The new war demands new strategies and new warriors. In the thirty years since the end of the Cold War, no U.S. president has confronted China as openly and decisively as President Donald Trump.

Trump's MAGA movement is more than just a domestic renewal—it is also the best U.S.–China policy. China's transformation from a Communist wasteland to a global power capable of challenging American supremacy was made possible by U.S. political leaders and elites who put America last by prioritizing their own wealth and power over the nation's interests. That era is over. No more selling out America or the Chinese people!

During his 2025 inaugural address, President Trump directly named Communist China as the greatest threat to the United States. His new administration is defined by hard-line China hawks. This marks a historic shift: America is no longer appeasing China—it is confronting it head-on.

President Trump's battle is not only against Chinese Communism; it is also against the Marxist ideological subversion within America itself. He is the first U.S. president to take a direct stand against domestic Communism. Upon taking office, he immediately abolished all DEI policies and programs in the executive branch of the federal government, recognizing them as a tenet of Cultural Marxism—an internal threat designed to weaken the nation from within. The fight against Communism abroad and at home has become a core mission of the MAGA movement.

The connection is clear: Most if not all of the American left and Communist China's totalitarianism are fundamentally linked—they share the same ideological essence, both following the "road to serfdom" described by the great economist Friedrich Hayek. Their differences lie in how they manifest across different nations, cultures, and historical stages.

Just as President Ronald Reagan oversaw the collapse of the Soviet Union, President Donald Trump has set in motion the downfall of both Communist China and American Communism. In his own words: "This is the final battle. Either the Communists win and destroy America, or we destroy the Communists."[26]

If successful, his presidency will be remembered not just for restoring American strength, but for ensuring that Communism, whether foreign or domestic, has no place in the land of the free. If America is to survive, Communism must be defeated.

That could be Trump's legacy.

ACKNOWLEDGMENTS

I am grateful to my friends and fellow patriots, Steven Nelson Jonnes and Richard Hassen, whose insights and editorial assistance greatly enriched this book.

NOTES

Chapter 1: The CCP's War on America

1. Paul Theroux, *Deep South: Four Seasons on Back Roads* (Eamon Dolan/Houghton, 2015), 440.

2. Theroux, *Deep South.*

3. Theroux, *Deep South*, 408.

4. Chris Morris, "10 Iconic American Companies Owned by Chinese Investors," CNBC, China in Transition, May 11, 2017, https://www.cnbc.com/2017/05/11/10-iconic-american-companies-owned-by-chinese-investors.html.

5. "What is a community with a shared future for mankind?," Central Commission for Discipline Inspection and Supervision, January 17, 2018, https://www.ccdi.gov.cn/special/zmsjd/zm19da_zm19da/201801/t20180116_161970.html.

6. Alex Luck, "Chinese Naval Task Force Circumnavigates Australia, Creates Local Stir," Naval News, March 7, 2025, https://www.navalnews.com/naval-news/2025/03/chinese-task-force-circumnavigates-australia-causing-local-stir/.

7. Ana Swanson, "Trump Presses World Trade Organization on China," *New York Times*, July 26, 2019, https://www.nytimes.com/2019/07/26/us/politics/trump-wto-china.html?searchResultPosition=1.

8. "China Withdraws Bid for Greenland Airport Projects: Sermitsiaq Newspaper," Reuters, June 4, 2019, https://www.reuters.com/article/business/china-withdraws-bid-for-greenland-airport-projects-sermitsiaq-newspaper-idUSKCN1T5190/.

9. "China Arming Houthi Rebels in Yemen in Exchange For Unimpeded Red Sea Passage," Foundation for Defense of Democracies, January 2, 2025, https://www.fdd.org/analysis/2025/01/02/china-arming-houthi-rebels-in-yemen-in-exchange-for-unimpeded-red-sea-passage/.

10. Guermantes Lailari, "China's Support of Hamas: Evidence and Actions," Jewish Policy Center, April 2, 2024, https://www.jewishpolicycenter.org/2024/04/02/chinas-support-of-hamas-evidence-and-actions/.

11. Brendan Cole, "Chinese Soldiers Quietly Creep into Ukraine War," *Newsweek*, April 12, 2025, https://www.newsweek.com/chinese-soldiers-quietly-creep-russia-ukraine-war-2058954.

12. Michael Dorgan, "Chinese Firm Aiding Houthi Attacks on US Vessels, as Airstrikes Kill 74," Fox News, April 18, 2025, https://www.foxnews.com/world/chinese-firm-aiding-houthi-attacks-us-vessels-airstrikes-kill-74.

13. Madeline Osburn, "Chinese Organization with Communist Party Ties Funds Black Lives Matter Ventures," The Federalist, September 16, 2020, https://thefederalist.com/2020/09/16/chinese-organization-with-communist-party-ties-funds-black-lives-matter-ventures/.

14. Daniel Flesch, "The Pro-Hamas Movement's Threat to America," The Heritage Foundation, June 14, 2024, https://www.heritage.org/middle-east/commentary/the-pro-hamas-movements-threat-america.

15. "S Korea Returns Remains of Chinese Soldiers Killed in Korean War," Al Jazeera, September 16, 2022, https://www.aljazeera.com/news/2022/9/16/s-korea-returns-remains-of-chinese-soldiers-killed-in-korean-war#:~:text=Casualty%20figures%20remain%20disputed%20but,US%20Aggression%20and%20Aid%20Korea.

16. Cai Yongmei, "The Truth About the CCP's Involvement in the War in Indochina," Independent Chinese PEN Center, February 3, 2017, https://www.chinesepen.org/blog/archives/61778.

17. "Are Fentanyl Overdose Deaths Rising in the US?," USA Facts, September 27, 2023, https://usafacts.org/articles/are-fentanyl-overdose-deaths-rising-in-the-us/.

18. "Select Committee Unveils Findings into CCP's Role in American Fentanyl Epidemic—Report & Hearing," Press Release, April 16, 2024, https://selectcommitteeontheccp.house.gov/media/press-releases/select-committee-unveils-findings-ccps-role-american-fentanyl-epidemic-report.

19. "China 'Made a Strategic Decision to Allow Their Fentanyl Operations to Continue,'" Federal Newswire, September 16, 2024, https://thefederalnewswire.com/stories/664263599-gatestone-institute-board-of-governors-member-china-made-a-strategic-decision-to-allow-their-fentanyl-operations-to-continue.

20. John Elflein, "Total Number of Cases and Deaths from COVID-19 in the United States as of April 26, 2023," Statistica, August 29, 2023, https://www.statista.com/statistics/1101932/coronavirus-covid19-cases-and-deaths-number-us-americans/.

21. "CIA Now Says COVID Most Likely Originated from a Lab Leak but Has 'Low Confidence' in Its Assessment," CBS News, January 27, 2025, https://www.cbsnews.com/news/cia-covid-likely-originated-lab-low-confidence-assessment/.

22. "The Heritage Foundation's Nonpartisan Commission on China and COVID-19 Unveils Seismic Report on China's Negligence During Pandemic Resulting in $18 Trillion in Economic Damages to Americans," Heritage.org, July 8, 2024, https://www.heritage.org/press/the-heritage-foundations-nonpartisan-commission-china-and-covid-19-unveils-seismic-report.

23. "China Will Attack America," Congressional Record (Bound Edition), Volume 148 (2002), Part 17, November 14, 2002, https://www.govinfo.gov/content/pkg/CRECB-2002-pt17/html/CRECB-2002-pt17-Pg22782-4.htm.

24. Zhi Ming, "The CCP's Nazi Militarism Has Rapidly Become Public, and the 'Dawn Project' to Devour the World Is Being Carried Out in Secret?," *Epoch Times*, October 13, 2009, https://www.epochtimes.com/gb/9/10/13/n2687327.htm.

25. Uy Hoang, "BMA Warns of Arrival of Genetic Weapons," *BMJ* 318 no. 7179 (1999): 283, https://pmc.ncbi.nlm.nih.gov/articles/PMC1114775/.

26. "Chinese Nationals Charged with Conspiracy and Smuggling a Dangerous Biological Pathogen into the U.S. for their Work at a University of Michigan Laboratory," Press Release, U.S. Attorney's Office, Eastern District of Michigan, June 3, 2025, https://www

.justice.gov/usao-edmi/pr/chinese-nationals-charged-conspiracy-and-smuggling-dangerous-biological-pathogen-us.

Chapter 2: Abandoning America for Russia

1. "History of the U.S. and China: U.S. Merchants Look to China," U.S. Embassy & Consulates in China, n.d., https://china.usembassy-china.org.cn/history-of-the-u-s-and-china/#century.

2. David Barboza, "Zuoyue Wang on the History of Chinese Students at U.S. Universities," The Wire China, July 18, 2021, https://www.thewirechina.com/2021/07/18/zuoyue-wang-on-the-history-of-chinese-students-at-u-s-universities/.

3. "The 164th Anniversary of Emory Alumnus Young John Allen, Sailing to China," Emory University Libraries blog, December 15, 2023, https://scholarblogs.emory.edu/woodruff/news/164th-anniversary-emory-alumnus-young-john-allen-sailing-to-china.

4. Adrian A. Bennett, *Missionary Journalist in China: Young J. Allen and His Magazines, 1860–1883* (The University Of Georgia Press, 1983), 181–182.

5. Hu Xiaojin, "The Translation and Dissemination of the American Constitution in China during the Late Qing Dynasty and Early Republic of China," (originally published in *Journal of East China University of Political Science and Law* [Shanghai], 2015, No. 20153) http://iqh.ruc.edu.cn/old/qdzwgxyj/zwgx_yjqy/wh/87f69a97d2844e4f98ad7b4f4ef6bb12.htm.

6. Tien-yi Li, *Woodrow Wilson's China Policy: 1913–1917* (Octagon Book, 1969), 77.

7. Yan Quan, *The Legacy of Failure: China's First Congressional Constitution* (Guangxi Normal University Press, 2007), 45–51.

8. Yan Quan, *The Legacy of Failure*, 6, 18–20.

9. H. G. Wells, *The Shape of Things to Come: The Ultimate Revolution* (Hutchinson, 1933), 96.

10. Lorraine Boissoneault, "The Surprisingly Important Role China Played in WWI," *Smithsonian Magazine*, August 17, 2017, https://www.smithsonianmag.com/history/surprisingly-important-role-china-played-world-war-i-180964532/.

11. Bruce A. Elleman, *Wilson and China: A Revised History of the Shandong Question* (Routledge, Taylor & Francis Ltd, 2015), 74.

12. Elleman, *Wilson and China*, 74.

13. Frances Wood and Christopher Arnander, *Betrayed Ally: China in the Great War* (Pen & Sword Military, 2016), 136.

14. Elleman, *Wilson and China*, 124.

15. Patrick J. Buchanan, *Churchill, Hitler, and "The Unnecessary War": How Britain Lost Its Empire and the West Lost the World* (Crown Publishing Group, 1st ed. 2008), xv.

16. Erez Manela, *The Wilsonian Moment: Self-Determination and the International Origins of Anticolonial Nationalism* (Oxford University Press, 2007), 184.

17. Manela, *The Wilsonian Moment*, 185–186.

18. Manela, *The Wilsonian Moment*, 184.

19. "Karakhan Manifesto," Britannica.com, https://www.britannica.com/event/Karakhan-Manifesto.

20. Elleman, *Wilson and China*, 74.

21. Xu Deheng, "The 100th Anniversary of the May Fourth Movement: Witnessing the May Fourth Movement," The National Committee of the Chinese People's Political Consultative Conference, May 9, 2019, http://www.cppcc.gov.cn/zxww/2019/05/09/ARTI1557361217451103.shtml.

22. "Zhou Enlai was arrested and imprisoned in his early years," Sohu.com, December 22, 2018, https://www.sohu.com/a/283682859_100148674.

23. Wang Shuren, "Famous Communists Who Participated in the May Fourth Movement," Chinaflagnet.com, May 4, 2023, https://www.chinaflagnet.com/post.html?id=64534d83be9bd963cb1770cb.

24. Li Zehou, "The Dual Variation of Enlightenment and Nationalism," *Journal of Modern Chinese Culture and Literature*, 1986. https://www.tandfonline.com/doi/abs/10.2753/CSP1097-1467310240.

25. Zhang Jinchao, "Southern Government and the Paris Peace Conference—A Discussion Centered on the Representation Issue," *Journal of Macau Polytechnic Institute*, Issue 2, 2014.

26. Chen Yongfa, *Seventy Years of the Chinese Communist Revolution*, Volume 1 (United Publishing, 2002), 69–70.

27. Mao Zedong, "On the People's Democratic Dictatorship," In Commemoration of the Twenty-eighth Anniversary of the Communist Party of China, June 30, 1949.

28. Arif Dirlik, *The Origins of Chinese Communism* (Oxford University Press, 1989), 191.

29. Zheng Xuejia, *History of the Chinese Communist Movement*, Volume 2 (National Chengchi University Press, 2019), 143.

30. Ishikawa Yoshihiro and Joshua A. Fogel, *The Formation of the Chinese Communist Party* (Columbia University Press, 2012), 237.

31. Cai Guoyu and Xiao Yu, *History of the Chinese Communist Party 1921–1949* (Wunan Publishing, 2020), 29.

32. Han Yuexiang, "Reflection on the Rationale of the Anti-Christian Movement to Reclaim Educational Rights in Modern China," *Journal of Research for Christianity in China*, 2017, 8.

33. C. Martin Wilbur, *Sun Yat-Sen: Frustrated Patriot (Studies of the East Asian Institute, Columbia University)* (Columbia University Press, 1976), 188.

34. Jessie Gregory Lutz, *Chinese Politics and Christian Missions: The Anti-Christian Movements of 1920–28* (Cross Roads Books, 1988), 96.

35. Viktor Usov, *Soviet Intelligence Agencies in China* (People's Liberation Army Press, 2007), 34–35 (Chinese translation).

36. Li Sida, "Revealed: How did Mao Zedong become the Minister of the Central Propaganda Department of the Kuomintang?" Ifeng.com, August 10, 2016, https://news.ifeng.com/a/20160810/49750822_0.shtml.

37. Dan N. Jacobs, *Borodin: Stalin's Man in China* (Harvard University Press, 1981), 143.

38. Yang Tianshi, *Chiang Kai-shek's Rise and the Northern Expedition* (Fengyun Era, 2009), 168.

39. S. N. Naumov, *Whampoa Military Academy*, translated by the Modern History Research Office of the Chinese Academy of Social Sciences (China Social Sciences Press, 1980), 112.

40. Yang Kuisong, *The Kuomintang's "Alliance with" and "Anti-Communism"* (Social Sciences Academic Press, 2008), 29–33, 45–48.

41. Zhang Yufa, *History of the Republic of China* (Lianjing, 2001), 157–158.

42. Zhang Yufa, *History of the Republic of China,* 89–95.

43. Li Yunhan, *From the Communist Party to the Party Purge* (China Academic Works Award Committee, 1977), 545.

Chapter 3: "Old Friends of the Chinese People"

1. Kevin Peraino, *A Force So Swift: Mao, Truman, and the Birth of Modern China, 1949* (Crown, 2017), 59.

2. Lloyd E. Eastman, *The Abortive Revolution: China under Nationalist Rule, 1927–1937* (Harvard University Press, 1974), 39.

3. Gerard H. Corr, *The Chinese Red Army: Campaigns and Politics Since 1949* (Schocken Books, 1974), 34.

4. Don Lawson, *The Long March: Red China Under Chairman Mao* (Thomas Y. Crowell, 1983), 49, 89.

5. Xie Tianqi, Official CCP records show Mao Zedong thanked Japan at least six times for invading China, *Epoch Times*, January 13, 2017, https://www.epochtimes.com/gb/17/1/12/n8697723.htm.

6. S. Bernard Thomas, *Season of High Adventure: Edgar Snow in China* (University of California Press, 1996), 91–92.

7. Thomas, *Season of High Adventure*, 90.

8. Edgar Snow, *Red Star over China* (Grove Press, Inc., 1938), 65–66.

9. Snow, *Red Star over China*, 69–70.

10. Gao Hua, *How the Red Sun Rose: The Origins and Development of the Yan'an Rectification Movement* (Chinese University of Hong Kong Press, 2000), 154.

11. Jung Chang and Jon Halliday, *Mao: The Unknown Story* (Alfred A. Knopf, 2005), 240.

12. "Bernie Sanders Defends Private Jet Use: 'No Apologies,'" *Fox and Friends*, May 8, 2025, https://www.foxnews.com/video/6372518325112.

13. Wang Shiwei, "Wild Lilies," March 17, 1942, https://www.marxists.org/chinese/reference-books/yanan1942/1-02.htm.

14. Gao Hua, *The Revolutionary Era* (Guangdong People's Publishing House, 2010), 140–141.

15. Thomas, *Season of High Adventure*, 173.

16. Edgar Snow, *The Other Side of the River: Red China Today* (Random House, 1961), 620.

17. National Security Archive Electronic Briefing Book No. 145, https://nsarchive2.gwu.edu/NSAEBB/NSAEBB145/index.htm.

18. Thomas, *Season of High Adventure*, 320–322.

19. Amy Qin, "From Following the Red Star to Criticizing the CCP: Mrs. Snow Was 'Changed' by June 4," *New York Times* Chinese Edition, April 12, 2018, https://cn.nytimes.com/obits/20180412/lois-wheeler-snow-dies/zh-hant/.

20. Amy Qin, "Lois Wheeler Snow, Critic of Human Rights Abuses in China, Dies at 97," *New York Times* (online), April 11, 2018.

21. Janice R. MacKinnon and Stephen R. MacKinnon, *Agnes Smedley: The Life and Times of an American Radical* (University of California Press, 1988), 177.

22. MacKinnon and MacKinnon, *Agnes Smedley*, 177–178.

23. MacKinnon and MacKinnon, *Agnes Smedley*, 172–173.

24. MacKinnon and MacKinnon, *Agnes Smedley*, 184.

25. Helen Foster Snow, *My China Years: A Memoir*, 1st ed. (William Morrow, 1984), 267.

26. Ruth Price, *The Lives of Agnes Smedley* (Oxford University Press, 2005), 130.

27. Price, *The Lives of Agnes Smedley*, 131.

28. MacKinnon and MacKinnon, *Agnes Smedley*, 188–192.

29. Price, *The Lives of Agnes Smedley*, 316–317.

30. MacKinnon and MacKinnon, *Agnes Smedley*, 212.

31. Barbara W. Tuchman, *Stilwell and the American Experience in China, 1911–45* (Macmillan, 1971), 168, 182.

32. Shan Wei, "Anna Louise Strong: 'China is the ideal place to be,'" Party History and Literature Research Institute of the CCP Central Committee, June 21, 2022, https://www.dswxyjy.org.cn/n1/2022/0621/c244516-32452516.html.

33. Banma Gengzhu, "Why Did an American Female Journalist Write 'A Million Slaves Stood Up' 65 Years Ago?" Chinanews.com, March 28, 2024, https://m.chinanews.com/wap/detail/cht/zw/ft10189016.shtml.

34. Joyce Hoffmann, *Theodore H. White and Journalism as Illusion* (University of Missouri Press, 1995), 72.

35. Theodore H. White, *In Search of History: A Personal Adventure* (Warner Books, 1979), 125.

36. Liu Dong, "A View from Abroad," Global Times, October 10, 2012, https://www.globaltimes.cn/content/737470.shtml.

37. "Yan'an: A 'Lab of Democracy'—Gunther Stein Tells the Story of Beans," May 14, 2021, Global Times, https://www.globaltimes.cn/page/202105/1223486.shtml.

38. Gunther Stein, *The Challenge of Red China* (Whittlesey House, 1945), 109.

39. Lu Shunmin, "Memories of Land Reform: Sons Fighting Fathers, Parading Through Streets with Iron Wire Through Nostrils," Folk History Sponsored by the Centre for Chinese Studies, The Chinese University of Hong Kong, June 4, 1989, https://nodebe4.github.io/mjlsh/1989-06-04/鲁顺民-土改记忆-儿斗父-铁丝穿进鼻孔去游街/.

40. "American Expert Han Ding: The First to Introduce China's Land Revolution to the West," xinhuanet.com, August 4, 2015, http://www.xinhuanet.com/world/2015-08/04/c_128089864.htm.

41. Gerald Imray, "'Into the Mouth of Trump Hell'? South African President Says White House Meeting Wasn't So Dramatic," AP, May 21, 2025, https://apnews.com/article/ramaphosa-trump-white-house-south-africa-61f31db77b3650cbb2abfa8945d365b5.

Chapter 4: Losing China to Communism

1. Barbara W. Tuchman, *Stilwell and the American Experience in China*, 320.

2. Tuchman, *Stilwell and the American Experience in China*, 463.

3. Tuchman, *Stilwell and the American Experience in China*, 485.

4. Tuchman, *Stilwell and the American Experience in China*, 485.

5. "Xi Jinping Wrote Back to General Stilwell's Descendants," Chinese Ministry of Foreign Affairs, August 31, 2023, https://www.fmprc.gov.cn/web/zyxw/202308/t20230831_11136016.shtml.

6. S. Bernard Thomas, *Season of High Adventure*, 172.

7. Tuchman, *Stilwell and the American Experience in China*, 464.

8. Richard Bernstein, *China 1945: Mao's Revolution and America's Fateful Choice* (Penguin Random House, 2014), 350.

9. Albert C. Wedemeyer, *Wedemeyer Reports!* (Henry Holt & Company, 1958), 314.

10. Wedemeyer, *Wedemeyer Reports!*, 198.

11. Wedemeyer, *Wedemeyer Reports!*, 290.

12. Joseph W. Esherick and John S. Service, *Lost Chance in China: The World War II Despatches of John S. Service* (Random House, 1974), 371.

13. Bernstein, *China 1945: Mao's Revolution and America's Fateful Choice*, 118.

14. "Service, John S. (John Stewart) (1909–1999)," UMKC University Libraries, https://finding-aids.library.umkc.edu/agents/people/623.

15. Yang Dongquan, "Several Questions about the US Military Observation Group's Inspection of Yan'an in 1944," China Communist Party News Network, September 29, 2015, http://cpc.people.com.cn/n/2015/0929/c69120-27647989.html.

16. *Dixie Mission: The United States Army Observer Group in Yan'an* (Institute of East Asian Studies, 2004), 82–83.

17. *Dixie Mission*, 84.

18. John Byron and Robert Pack, *The Claws of the Dragon: Kang Sheng—The Evil Genius Behind Mao–and His Legacy of Terror in People's China* (Simon & Schuster, 1992), 18, 157, 186.

19. *Zhang Guotao: My Memoirs*, Volume 3 (Ming Pao Monthly, Hong Kong, 1974), 1967.

20. *Chinese Revolution*, Volume 2 (Renmin University of China Press, 1980), 764, 767.

21. "Si Yang, In the Fight Against Japan, Is It the 'Mainstay' or the Preservation of Strength?" Voice of America, June 20, 2021, https://www.voachinese.com/a/distorted-facts-ccp-history-part-4-anti-Japanese-war-20210620/5932547.html.

22. Carolle J. Carter and Michael Schaller, *Mission to Yenan: American Liaison with the Chinese Communists, 1944–1947* (University Press of Kentucky, 1997), 205–206.

23. Wilbur J. Peterkin, *Inside China 1943–1945: An Eyewitness Account of America's Mission to Yenan* (Dixie Mission Books, 1992), 118.

24. Lin Hui, "The Story Behind the US Military Being Deceived into Airlifting 20 Senior PLA Generals," *Epoch Times*, August 11, 2023, https://www.epochtimes.com/gb/23/8/11/n14052185.htm.

25. S. M. Plokhy, *Yalta: The Price of Peace* (Penguin Books, 2014), 218.

26. Plokhy, *Yalta*, 16.

27. Plokhy, *Yalta*, 288.

28. Wedemeyer, *Wedemeyer Reports!*, 428.

29. Li Yingjie, "Exhibition of Japanese Southern Manchuria Arsenal Opens to the Public," People's Information, September 16, 2021, https://baijiahao.baidu.com/s?id=1711094774859294014.

30. Richard C. Thornton, *China: A Political History, 1917–1980* (Westview Press, 1982), 206–207.

31. Zhang Guocheng, *American Decision* (Baqi Culture, 2020), 262.

32. Daniel Kurtz-Phelan, *The China Mission: George Marshall's Unfinished War, 1945–1947* (W. W. Norton & Company, 2018), 2.

33. Debi Unger, Irwin Unger, and Stanley Hirshson, *George Marshall: A Biography* (Harper, 2014), 381–382.

34. Kurtz-Phelan, *The China Mission*, 321.

35. Kurtz-Phelan, *The China Mission*, 319–321.

36. Thornton, *China: A Political History*, 208.

37. John Leighton Stuart, *Fifty Years in China: The Memoirs of John Leighton Stuart, Missionary and Ambassador* (Random House, 1946), xviii–xx.

38. "Nation Mourns Top Soldier," The George C. Marshall Foundation, October 11, 2023, https://www.marshallfoundation.org/articles-and-features/nation-mourns-top-soldier/.

39. Kurtz-Phelan, *The China Mission*, 350–351.

40. William Manchester, *American Caesar: Douglas MacArthur 1880–1964* (Little, Brown and Company, 1978), 802.

41. John J. McLaughlin, *General Albert C. Wedemeyer: America's Unsung Strategist in World War II* (Casemate, 2012), 146.

42. McLaughlin, *General Albert C. Wedemeyer*, 151.

43. Stuart, *Fifty Years in China*, 155.

44. Stuart, *Fifty Years in China*, 220.

45. Stuart, *Fifty Years in China*, 75.

46. Bibliographic Dictionary of Chinese Christianity, https://web.archive.org/web/20141013174158/http://www.bdcconline.net/en/stories/s/sailer-randolph-c.php.

47. Stuart, *Fifty Years in China*, 211–12.

48. Stuart, *Fifty Years in China*, 247–248.

49. Lu Zhiwei, "Proud Integrity, Seeking Only a Clear Conscience," Guangming Daily Online, September 3, 2011, https://web.archive.org/web/20131203140819/http://history.gmw.cn/2011-09/03/content_2579679.htm.

Chapter 5: The Opening That Saved the Party

1. Andrew Bernstein, "The Vindication of Joseph McCarthy," The Objective Standard, November 19, 2016, https://www.theobjectivestandard.com/p/vindication-joseph-mccarthy.

2. Tan Song, *Bloody Red Land: Interviews on the CCP Land Reform* (Asia-Pacific Political Philosophy and Culture Publishing House, 2019), 75.

3. "The Brutality of the CCP's Land Reform Continues to This Day," Radio Free China, February 8, 2019, https://www.rfa.org/mandarin/yataibaodao/shehui/yl-02082019115356.html.

4. Lin Hui, "How Many Landlords Were Suppressed in The Early Days of the CCP?" *Epoch Times*, August 13, 2011, https://www.epochtimes.com/gb/11/8/13/n3342975.htm.

5. Frank Dikötter, *Mao's Great Famine: The History of China's Most Devastating Catastrophe, 1958–1962* (Walker & Company, 2010), 325.

6. Li Jingduan, "Reminiscing About the Ideological Reform of Teachers 60 Years Ago," China Writers Network, December 31, 2013, https://www.chinawriter.com.cn/2013/2013-12-31/186871.html.

7. Li Yang, "The Ins and Outs of the First Ideological Reform Movement after the Founding of the People's Republic of China," Internet Archive, August 5, 2012, (originally published in *China Social Guide*, Issue 11, 2004) https://web.archive.org/web/20160519053222/http://www.21ccom.net/articles/lsjd/lsjj/article_2012080565105.html.

8. Edward, "A Record of Communist Tyranny: The Anti-Rightist Movement," *Epoch Times*, Janurary 10, 2018, https://www.epochtimes.com/b5/18/1/10/n10044605.htm.

9. "He Ke, Niu Youlan, an Enlightened Gentry in Land Reform," www.CND.org, December 5, 2020, http://hx.cnd.org/?p=191071.

10. William J. Tompson, *Khrushchev: A Political Life* (Palgrave Macmillan, 1997), 208.

11. "Qian Xuesen: The Man the US Deported—Who Then Helped China Into Space," BBC, October 26, 2020, https://www.bbc.com/news/stories-54695598.

12. Sergey Radchenko, "The Island That Changed History," *New York Times*, March 2, 2019, https://www.nytimes.com/2019/03/02/opinion/soviet-russia-china-war.html.

13. S. Bernard Thomas, *Season of High Adventure*, 329.

14. John P. Glennon and Harriet D. Schwar, *Foreign Relations of the United States, 1955–1957* (United States Government Printing Office, Volume 2, 1986), 422.

15. Glennon and Schwar, *Foreign Relations.*

16. "Address by the Secretary of State, San Francisco, June 28, 1957," Department of State, Office of the Historian, https://history.state.gov/historicaldocuments/frus1955-57v03/d268.

17. John Lewis Gaddis, *Strategies of Containment: A Critical Appraisal of American National Security Policy During the Cold War* (Oxford University Press, 2005), 33.

18. Gaddis, *Strategies of Containment*, 114.

19. Gaddis, *Strategies of Containment*, 285.

20. Gaddis, *Strategies of Containment*, 282.

21. James Mann, *About Face: A History of America's Curious Relationship with China, from Nixon to Clinton* (Alfred Knopf, First Vintage Books edition, 2000), 8.

22. "People's Daily and Christopher Nixon Cox Discuss US–China Relations in New Documentary Series," PR Newswire, January 24, 2020, https://www.prnewswire.com/news-releases/peoples-daily-and-christopher-nixon-cox-discuss-us-china-relations-in-new-documentary-series-300992946.html.

Chapter 6: From Misjudgment to Surrender: Presidential Failures on China

1. "Trump Says Nixon Helping Open China Is 'Worst Thing' He Ever Did," Forbes Breaking News, YouTube.com, https://www.youtube.com/watch?v=GELiBIgz9-Y.

2. Literature Research Office of the CPC Central Committee, *Biography of Mao Zedong 1949–1976* (Central Literature Publishing House, 2003), 939.

3. "336 Million Chinese Abortions in 40 Years," Al Jazeera, March 16, 2013, https://www.aljazeera.com/news/2013/3/16/336-million-chinese-abortions-in-40-years#:~:text=Data%20posted%20on%20the%20health,have%20performed%20336%20million%20abortions.

4. "Answers to the Italian Journalist Oriana Fallaci," The Selected Works of Deng Ziaoping, August 21 and 23, 1980, https://dengxiaopingworks.wordpress.com/2013/02/25/answers-to-the-italian-journalist-oriana-fallaci/.

5. Patrick E. Tyler, "Deng Xiaoping: A Political Wizard Who Put China on the Capitalist Road," *New York Times*, February 20, 1997.

6. Jimmy Carter, 39th President of the United States: 1977–1981, Address at Commencement Exercises at the University of Notre Dame.

7. Huang Xiang: Democracy Wall and China's New Poetry Movement (Part 2), *Epoch Times*, December 10, 2006, https://www.epochtimes.com/gb/6/12/9/n1551070.htm.

8. James Chau, "39 on 40: An Interview with Jimmy Carter," China-U.S. Focus, January 21, 2019, https://www.chinausfocus.com/foreign-policy/39-on-40-an-interview-with-jimmy-carter.

9. Ronald Reagan, Address at Commencement Exercises at the University of Notre Dame, May 17, 1981.

10. Reagan Doctrine, 1985, U.S. Department of State Archive, https://2001-2009.state.gov/r/pa/ho/time/rd/17741.htm.

11. James Mann, *About Face* (Knopf Doubleday, 2000), 55.

12. "Remarks Upon Returning from China," Ronald Reagan Presidential Library, May 1, 1984, https://www.reaganlibrary.gov/archives/speech/remarks-upon-returning-china.

13. Robert Service, *The End of the Cold War: 1985–1991* (Hachette, 2015), 94.

14. Ezra F. Vogel, *Deng Xiaoping and the Transformation of China* (Harvard University Press, 2011), 649.

15. Vogel, *Deng Xiaoping and the Transformation of China*, 650.

16. Ted Galen Carpenter, "George H.W. Bush's Shameful Kowtow to China: a Cautionary Tale," Cato Institute, May 27, 2020, https://www.cato.org/commentary/george-hw-bushs-shameful-kowtow-china-cautionary-tale.

17. Isaac Stone Fish, *America Second: How America's Elites Are Making China Stronger* (Knopf, first edition, 2022), 42.

18. Service, *The End of the Cold War*, 446.

19. "After 50 Years of Denial, an Apology," *Tampa Bay Times*, April 14, 1990, https://www.tampabay.com/archive/1990/04/14/after-50-years-of-denial-an-apology/.

20. "Looking for China's Gorbachev: The Tiananmen Square Incident That Turned into Tanks Suppressing Students," Apollo Network, August 31, 2020, https://www.aboluowang.com/2022/0831/1796863.html.

21. Fish, *America Second*, 62.

22. Nicholas D. Kristof, "Martial Law Ends in Tibet's Capital," *New York Times*, May 1, 1990, A13.

23. Hai Yan, "Chinese Media Generally Have a Favorable Impression of Bush Sr. and Call Him an Old Friend," Voice of America, December 2, 2018, https://www.voachinese.com/a/China-Reaction-To-Death-Of-Bush-Senior-20181202/4683387.html.

24. Li Jingjing, "Will China and U.S. get along?," YouTube, September 20, 2024, https://www.youtube.com/watch?v=vOSp-Lyfob4.

25. "Candidates Play It Safe When It Comes to China," *New York Times* (online), April 15, 2008.

26. Lena H. Sun, "Chinese Rebuff Christopher on Human Rights; Dissident Movement Makes Comeback-In Small Units," *Washington Post*, March 13, 1994, A01.

27. Jim Mann, "Clinton to Set Human Rights Guidelines for Firms Overseas Policy: Principles Drawn Up with China in Mind Have Been Broadened. Support from U.S. Business Leaders Is Paltry," *Los Angeles Times*, January 13, 1995.

28. Bill Clinton, *My Life* (Vintage, Penguin Random House, 2013), 793.

29. Adam Taylor, "The Failed Boycott of the 2008 Beijing Olympics Hangs over This Year's Boycott," *Washington Post*, February 3, 2022.

30. George W. Bush, *Decision Points* (Penguin Random House, 2010), 429.

31. "Survey: Most Americans Now Have an Unfavorable Impression of China," USC U.S.–China Institute, March 5, 2008, https://china.usc.edu/survey-most-americans-now-have-unfavorable-impression-china.

32. Gordon Lubold, "Obama Says U.S. Will No Longer Be the World's Policeman," *Foreign Policy*, May 28, 2014, https://foreignpolicy.com/2014/05/28/obama-says-u-s-will-no-longer-be-the-worlds-policeman/.

33. Linda Feldmann, "Chaos in Copenhagen: Behind the Scenes at Global Warming Summit," *Christian Science Monitor*, December 20, 2009, https://www.csmonitor.com/USA/Politics/The-Vote/2009/1220/Chaos-in-Copenhagen-behind-the-scenes-at-global-warming-summit.

34. Michael Wines and Sharon LaFraniere, "During Visit, Obama Skirts Chinese Political Sensitivities," *New York Times* (online), November 17, 2009.

35. "Xi, Obama Meeting: A Lively History Lesson," *China Daily*, November 15, 2014, https://www.chinadaily.com.cn/china/2014-11/15/content_18920403.htm.

36. Mark Landler and Jane Perlez, "Obama Plays Down Confrontation with China Over His Plane's Stairs," *New York Times*, September 5, 2016.

37. "Trump Says He Would Have Left G-20 Summit in China Over Obama Staircase Flap," *Chicago Tribune*, August 22, 2019, https://www.chicagotribune.com/2016/09/05/trump-says-he-would-have-left-g-20-summit-in-china-over-obama-staircase-flap/.

38. Jane Perlez, "Muted U.S. Response to China's Seizure of Drone Worries Asian Allies," *New York Times*, December 18, 2016, https://www.nytimes.com/2016/12/18/world/asia/muted-us-response-to-chinas-seizure-of-drone-worries-asian-allies.html.

39. The full text of the China–U.S. talks is here: https://www.kunlunce.com/ssjj/guojipinglun/2021-03-20/151161.html.

Chapter 7: The Rise of the CCP's Wealth

1. Xi Jinping, Speech at the Celebration of the 40th Anniversary of Reform and Opening Up, http://www.xinhuanet.com/politics/leaders/2018-12/18/c_1123868586.htm.

2. Lu Feng, "Quantitative Estimation of Wages of Migrant Workers in China (1979–2010)," National School of Development, Peking University, November 28, 2011, https://nsd.pku.edu.cn/pub/chnsd/attachments/6548c6f9e6314a4fb20a4efdec5ff4a2.pdf.

3. Aditya Chakrabortty, "The Woman Who Nearly Died Making Your iPad," *The Guardian*, August 13, 2025, https://www.theguardian.com/commentisfree/2013/aug/05/woman-nearly-died-making-ipad.

4. Dennis Normile, "One in Three Chinese Children Faces an Education Apocalypse. An Ambitious Experiment Hopes to Save Them," *Science*, September 21, 2017, https://www.science.org/content/article/one-three-chinese-children-faces-education-apocalypse-ambitious-experiment-hopes-save.

5. Chris Buckley, "Why Parts of Beijing Look Like a Devastated War Zone," *New York Times*, November 30, 2017, https://www.nytimes.com/2017/11/30/world/asia/china-beijing-migrants.html.

6. Scott Neuman, "SOS Note, Prison ID Reportedly Found in Chinese-Made Pants," The Two-Way, NPR, June 25, 2014, https://www.npr.org/sections/thetwo-way/2014/06/25/325633408/sos-note-prison-id-reportedly-found-in-chinese-made-pants.

7. Laurel Wamsley, "6-Year-Old Finds Message Alleging Chinese Prison Labor in Box of Christmas Cards," NPR, December 23, 2019, https://www.npr.org/2019/12/23/790832681/6-year-old-finds-message-alleging-chinese-prison-labor-in-box-of-christmas-cards.

8. Hal Brands, "China Is Running out of Water and That's Scary for Asia," American Enterprise Institute, December 29, 2021, https://www.aei.org/op-eds/china-is-running-out-of-water-and-thats-scary-for-asia/.

9. "China to Shut Factories Ahead of Olympics—Sources," Reuters, July 4, 2008, https://www.reuters.com/article/economy/china-to-shut-factories-ahead-of-olympics-sources-idUSSP38342/.

10. Steve Scauzillo, "Air Pollution from China Undermining Gains in California, Western States," *San Gabriel Valley Tribune*, August 30, 2017, https://www.sgvtribune.com/2015/08/11/air-pollution-from-china-undermining-gains-in-california-western-states/.

11. Andrew Gregory, "Lung Cancer Diagnoses on the Rise Among Never-Smokers Worldwide," *The Guardian*, February 3, 2025, https://www.theguardian.com/society/2025/feb/03/lung-cancer-never-smokers-rise-worldwide-air-pollution.

12. Tim Pearce, "Trump Is Right: China Is Literally Building an Island Made of Trash," Daily Wire, April 23, 2025, https://www.dailywire.com/news/trump-is-right-china-is-literally-building-an-island-made-of-trash.

13. Jeff Ferry, "Top Ten Cases of Chinese IP Theft," Coalition for a Prosperous America, May 1, 2018, https://prosperousamerica.org/top-ten-cases-of-chinese-ip-theft/.

14. Matt Ridley, *How Innovation Works: And Why It Flourishes in Freedom* (HarperCollins, 2020), 360, 373.

15. Pratik Jakhar, "Who really came up with China's 'four new inventions'?," BBC, April 2, 2018, https://www.bbc.com/news/world-asia-china-43406560.

16. "China 'Copycat' Ninebot Buys Segway," Industry Week, April 15, 2015, https://www.industryweek.com/innovation/intellectual-property/article/21964979/china-copycat-ninebot-buys-segway.

17. Ben Penn and Patricia Hurtado, "Tesla Trade Secrets Stolen by Chinese Company's Owners, US Says," Bloomberg Law, March 19, 2024, https://news.bloomberglaw.com/us-law-week/tesla-trade-secrets-stolen-by-chinese-companys-owners-us-says.

18. Leo Timm, "Quality, Safety Concerns of Chinese-made EVs Come to the Fore," Vision Times, May 29, 2024, https://www.visiontimes.com/2024/05/29/quality-safety-concerns-of-chinese-made-evs-come-to-the-fore.html.

19. Brandon J. Weichert, "The Curious Case of China's Quest for 'Invisibility Cloak,'" Asia Times, July 30, 2021, https://asiatimes.com/2021/07/the-curious-case-of-chinas-quest-for-invisibility-cloak/?utm_source=chatgpt.com#.

20. Jianli Yang, "How COVID-19 Affects U.S.-China Trade Deal," Washington International Trade Association, August 7, 2020, https://www.wita.org/blogs/how-covid-19-affects-u-s-china/.

21. Diyar Guldogan, "Boeing 'Should Default China' for Not Taking Planes: Trump," Anadolu Agency, April 24, 2025, https://www.aa.com.tr/en/americas/boeing-should-default-china-for-not-taking-planes-trump/3547873.

22. Emma Farge, "Exclusive: US Pauses Financial Contributions to WTO, Trade Sources Say," Reuters, March 27, 2025, https://www.reuters.com/world/us-suspends-financial-contributions-wto-trade-sources-say-2025-03-27/.

23. Chay Bowes (@BowesChay), X, January 17, 2025, https://x.com/BowesChay/status/1880210578825965737.

24. Liu Ruifu, "The Fundamental Difference Between China's Independent and Fair Judiciary and Western Countries' 'Judicial Independence,'" Chinese Communist Party Online, December 26, 2014, http://theory.people.com.cn/n/2014/1226/c143844-26280659-2.html.

25. "Beijing Issues Order to Demolish Petition Village, Human Rights Groups Call for Halt," Voice of America, September 6, 2007, https://www.voachinese.com/a/a-21-w2007-09-06-voa29-63222062/970470.html.

26. Li Xin'an, "709 Case: The Third Climax of the CCP's Persecution of Human Rights Lawyers," *Epoch Times*, July 11, 2018, https://www.epochtimes.com/gb/18/7/9/n10549209.htm.

27. Jason Smith (@shangguanjiewen), X, January 20, 2025, https://x.com/shangguanjiewen/status/1881508695282221191?t=FCcFwC0GnxUo6db5l0E-Fg.

28. Nicholas Yong, "Jack Ma: Alibaba Founder Seen in China after Long Absence," BBC, March 27, 2023, https://www.bbc.com/news/world-asia-china-65084344.

29. Ou Xifu, "China's Stability Maintenance Fees Continue to Rise," Institute for National Defense and Security Research, March 22, 2019, https://indsr.org.tw/respublicationcon?uid=12&resid=692&pid=2366.

30. "China Keeps Parade Costs Secret While Rewarding Attending Nations," Voice of America, September 6, 2015, https://www.voachinese.com/a/china-parade-20150906/2949766.html.

31. "Jiang Zemin's Family Stole Huge Amounts of State Assets and Hid Them Overseas," *Epoch Times*, June 3, 2019, https://www.epochtimes.com/gb/19/6/2/n11294864.htm.

32. Nick Koutsobinas, "China President Xi Worth $700 Million, Congressional Report Says," Newsmax, June 9, 2024, https://www.newsmax.com/newsfront/xi-jinping-china-corruption/2024/06/09/id/1168077/.

33. Zhang Jing, "The CCP's Sky-High Stability Maintenance Fees Have Long Become a Black Industry Chain," *Epoch Times*, December 1, 2024, https://www.epochtimes.com/gb/24/11/30/n14382086.htm.

34. Li Keqiang, "600 Million People in China Have a Monthly Income of 1,000 Yuan, with an Average Annual Income of 30,000 Yuan," huanqiu.com, May 28, 2020, https://china.huanqiu.com/article/3yQjRYQnUhh.

35. Sean McMeekin, *To Overthrow the World: The Rise and Fall and Rise of Communism* (Basic Books, 2024), 415.

36. Nate Cardozo and Sophia Cope, "Cisco's Latest Attempt to Dodge Responsibility for Facilitating Human Rights Abuses: Export Rules," Electronic Frontier Foundation, April

18, 2016, https://www.eff.org/deeplinks/2016/04/ciscos-latest-attempt-dodge-responsibility-facilitating-human-rights-abuses-export.

37. Travis Kliever, "China's Social Credit System [Punishments & Rewards] in 2025", Remote Pad, October 13, 2025, https://globalizationpedia.com/china-social-credit-system-advanced-guide/.

Chapter 8: Claws of the Dragon Reaching Inside America

1. Jonathan Manthorpe, *Claws of the Panda: Beijing's Campaign of Influence and Intimidation in Canada* (Cormorant Books Incorporated, first edition, 2019), 44.

2. "Putting Money in the Party's Mouth: How China Mobilizes Funding for United Front Work," Center for Security and Emerging Technology, Georgetown University, September 16, 2020, https://cset.georgetown.edu/article/putting-money-in-the-partys-mouth-how-china-mobilizes-funding-for-united-front-work/.

3. Yi-Zheng Lian, "China Has a Vast Influence Machine, and You Don't Even Know It," *New York Times* (online), May 21, 2018.

4. Frank Dikötter, *China After Mao: The Rise of a Superpower* (Bloomsbury Publishing, 2022), 145.

5. James T. Areddy and Charles Hutzler, "In China, Henry Kissinger Was the Ultimate Door-Opener," *Wall Street Journal*, November 30, 2023.

6. Barbara Starr and Ryan Browne, "Trump Administration Removes Experts from Defense Policy Board," CNN, November 26, 2020, https://www.cnn.com/2020/11/26/politics/trump-administration-defense-policy-board/index.html.

7. John Kirby, "'Unfortunate' Kissinger Has More Attention in China," Yahoo!News (video), July 21, 2023, https://www.yahoo.com/news/kirby-unfortunate-kissinger-more-attention-090302110.html.

8. "Di Dongsheng Reveals That the CCP Is Infiltrating the United States," *Epoch Times*, December 8, 2020, https://www.epochtimes.com/gb/20/12/8/n12603896.htm.

9. "The Bidens' Influence Peddling Timeline," Committee on Oversight and Government Reform, n.d., https://oversight.house.gov/the-bidens-influence-peddling-timeline/.

10. "Joe Biden Met Nearly Every Foreign Associate Funneling His Family Millions," Committee on Oversight and Government Reform, February 14, 2024, https://oversight.house.gov/blog/joe-biden-met-nearly-every-foreign-associate-funneling-his-family-millions%EF%BF%BC/.

11. Kelly Laco, "Joe Biden Met with Now-Missing Chinese Oil Giant Chairman Ye Jianming But Claimed He Was Just 'Checking In' on Drug Addict Son, According to Hunter's Business Partner," *Daily Mail*, January 29, 2024, https://www.dailymail.co.uk/news/article-13019339/joe-biden-chinese-oil-chairman-ye-jianming-hunter-biden.html.

12. Joe Schoffstall and Cameron Cawthorne, "UPenn, Which Hosts Biden's Think Tank, Sees Chinese Donations Soar, Including from CCP-Linked Sources," Fox News, January 18, 2024, https://www.foxnews.com/politics/university-housing-bidens-think-tank-recently-experienced-a-surge-of-chinese-donations-records-show.

13. Anna Gronewold, "Pompeo To Governors: China Is Watching You," Politico, February 8, 2020, https://www.politico.com/news/2020/02/08/mike-pompeo-governors-china-112539.

14. Steven W. Mosher, "Tim Walz Defended Communism in China to His Students: 'Everyone Is the Same and Everyone Shares,'" Population Research Institute, August 26, 2024, https://www.pop.org/tim-walz-defended-communism-in-china-to-his-students-everyone-is-the-same-and-everyone-shares/.

15. Alana Goodman, "Walz Praised Chinese Communism as a System Where 'Everyone Shares,'"Washington Free Beacon, August 19, 2024, https://freebeacon.com/elections/walz-praised-chinese-communism-as-a-system-where-everyone-shares/.

16. Dan Swinhoe, "Apple Officially Opens Data Center in China," DCD, May 28, 2021, https://www.datacenterdynamics.com/en/news/apple-officially-opens-data-center-in-china/.

17. Wes Davis, "Apple Is Locking Down the iPhone App Store to Comply with a New Law in China," The Verge, October 3, 2023, https://www.theverge.com/2023/10/3/23901205/apple-app-store-government-license-china.

18. "Apple Boss Hails China Ties," RT, March 26, 2023, https://www.rt.com/business/573614-apple-cook-ties-china/.

19. "Report: China Steps Up Nationwide Ban on iPhones," PYMNTS, December 17, 2023, https://www.pymnts.com/apple/2023/report-china-steps-up-nationwide-ban-on-iphones.

20. Andy Hirschfeld, "Apple to Move Assembly of US Phones to India in Shift Away from China," Al Jazeera, April 25, 2025, https://www.aljazeera.com/economy/2025/4/25/apple-to-move-assembly-of-us-phones-to-india-in-shift-away-from-china.

21. Joanna Chiu, "China: Report reveals Microsoft & Google incubator programmes backed surveillance startups, sparking human rights concerns," Business and Human Rights Resource Centre, November 19, 2024, https://www.business-humanrights.org/en/latest-news/china-report-reveals-microsoft-and-google-incubators-backed-surveillance-startups-sparking-human-rights-concerns/.

22. Marcus Gilmer, "Mark Zuckerberg Talked Baby Names with the President of China During Facebook's Charm Campaign," Mashable, September 18, 2017, https://mashable.com/article/zuckerberg-chinese-president-baby-names.

23. "Mark Zuckerberg Keeps a Book Written by the President of China on His Desk," Business Insider, December 8, 2014, https://www.businessinsider.com/mark-zuckerberg-keeps-a-book-written-by-the-president-of-china-on-his-desk-2014-12.

24. Katie Razzall and Sarah Bell, "Facebook Was 'Hand in Glove' With China, BBC Told," BBC, March 10, 2025, https://www.bbc.com/news/articles/cly820v99ppo.

25. Matt Pottinger, "A U.S. Flop, American's Book on Jiang Zemin Wows China," *Wall Street Journal*, Eastern edition, March 9, 2005, B.1.

26. Robert Lawrence Kuhn and Bruce Gilley, "One Country, Two Prisms," *Foreign Affairs*, January/February 2006, https://www.foreignaffairs.com/articles/asia/2006-01-01/one-country-two-prisms.

27. Michael Forsythe and Eric Lipton, "For the Chao Family, Deep Ties to the World's 2 Largest Economies," *New York Times*, June 2, 2019, https://www.nytimes.com/2019/06/02/us/politics/transportation-secretary-elaine-chao.html.

28. Peter Schweizer, *Secret Empires: How the American Political Class Hides Corruption and Enriches Family and Friends* (Harper, first edition, 2018), 75–76.

29. Schweizer, *Secret Empires*, 87.

30. Michael Stumo, "How McConnell and Chao Used Political Power to Make Their Family Rich," Coalition for a Prosperous America, March 19, 2018, https://prosperousamerica.org/how-mcconnell-and-chao-used-political-power-to-make-their-family-rich/.

31. Full Text of Xi Jinping's Report at 19th CPC National Congress, *China Daily*, November 4, 2017, https://www.chinadaily.com.cn/china/19thcpcnationalcongress/2017-11/04/content_34115212.htm.

32. Dan Hart, "Boston Mayor Michelle Wu Received $300K in Campaign Funds from CCP Operative," Washington Stand, April 16, 2025, https://washingtonstand.com/news/report-boston-mayor-michelle-wu-received-300k-in-campaign-funds-from-ccp-operative.

33. Philip Lenczycki, "EXCLUSIVE: How Chinese Intel Infiltrated LA Mayor Karen Bass' Camp," Daily Caller, June 16, 2025, https://www.aol.com/exclusive-chinese-intel-infiltrated-la-220002793.html.

34. James T. Areddy, "How Beijing Recruited New York Chinatowns for Influence Campaign," *Wall Street Journal* (online), October 22, 2024.

35. Didi Kirsten Tatlow, "Exclusive: 600 U.S. Groups Linked to Chinese Communist Party Influence Effort with Ambition Beyond Election," *Newsweek*, October 26, 2020, https://www.newsweek.com/2020/11/13/exclusive-600-us-groups-linked-chinese-communist-party-influence-effort-ambition-beyond-1541624.html.

36. Randall, "Asian American Groups Condemn House Passage of China Initiative," AsAm News, September 12, 2024, https://asamnews.com/2024/09/12/anti-china-racial-profiling-legislation-gop-china-week/.

37. "Asian Americans Advancing Justice—AAJC Submits Letter Opposing Reauthorization of the House Select Committee on the Chinese Communist Party in Upcoming Congress," Asian Americans Advancing Justice, December 10, 2024, https://www.advancingjustice-aajc.org/press-release/asian-americans-advancing-justice-aajc-submits-letter-opposing-reauthorization-house.

38. "Asian American Community and Allies Rally Against Florida's Anti-Chinese Land Law After Court Hearings," Stop AAPI Hate, April 19, 2024, https://stopaapihate.org/2024/04/19/asian-american-community-and-allies-rally-against-floridas-anti-chinese-land-law-after-court-hearings/.

39. "Twitter's Hiring of China-Linked AI Expert Sparks Concern," Radio Free Asia, May 20, 2020, https://www.rfa.org/english/news/china/concern-05202020134312.html.

40. Xiang Ling, "Spy Cases Continue. The CCP Has Extensively Infiltrated the Overseas Chinese Democracy Movement," Voice of America, August 23, 2024, https://www.voachinese.com/a/observing-the-ccps-infiltration-of-overseas-democratic-movements-through-shujun-wangs-case-20240820/7750206.html.

41. "Chinese Communist Leaders Denounce U.S. Values but Send Children to U.S. Colleges," *Washington Post*, May 19, 2012.

42. Steven Erlanger, "The Jiang Visit: The Overview; China's President Draws Applause at Harvard Talk," *New York Times*, November 2, 1997.

43. William J. Dobson, "The East Is Crimson," Slate, May 23, 2012, https://www.slate.com/articles/news_and_politics/foreigners/2012/05/harvard_and_the_chinese_communist_party_top_chinese_officials_are_studying_at_elite_u_s_universities_in_large_numbers_.html?utm_source=chatgpt.com.

44. Jessica Costescu, "Harvard Quietly Trained Members of Chinese 'Paramilitary Organization'—After the US Sanctioned It Over Uyghur Genocide," Washington Free Beacon, April 28, 2025, https://freebeacon.com/campus/harvard-quietly-trained-members-of-chinese-paramilitary-organization-after-the-us-sanctioned-it-over-uyghur-genocide/.

45. "Harvard Accused of Bias for Punishing Anti-CCP Protesters while Apologising to Pro-CCP Attacker, Reveals US Committee," Asian News International, May 24, 2025, https://aninews.in/news/world/asia/harvard-accused-of-bias-for-punishing-anti-ccp-protesters-while-apologising-to-pro-ccp-attacker-reveals-us-committee20250524142149/.

46. Costescu, "Harvard Quietly Trained..."

47. "Confucius Institutes Have Been Running for Decades, with an Investment of Nearly US$1 Billion," Guangzhou NetEase Computer System Co., March 7, 2022, https://www.163.com/dy/article/H1ROSHUS0552C574.html.

48. Aleks Phillips, "China's Influence in U.S. Public Schools: What We Know, What We Don't," *Newsweek*, September 20, 2023, https://www.newsweek.com/chinese-influence-us-public-schools-what-we-know-1828571.

49. "Little Red Classrooms," Defending Education, July 26, 2023, https://defendinged.org/investigations/little-red-classrooms-china-infiltration-of-american-k-12-schools/.

50. Lin Xiaoyi, "Xi's Letter Strengthens Decades-Long Friendship with Muscatine Residents, Boosts China–US Youth Exchanges," Global Times, March 14, 2024, https://www.globaltimes.cn/page/202403/1308868.shtml.

51. "Two Major Methods Used by the CCP to Infiltrate the United States," Vision Times, April 5, 2024, https://www.secretchina.com/news/gb/2024/04/05/1058857.html.

52. Dikötter, *China After Mao*, 145.

53. Evelyn Cheng, "How an Interview with One Chinese Billionaire Threw a US Broadcaster into Turmoil," CNBC, June 9, 2017, https://www.cnbc.com/2017/06/09/interview-with-guo-wengui-throws-voice-of-america-into-turmoil.html.

54. Sasha Gong, "Voice of America Lost: A Decline in Mission and Influence," American Greatness, March 12, 2025, https://amgreatness.com/2025/03/12/voice-of-america-lost-a-decline-in-mission-and-influence/.

55. Isaac Stone Fish, "Chinese Ownership Is Raising Questions About the Editorial Independence of a Major U.S. Magazine," *Washington Post*, December 14, 2017, https://www.washingtonpost.com/news/democracy-post/wp/2017/12/14/chinese-ownership-is-raising-questions-about-the-editorial-independence-of-a-major-u-s-magazine/.

56. Christopher Paul, "How China Plays By Different Rules—At Everyone Else's Expense," *The Hill*, February 6, 2022, https://thehill.com/opinion/technology/592998-how-china-plays-by-different-rules-at-everyone-elses-expense/.

57. Shannon Bond, "China Is Pushing Divisive Political Messages Online Using Fake U.S. Voters," KPBS/NPR, September 3, 2024, https://www.kpbs.org/news/national/2024/09/03/china-is-pushing-divisive-political-messages-online-using-fake-u-s-voters.

58. Ziva Dahl, "China Uses Hollywood in Its Information Warfare Campaign," *Newsweek*, February 3, 2021, https://www.newsweek.com/china-uses-hollywood-its-information-warfare-campaign-opinion-1566300.

59. Tatiana Siegel, "Richard Gere's Studio Exile: Why His Hollywood Career Took an Indie Turn," *Hollywood Reporter*, April 18, 2017, https://www.hollywoodreporter.com/movies/movie-features/richard-geres-studio-exile-why-his-hollywood-career-took-an-indie-turn-992258/.

60. Mark Alan Burger, "That Time Brad Pitt Was Banned from China," *Interview*, December 20, 2019, https://www.interviewmagazine.com/film/that-time-brad-pitt-was-banned-in-china-seven-years-in-tibet.

61. Daniel Victor, "N.B.A.'s Warriors Disavow Part-Owner's Uyghur Comments," *New York Times*, January 18, 2022, https://www.nytimes.com/2022/01/18/sports/basketball/warriors-chamath-palihapitiya-uyghurs-nba.html.

62. Dawn Liu and Linda Givetash, "NBA Fan Event in China Canceled Amid Fallout over Hong Kong Tweet," NBC News, October 9, 2019, https://www.nbcnews.com/news/world/nba-fan-event-china-canceled-amid-fallout-over-hong-kong-n1064101.

63. "James Harden Apologizes as Controversy Grows: 'We love China,'" ESPN, October 6, 2019, https://www.espn.com/nba/story/_/id/27787634/james-harden-apologizes-controversy-grows-love-china.

64. Billie Thomson, "Houston Rockets Player Russell Westbrook Is Hailed as a Hero in China After Wearing a Traditional Chinese Coat to a Press Conference Amid Intensifying Row Between Beijing and the NBA Over Hong Kong Protests," *Daily Mail*, October 9, 2019, https://www.dailymail.co.uk/news/article-7554615/Houston-Rockets-player-Russell-Westbrook-hailed-hero-China-wearing-Chinese-top.html.

65. Peter Mattis, "PRC Malign Influence at Home and Abroad—Peter Mattis's Testimony Before the Senate Foreign Relations Committee," Jamestown Perspectives, The Jamestown Foundation, March 31, 2025, https://jamestown.org/program/prc-malign-influence-at-home-and-abroad-peter-mattiss-testimony-before-the-senate-foreign-relations-committee/.

Chapter 9: Taiwan: The Betrayal and Great Triumph

1. Lee Teng-Hui, *The Road to Democracy: Taiwan's Pursuit of Identity* (PHP Institute, Inc., 1999), 36.

2. George H. Kerr, *Formosa Betrayed* (Houghton Mifflin, 1965), 39.

3. Du Zujian, ed., *An Island's Confidant: Taiwan Expert George H. Kerr and His Story* (Avant-Garde Publishing, 2022), 37.

4. Sulmaan Wasif Khan, *The Struggle for Taiwan: A History of America, China and the Island Caught Between* (Basic Books, 2024), 47. (EPUB)

5. Statement by the President on the Situation in Korea, June 27, 1950, Harry S. Truman Library and Museum, https://www.trumanlibrary.gov/library/public-papers/173/statement-president-situation-korea.

6. William Manchester, *American Caesar* (Little, Brown and Company, 1978), 568.

7. Manchester, *American Caesar*, 498.

8. Manchester, *American Caesar*, 557.

9. Manchester, *American Caesar*, 563.

10. Manchester, *American Caesar*, 639.

11. Chiang Kai-shek, Mourning for the late US Marshal MacArthur, Chiang Kai-shek Cultural and Educational Foundation, April 10, 1964, http://www.ccfd.org.tw/ccef001/index.php?option=com_content&view=article&id=439:0002-145&catid=349&Itemid=256.

12. Jonathan Fenby, *Generalissimo: Chiang Kai-Shek and the China He Lost* (Da Capo Press, 2010), 62–63.

13. Lee Teng-Hui, *The Road to Democracy*, (Dell Publishing Company, 1st ed., 1999), 39-40.

14. Yu Jie, *Reformers in Disguise: Deciphering the Myths of Deng Xiaoping and Chiang Ching-kuo* (Eight Banners Culture, 2022), 128–129.

15. Chen Cuilian, *Reexamining Postwar Taiwan's Political History: The Three-Way Struggle Between the U.S., the KMT Government, and Taiwanese Society* (Chunshan Publishing, 2023), 275.

16. Gerrit van der Wees, "In Memoriam Lee Teng-hui, 1923–2020," University of Nottingham Taiwan Research Hub, August 4, 2020, https://taiwaninsight.org/2020/08/04/in-memoriam-lee-teng-hui-1923-2020/.

17. "Taiwan Remains 1st in Asia, 10th Globally in EIU Democracy Index," Taipei Economic and Cultural Office in Thailand, Taiwan Republic of China, February 19, 2024, https://www.roc-taiwan.org/th_en/post/6470.html.

18. Huang Tai-lin, "White Terror Exhibit Unveils Part of the Truth," *Taipei Times*, May 20, 2005, https://www.taipeitimes.com/News/taiwan/archives/2005/05/20/2003255840.

19. Michael Turton, "Notes from Central Taiwan: Formosa in German Colonial Dreams," *Taipei Times*, June 27, 2022, https://www.taipeitimes.com/News/feat/archives/2022/06/27/2003780629.

20. Michael Turton, "America, Taiwan, and the Inevitability of History," Medium, June 16, 2018, https://medium.com/american-citizens-for-taiwan/america-taiwan-and-the-inevitability-of-history-9b5f8eba2f09.

21. Treaty of Peace with Japan, Taiwan Documents Project, http://www.taiwandocuments.org/sanfrancisco01.htm#:~:text=San%20Francisco%20Peace%20Treaty&text=Note%3A%20Neither%20the%20Republic%20of,Peace%20with%20Japan%20in%201952.

22. Chen Cuilian, *Reexamining Postwar Taiwan's Political History: The Three-Way Struggle Between the U.S., the KMT Government, and Taiwanese Society* (Chunshan Publishing, 2023), 118, 134.

23. Turton, "America, Taiwan, and the Inevitability of History."

24. "The Taiwan Strait Crises: 1954–55 and 1958", U.S. Department of State Archive, n.d., https://2001-2009.state.gov/r/pa/ho/time/lw/88751.htm.

25. "The Taiwan Strait Crisis of 1958," *Taiwan Today*, original publication August 1, 1959, https://taiwantoday.tw/news.php?unit=4&post=7540.

26. "Agri Economic Development Corporation (AEDC): Flagship Mission Project," The Morung Express, September 30, 2020, https://morungexpress.com/agri-economic-development-corporation-aedc-flagship-mission-project.

27. Denny Roy, *Taiwan: A Political History* (Cornell University Press, 2003), 131.

28. Roy, *Taiwan*, 131.

29. Henry Scott-Stokes, "Taiwan Leaders Respond to U.S. Move with Calm," *New York Times*, December 17, 1978, https://www.nytimes.com/1978/12/17/archives/taiwan-leaders-respond-to-us-move-with-calm-tremendous-adverse.html.

30. Donald J. Trump (@realdonaldtrump), X, December 2, 2016, https://x.com/realDonaldTrump/status/804863098138005504.

31. Michael R. Pompeo, "Lifting Self-Imposed Restrictions on the U.S.-Taiwan Relationship," U.S. Department of State, January 9, 2021, https://2017-2021.state.gov/lifting-self-imposed-restrictions-on-the-u-s-taiwan-relationship/.

32. "Taiwan Government Thanks the U.S. Government for Announcing A New Batch of Arms Sales to Taiwan Related to Tanks and Missiles," Institute of Diplomacy and International Affairs, Ministry of Foreign Affairs, Republic of China, July 9, 2019, https://subsite.mofa.gov.tw/idia/News_Content.aspx?n=6073&sms=1689&s=111351.

33. Nancy A. Youssef and Chun Han Wong, "Hegseth Warns of 'Devastating Consequences' Should China Seek to 'Conquer' Taiwan; The Defense Secretary Said Asia Is the Administration's Priority Region," *Wall Street Journal* (online), May 31, 2025.

34. "China's United Front Exposed: Officials' Leaked Calls and Tactics to Buy Off Taiwanese Influencers," FunTV, YouTube.com, https://www.youtube.com/watch?v=IXndeTRH8tU; and "Documentary on China's United Front (Part 2): 200,000 Taiwanese Obtain CCP Passports!," FunTV, YouTube.com, https://www.youtube.com/watch?v=ZCyWe3Ib7DI.

35. Helen Davidson, "Taiwan Jails Four Soldiers, Including Three Who Worked in Presidential Office, for Spying for China," *The Guardian*, March 27, 2025, https://www.theguardian.com/world/2025/mar/27/taiwan-jails-four-soldiers-including-three-who-worked-in-presidential-office-for-spying-for-china.

36. Christy Choi and Wayne Chang, "Drag Queen Nymphia Wind Performs at Taiwan's Presidential Office," CNN, May 16, 2024, https://www.cnn.com/2024/05/16/style/drag-queen-nymphia-wind-taiwan-president-intl-hnk/index.html.

Chapter 10: The Trump Reversal: America Fights Back

1. Donald J. Trump, *Crippled America: How to Make America Great Again* (Threshold Editions, 2015), 43.

2. "China Theft of Technology Is Biggest Law Enforcement Threat to US, FBI Says," *The Guardian*, February 6, 2020, https://www.theguardian.com/world/2020/feb/06/china-technology-theft-fbi-biggest-threat.

3. Andrew Wong, "China: We Are a 'Near-Arctic State' and We Want a 'Polar Silk Road,'" CNBC, February 14, 2018, https://www.cnbc.com/2018/02/14/china-we-are-a-near-arctic-state-and-we-want-a-polar-silk-road.html.

4. Amrith Ramkumar, Natalie Andrews, and Rolfe Winkler, "Trump Exempts Tech Companies That Invest in U.S. From 100% Chip Tariffs; Step offers relief to Apple, which announced another $100 billion investment," *Wall Street Journal* (Online), Dow Jones & Company Inc., August 6, 2025.

5. Edward Helmore, "Trump calls for resignation of Intel chief a day after 100% chip tariff threat," *The Guardian*, August 7, 2025.

6. Xia Baolong, "Ensuring High-quality Development with High-level Security, Continuously Composing a New Chapter in the Practice of 'One Country, Two Systems,'" Hong Kong and Macao Work Office of the CPC Central Committee, April 15, 2025, https://www.hmo.gov.cn/gab/bld/xbl/gzdt/202504/t20250415_40714.html.

7. "Presidential Message on the National Day for the Victims of Communism," Trump White House Archives, November 7, 2020, https://trumpwhitehouse.archives.gov/briefings-statements/presidential-message-national-day-victims-communism-110720/.

8. James Bickerton, "Is Kamala Harris a Marxist? We Asked Actual Communists," *Newsweek*, September 13, 2024, https://www.newsweek.com/kamala-harris-marxist-we-asked-actual-communists-1953534.

9. Rachel Scully, "Walz Defends Using the Term 'Socialism': 'It's What the Right Uses,'" *The Hill*, October 13, 2024, https://thehill.com/homenews/campaign/4930881-walz-defends-socialism-capitalism/.

10. Thomas P. Hughes, "How America Helped Build the Soviet Machine," *American Heritage*, December 1988, Volume 39, Issue 8, https://www.americanheritage.com/how-america-helped-build-soviet-machine.

11. Hughes, "How America Helped Build the Soviet Machine."

12. Hughes, "How America Helped Build the Soviet Machine."

13. Sean McMeekin, *To Overthrow the World* (Basic Books, 2024), 452–453.

14. "The Greatest Humanitarian Mission in History: America's 1921 Famine Relief Expedition to Soviet Russia," The Heritage Foundation, December 2, 2021, https://www.heritage.org/civil-society/event/the-greatest-humanitarian-mission-history-americas-1921-famine-relief.

15. "World War II Allies: U.S. Lend-Lease to the Soviet Union, 1941–1945," https://ru.usembassy.gov/world-war-ii-allies-u-s-lend-lease-to-the-soviet-union-1941-1945/.

16. Rossana Cambron, "Maintaining Momentum: Next Steps in Building the CPUSA," Communist Party USA, April 20, 2021, https://www.cpusa.org/article/maintaining-momentum-next-steps-in-building-the-cpusa/.

17. Azri Azizan, "'We Don't Care, China Has Been Here for 5,000 Years'—Chinese Analyst on Possibility of Losing the US Market," World of Buzz, April 26, 2025, https://worldofbuzz.com/we-dont-care-china-has-been-here-for-5000-years-chinese-analyst-on-possibility-of-losing-the-us-market/.

18. Yang Guang, "Chairman Mao's Humorous Self-Portrait: 'Marx Plus Qin Shi Huang,'" Red Song Club QQ Group, December 12, 2022, https://mzd.szhgh.com/pingshu/2022-12-12/317331.html.

19. Meng Zhe, Xu-Pan Yiru, and Ge Xinge, "Mearsheimer on China-US: Hot War Is Possible," *China Daily*, October 30, 2024, https://www.chinadaily.com.cn/a/202410/30/WS6721e351a310f1265a1ca7e6.html.

20. "The World Is Undergoing Major Changes Unseen in a Century. Where Are the Changes Happening?," Communist Party Member Network, August 4, 2021, https://www.12371.cn/2021/08/04/ARTI1628057666635370.shtml.

21. Melissa Zhu, "Nancy Pelosi's Long History of Opposing Beijing," BBC News, August 2, 2022, https://www.bbc.com/news/world-asia-china-62343675.

22. "Sen. Rand Paul on Trump tariffs: Trade is an integral part of capitalism," CNBC TV, YouTube.com, https://www.youtube.com/watch?v=iuUECPxrjVU.

23. Xi Van Fleet (@XVanFleet), X, April 29, 2025, https://x.com/XVanFleet/status/1917245584265580743.

24. "VOA Exclusive: Greta Van Susteren Interviews Former US President Jimmy Carter," Voice of America, YouTube.com, https://www.youtube.com/watch?v=yhIQlAFE0Co.

25. "Remarks by President Barack Obama at Town Hall Meeting with Future Chinese Leaders." Obama White House Archives, November16, 2009, https://obamawhitehouse.archives.gov/the-press-office/remarks-president-barack-obama-town-hall-meeting-with-future-chinese-leaders.

26. Glenn C. Altschuler, "Trump Is Right That America Is in Mortal Danger. He's Dead Wrong About the Cause," *The Hill*, June 12, 2023, https://thehill.com/opinion/campaign/4046146-trump-is-right-that-america-is-in-mortal-danger-hes-dead-wrong-about-the-cause/.

INDEX

ABOUT THE AUTHORS

XI VAN FLEET

Xi Van Fleet was born in Chengdu, China, in 1959—at the height of Mao's most deadly political campaign, the Great Leap Forward, which ultimately led to the Great Famine killing up to 50 million Chinese, the horrors of which she later learned through her mother's stories.

She would later live through Mao's final and most destructive campaign—the Chinese Cultural Revolution. Spanning a full decade from 1966 to 1976, it coincided exactly with her ten years of schooling, from elementary through high school.

She not only witnessed the destruction, devastation, and human suffering brought about by the Cultural Revolution, but was also deeply indoctrinated by radical Maoist ideology—leaving her unable to think independently or critically. Years later, she would raise the alarm about a similar pattern of ideological indoctrination taking root in American schools.

At age sixteen, after graduating from high school, she—like all urban youths—was sent to the countryside for "reeducation," a euphemism for forced labor under harsh and primitive conditions.

It was only after Mao's death and the end of the Cultural Revolution that she was able to attend college, where she studied English. In 1986, with the help of an American teacher she met in China, she came to the United States as a graduate student.

Like many immigrants from Communist countries, she initially naïvely believed she had left Communism behind for good—freedom in America, she thought, was a given. Her political awakening came later, as she began to notice troubling signs that echoed the Cultural Revolution she had lived through in China: political correctness, identity politics, censorship, and an increasing pressure to conform ideologically.

The watershed moment for her came in 2020, when the BLM riots swept across America. It became undeniably clear to her: This was a full-blown Marxist revolution—history repeating itself before her eyes.

In 2021, she delivered a school board speech in Loudoun County, Virginia, against critical race theory that went viral and ignited national conservative media attention.

In 2022, she quit her job and dedicated herself to writing a book—something she never imagined doing. Her goal was to compare the Woke Revolution to Mao's Cultural Revolution and sound the alarm for the American people. *Mao's America: A Survivor's Warning* was well received and resonated deeply with the public.

Made in America is her second book, written in collaboration with author Yu Jie. Together, they tell a vitally important story: how the United States—through liberal journalists, misguided politicians, and, later, amoral Wall Street firms and multinational corporations—inadvertently fueled the rise of the Chinese Communist Party, ultimately putting America's own survival at risk.

Describing herself as "Chinese by birth, American by choice, survivor of Mao's Cultural Revolution, and defender of liberty," she has made it her life's mission to educate Americans about the evil of Communism and the grave threat it poses to the United States—and to the free world.

YU JIE

Yu Jie was born in 1973 in Pujiang County, Chengdu, Sichuan, China.

At sixteen, he learned the truth about the Tiananmen Massacre through foreign radio broadcasts, awakening his lifelong resistance to Communism and solidarity with the brave youth of Tiananmen Square.

In 1992, Yu entered Beijing University to study Chinese, later earning a master's degree. His 1998 book, *Fire and Ice*, a collection of essays and literary criticism, resonated deeply with China's youth, selling more than a million copies and becoming a staple in university dorms. Despite heavy censorship, Yu emerged as a leading voice for freedom among post-1989 Chinese intellectuals.

In 2000, the Chinese Communist Party blacklisted him from all academic and media positions. He publicly protested, earning support from hundreds of writers and scholars. From 2002 to 2006, he served as a board member and vice president of the Independent Chinese PEN (a worldwide association of writers founded in 1921) Center, led by Nobel laureate Liu Xiaobo, representing the organization at international PEN conferences and drawing global attention to China's repression of free expression.

In 2003, he visited the U.S. at the invitation of the State Department. In 2004, he and Liu Xiaobo were detained for their work on the *China Human Rights Report*. In 2006, Yu met President George W. Bush at the White House to discuss China's human rights crisis.

Yu continued to challenge the regime, publishing *China's Best Actor: Wen Jiabao* in 2010. That same year, on the day of Liu Xiaobo's Nobel Peace Prize ceremony, Yu was abducted and tortured by state security. He narrowly survived.

In 2012, Yu emigrated to the United States with his family. At a National Press Club conference in Washington, D.C., he exposed the brutality of the CCP and committed himself to its defeat. Now based in the D.C. area, he founded the Asia-Pacific Institute for Religious Freedom and Democratization. In 2018, he became a U.S. citizen.

In recent years, Yu has turned his attention to Western politics, identifying the rise of leftist ideology in America as a growing threat rooted in the same Communist origins he fought in China. To awaken the West, he has authored several books in support of President Trump and the MAGA movement, including *Governance with Common Sense*; *The Leftist Calamity in the West*; *Trump Moves Right, Xi Jinping Moves Left*; and *Trump: Saving America*.

Writing is both Yu Jie's profession and his calling. He has authored more than ninety books—totaling 15 million Chinese characters—across a wide range of subjects. His mission is to wield the power of words against Marxist-Leninist-Maoist-Xiist totalitarianism and to challenge Western leftist ideology, while advancing American conservative political philosophy within the Chinese-speaking world.

Partnering with fellow Chinese American author Xi Van Fleet on this book, Yu aims to share his message with a broad audience of American and English-speaking readers.